Mometrix
TEST PREPARATION

Virginia

SOL Virginia and U.S. History Secrets Study Guide

DEAR FUTURE EXAM SUCCESS STORY

First of all, **THANK YOU** for purchasing Mometrix study materials!

Second, congratulations! You are one of the few determined test-takers who are committed to doing whatever it takes to excel on your exam. **You have come to the right place.** We developed these study materials with one goal in mind: to deliver you the information you need in a format that's concise and easy to use.

In addition to optimizing your guide for the content of the test, we've outlined our recommended steps for breaking down the preparation process into small, attainable goals so you can make sure you stay on track.

We've also analyzed the entire test-taking process, identifying the most common pitfalls and showing how you can overcome them and be ready for any curveball the test throws you.

Standardized testing is one of the biggest obstacles on your road to success, which only increases the importance of doing well in the high-pressure, high-stakes environment of test day. Your results on this test could have a significant impact on your future, and this guide provides the information and practical advice to help you achieve your full potential on test day.

Your success is our success

We would love to hear from you! If you would like to share the story of your exam success or if you have any questions or comments in regard to our products, please contact us at **800-673-8175** or **support@mometrix.com**.

Thanks again for your business and we wish you continued success!

Sincerely,
The Mometrix Test Preparation Team

Need more help? Check out our flashcards at:
http://MometrixFlashcards.com/SOL

Written and edited by the Mometrix Exam Secrets Test Prep Team
Printed in the United States of America

TABLE OF CONTENTS

Introduction

Thank you for purchasing this resource! You have made the choice to prepare yourself for a test that could have a huge impact on your future, and this guide is designed to help you be fully ready for test day. Obviously, it's important to have a solid understanding of the test material, but you also need to be prepared for the unique environment and stressors of the test, so that you can perform to the best of your abilities.

For this purpose, the first section that appears in this guide is the **Secret Keys**. We've devoted countless hours to meticulously researching what works and what doesn't, and we've boiled down our findings to the five most impactful steps you can take to improve your performance on the test. We start at the beginning with study planning and move through the preparation process, all the way to the testing strategies that will help you get the most out of what you know when you're finally sitting in front of the test.

We recommend that you start preparing for your test as far in advance as possible. However, if you've bought this guide as a last-minute study resource and only have a few days before your test, we recommend that you skip over the first two Secret Keys since they address a long-term study plan.

If you struggle with **test anxiety**, we strongly encourage you to check out our recommendations for how you can overcome it. Test anxiety is a formidable foe, but it can be beaten, and we want to make sure you have the tools you need to defeat it.

Secret Key #1 – Plan Big, Study Small

There's a lot riding on your performance. If you want to ace this test, you're going to need to keep your skills sharp and the material fresh in your mind. You need a plan that lets you review everything you need to know while still fitting in your schedule. We'll break this strategy down into three categories.

Information Organization

Start with the information you already have: the official test outline. From this, you can make a complete list of all the concepts you need to cover before the test. Organize these concepts into groups that can be studied together, and create a list of any related vocabulary you need to learn so you can brush up on any difficult terms. You'll want to keep this vocabulary list handy once you actually start studying since you may need to add to it along the way.

Time Management

Once you have your set of study concepts, decide how to spread them out over the time you have left before the test. Break your study plan into small, clear goals so you have a manageable task for each day and know exactly what you're doing. Then just focus on one small step at a time. When you manage your time this way, you don't need to spend hours at a time studying. Studying a small block of content for a short period each day helps you retain information better and avoid stressing over how much you have left to do. You can relax knowing that you have a plan to cover everything in time. In order for this strategy to be effective though, you have to start studying early and stick to your schedule. Avoid the exhaustion and futility that comes from last-minute cramming!

Study Environment

The environment you study in has a big impact on your learning. Studying in a coffee shop, while probably more enjoyable, is not likely to be as fruitful as studying in a quiet room. It's important to keep distractions to a minimum. You're only planning to study for a short block of time, so make the most of it. Don't pause to check your phone or get up to find a snack. It's also important to **avoid multitasking**. Research has consistently shown that multitasking will make your studying dramatically less effective. Your study area should also be comfortable and well-lit so you don't have the distraction of straining your eyes or sitting on an uncomfortable chair.

The time of day you study is also important. You want to be rested and alert. Don't wait until just before bedtime. Study when you'll be most likely to comprehend and remember. Even better, if you know what time of day your test will be, set that time aside for study. That way your brain will be used to working on that subject at that specific time and you'll have a better chance of recalling information.

Finally, it can be helpful to team up with others who are studying for the same test. Your actual studying should be done in as isolated an environment as possible, but the work of organizing the information and setting up the study plan can be divided up. In between study sessions, you can discuss with your teammates the concepts that you're all studying and quiz each other on the details. Just be sure that your teammates are as serious about the test as you are. If you find that your study time is being replaced with social time, you might need to find a new team.

Secret Key #2 – Make Your Studying Count

You're devoting a lot of time and effort to preparing for this test, so you want to be absolutely certain it will pay off. This means doing more than just reading the content and hoping you can remember it on test day. It's important to make every minute of study count. There are two main areas you can focus on to make your studying count.

Retention

It doesn't matter how much time you study if you can't remember the material. You need to make sure you are retaining the concepts. To check your retention of the information you're learning, try recalling it at later times with minimal prompting. Try carrying around flashcards and glance at one or two from time to time or ask a friend who's also studying for the test to quiz you.

To enhance your retention, look for ways to put the information into practice so that you can apply it rather than simply recalling it. If you're using the information in practical ways, it will be much easier to remember. Similarly, it helps to solidify a concept in your mind if you're not only reading it to yourself but also explaining it to someone else. Ask a friend to let you teach them about a concept you're a little shaky on (or speak aloud to an imaginary audience if necessary). As you try to summarize, define, give examples, and answer your friend's questions, you'll understand the concepts better and they will stay with you longer. Finally, step back for a big picture view and ask yourself how each piece of information fits with the whole subject. When you link the different concepts together and see them working together as a whole, it's easier to remember the individual components.

Finally, practice showing your work on any multi-step problems, even if you're just studying. Writing out each step you take to solve a problem will help solidify the process in your mind, and you'll be more likely to remember it during the test.

Modality

Modality simply refers to the means or method by which you study. Choosing a study modality that fits your own individual learning style is crucial. No two people learn best in exactly the same way, so it's important to know your strengths and use them to your advantage.

For example, if you learn best by visualization, focus on visualizing a concept in your mind and draw an image or a diagram. Try color-coding your notes, illustrating them, or creating symbols that will trigger your mind to recall a learned concept. If you learn best by hearing or discussing information, find a study partner who learns the same way or read aloud to yourself. Think about how to put the information in your own words. Imagine that you are giving a lecture on the topic and record yourself so you can listen to it later.

For any learning style, flashcards can be helpful. Organize the information so you can take advantage of spare moments to review. Underline key words or phrases. Use different colors for different categories. Mnemonic devices (such as creating a short list in which every item starts with the same letter) can also help with retention. Find what works best for you and use it to store the information in your mind most effectively and easily.

Secret Key #3 – Practice the Right Way

Your success on test day depends not only on how many hours you put into preparing, but also on whether you prepared the right way. It's good to check along the way to see if your studying is paying off. One of the most effective ways to do this is by taking practice tests to evaluate your progress. Practice tests are useful because they show exactly where you need to improve. Every time you take a practice test, pay special attention to these three groups of questions:

- The questions you got wrong
- The questions you had to guess on, even if you guessed right
- The questions you found difficult or slow to work through

This will show you exactly what your weak areas are, and where you need to devote more study time. Ask yourself why each of these questions gave you trouble. Was it because you didn't understand the material? Was it because you didn't remember the vocabulary? Do you need more repetitions on this type of question to build speed and confidence? Dig into those questions and figure out how you can strengthen your weak areas as you go back to review the material.

Additionally, many practice tests have a section explaining the answer choices. It can be tempting to read the explanation and think that you now have a good understanding of the concept. However, an explanation likely only covers part of the question's broader context. Even if the explanation makes perfect sense, **go back and investigate** every concept related to the question until you're positive you have a thorough understanding.

As you go along, keep in mind that the practice test is just that: practice. Memorizing these questions and answers will not be very helpful on the actual test because it is unlikely to have any of the same exact questions. If you only know the right answers to the sample questions, you won't be prepared for the real thing. **Study the concepts** until you understand them fully, and then you'll be able to answer any question that shows up on the test.

It's important to wait on the practice tests until you're ready. If you take a test on your first day of study, you may be overwhelmed by the amount of material covered and how much you need to learn. Work up to it gradually.

On test day, you'll need to be prepared for answering questions, managing your time, and using the test-taking strategies you've learned. It's a lot to balance, like a mental marathon that will have a big impact on your future. Like training for a marathon, you'll need to start slowly and work your way up. When test day arrives, you'll be ready.

Start with the strategies you've read in the first two Secret Keys—plan your course and study in the way that works best for you. If you have time, consider using multiple study resources to get different approaches to the same concepts. It can be helpful to see difficult concepts from more than one angle. Then find a good source for practice tests. Many times, the test website will suggest potential study resources or provide sample tests.

Practice Test Strategy

If you're able to find at least three practice tests, we recommend this strategy:

Untimed and Open-Book Practice

Take the first test with no time constraints and with your notes and study guide handy. Take your time and focus on applying the strategies you've learned.

Timed and Open-Book Practice

Take the second practice test open-book as well, but set a timer and practice pacing yourself to finish in time.

Timed and Closed-Book Practice

Take any other practice tests as if it were test day. Set a timer and put away your study materials. Sit at a table or desk in a quiet room, imagine yourself at the testing center, and answer questions as quickly and accurately as possible.

Keep repeating timed and closed-book tests on a regular basis until you run out of practice tests or it's time for the actual test. Your mind will be ready for the schedule and stress of test day, and you'll be able to focus on recalling the material you've learned.

Secret Key #4 – Pace Yourself

Once you're fully prepared for the material on the test, your biggest challenge on test day will be managing your time. Just knowing that the clock is ticking can make you panic even if you have plenty of time left. Work on pacing yourself so you can build confidence against the time constraints of the exam. Pacing is a difficult skill to master, especially in a high-pressure environment, so **practice is vital**.

Set time expectations for your pace based on how much time is available. For example, if a section has 60 questions and the time limit is 30 minutes, you know you have to average 30 seconds or less per question in order to answer them all. Although 30 seconds is the hard limit, set 25 seconds per question as your goal, so you reserve extra time to spend on harder questions. When you budget extra time for the harder questions, you no longer have any reason to stress when those questions take longer to answer.

Don't let this time expectation distract you from working through the test at a calm, steady pace, but keep it in mind so you don't spend too much time on any one question. Recognize that taking extra time on one question you don't understand may keep you from answering two that you do understand later in the test. If your time limit for a question is up and you're still not sure of the answer, mark it and move on, and come back to it later if the time and the test format allow. If the testing format doesn't allow you to return to earlier questions, just make an educated guess; then put it out of your mind and move on.

On the easier questions, be careful not to rush. It may seem wise to hurry through them so you have more time for the challenging ones, but it's not worth missing one if you know the concept and just didn't take the time to read the question fully. Work efficiently but make sure you understand the question and have looked at all of the answer choices, since more than one may seem right at first.

Even if you're paying attention to the time, you may find yourself a little behind at some point. You should speed up to get back on track, but do so wisely. Don't panic; just take a few seconds less on each question until you're caught up. Don't guess without thinking, but do look through the answer choices and eliminate any you know are wrong. If you can get down to two choices, it is often worthwhile to guess from those. Once you've chosen an answer, move on and don't dwell on any that you skipped or had to hurry through. If a question was taking too long, chances are it was one of the harder ones, so you weren't as likely to get it right anyway.

On the other hand, if you find yourself getting ahead of schedule, it may be beneficial to slow down a little. The more quickly you work, the more likely you are to make a careless mistake that will affect your score. You've budgeted time for each question, so don't be afraid to spend that time. Practice an efficient but careful pace to get the most out of the time you have.

Secret Key #5 – Have a Plan for Guessing

When you're taking the test, you may find yourself stuck on a question. Some of the answer choices seem better than others, but you don't see the one answer choice that is obviously correct. What do you do?

The scenario described above is very common, yet most test takers have not effectively prepared for it. Developing and practicing a plan for guessing may be one of the single most effective uses of your time as you get ready for the exam.

In developing your plan for guessing, there are three questions to address:

- When should you start the guessing process?
- How should you narrow down the choices?
- Which answer should you choose?

When to Start the Guessing Process

Unless your plan for guessing is to select C every time (which, despite its merits, is not what we recommend), you need to leave yourself enough time to apply your answer elimination strategies. Since you have a limited amount of time for each question, that means that if you're going to give yourself the best shot at guessing correctly, you have to decide quickly whether or not you will guess.

Of course, the best-case scenario is that you don't have to guess at all, so first, see if you can answer the question based on your knowledge of the subject and basic reasoning skills. Focus on the key words in the question and try to jog your memory of related topics. Give yourself a chance to bring the knowledge to mind, but once you realize that you don't have (or you can't access) the knowledge you need to answer the question, it's time to start the guessing process.

It's almost always better to start the guessing process too early than too late. It only takes a few seconds to remember something and answer the question from knowledge. Carefully eliminating wrong answer choices takes longer. Plus, going through the process of eliminating answer choices can actually help jog your memory.

Summary: Start the guessing process as soon as you decide that you can't answer the question based on your knowledge.

How to Narrow Down the Choices

The next chapter in this book (**Test-Taking Strategies**) includes a wide range of strategies for how to approach questions and how to look for answer choices to eliminate. You will definitely want to read those carefully, practice them, and figure out which ones work best for you. Here though, we're going to address a mindset rather than a particular strategy.

Your odds of guessing an answer correctly depend on how many options you are choosing from.

Number of options left	5	4	3	2	1
Odds of guessing correctly	20%	25%	33%	50%	100%

You can see from this chart just how valuable it is to be able to eliminate incorrect answers and make an educated guess, but there are two things that many test takers do that cause them to miss out on the benefits of guessing:

- Accidentally eliminating the correct answer
- Selecting an answer based on an impression

We'll look at the first one here, and the second one in the next section.

To avoid accidentally eliminating the correct answer, we recommend a thought exercise called **the $5 challenge**. In this challenge, you only eliminate an answer choice from contention if you are willing to bet $5 on it being wrong. Why $5? Five dollars is a small but not insignificant amount of money. It's an amount you could afford to lose but wouldn't want to throw away. And while losing $5 once might not hurt too much, doing it twenty times will set you back $100. In the same way, each small decision you make—eliminating a choice here, guessing on a question there—won't by itself impact your score very much, but when you put them all together, they can make a big difference. By holding each answer choice elimination decision to a higher standard, you can reduce the risk of accidentally eliminating the correct answer.

The $5 challenge can also be applied in a positive sense: If you are willing to bet $5 that an answer choice *is* correct, go ahead and mark it as correct.

Summary: Only eliminate an answer choice if you are willing to bet $5 that it is wrong.

Which Answer to Choose

You're taking the test. You've run into a hard question and decided you'll have to guess. You've eliminated all the answer choices you're willing to bet $5 on. Now you have to pick an answer. Why do we even need to talk about this? Why can't you just pick whichever one you feel like when the time comes?

The answer to these questions is that if you don't come into the test with a plan, you'll rely on your impression to select an answer choice, and if you do that, you risk falling into a trap. The test writers know that everyone who takes their test will be guessing on some of the questions, so they intentionally write wrong answer choices to seem plausible. You still have to pick an answer though, and if the wrong answer choices are designed to look right, how can you ever be sure that you're not falling for their trap? The best solution we've found to this dilemma is to take the decision out of your hands entirely. Here is the process we recommend:

Once you've eliminated any choices that you are confident (willing to bet $5) are wrong, select the first remaining choice as your answer.

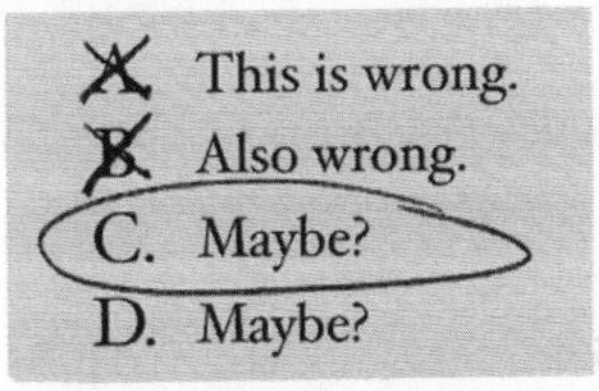

Whether you choose to select the first remaining choice, the second, or the last, the important thing is that you use some preselected standard. Using this approach guarantees that you will not be enticed into selecting an answer choice that looks right, because you are not basing your decision on how the answer choices look.

This is not meant to make you question your knowledge. Instead, it is to help you recognize the difference between your knowledge and your impressions. There's a huge difference between thinking an answer is right because of what you know, and thinking an answer is right because it looks or sounds like it should be right.

Summary: To ensure that your selection is appropriately random, make a predetermined selection from among all answer choices you have not eliminated.

Test-Taking Strategies

This section contains a list of test-taking strategies that you may find helpful as you work through the test. By taking what you know and applying logical thought, you can maximize your chances of answering any question correctly!

It is very important to realize that every question is different and every person is different: no single strategy will work on every question, and no single strategy will work for every person. That's why we've included all of them here, so you can try them out and determine which ones work best for different types of questions and which ones work best for you.

Question Strategies

⊘ Read Carefully

Read the question and the answer choices carefully. Don't miss the question because you misread the terms. You have plenty of time to read each question thoroughly and make sure you understand what is being asked. Yet a happy medium must be attained, so don't waste too much time. You must read carefully and efficiently.

⊘ Contextual Clues

Look for contextual clues. If the question includes a word you are not familiar with, look at the immediate context for some indication of what the word might mean. Contextual clues can often give you all the information you need to decipher the meaning of an unfamiliar word. Even if you can't determine the meaning, you may be able to narrow down the possibilities enough to make a solid guess at the answer to the question.

⊘ Prefixes

If you're having trouble with a word in the question or answer choices, try dissecting it. Take advantage of every clue that the word might include. Prefixes can be a huge help. Usually, they allow you to determine a basic meaning. *Pre-* means before, *post-* means after, *pro-* is positive, *de-* is negative. From prefixes, you can get an idea of the general meaning of the word and try to put it into context.

⊘ Hedge Words

Watch out for critical hedge words, such as *likely, may, can, often, almost, mostly, usually, generally, rarely,* and *sometimes.* Question writers insert these hedge phrases to cover every possibility. Often an answer choice will be wrong simply because it leaves no room for exception. Be on guard for answer choices that have definitive words such as *exactly* and *always.*

⊘ Switchback Words

Stay alert for *switchbacks*. These are the words and phrases frequently used to alert you to shifts in thought. The most common switchback words are *but, although,* and *however*. Others include *nevertheless, on the other hand, even though, while, in spite of, despite,* and *regardless of.* Switchback words are important to catch because they can change the direction of the question or an answer choice.

☑ FACE VALUE

When in doubt, use common sense. Accept the situation in the problem at face value. Don't read too much into it. These problems will not require you to make wild assumptions. If you have to go beyond creativity and warp time or space in order to have an answer choice fit the question, then you should move on and consider the other answer choices. These are normal problems rooted in reality. The applicable relationship or explanation may not be readily apparent, but it is there for you to figure out. Use your common sense to interpret anything that isn't clear.

Answer Choice Strategies

☑ ANSWER SELECTION

The most thorough way to pick an answer choice is to identify and eliminate wrong answers until only one is left, then confirm it is the correct answer. Sometimes an answer choice may immediately seem right, but be careful. The test writers will usually put more than one reasonable answer choice on each question, so take a second to read all of them and make sure that the other choices are not equally obvious. As long as you have time left, it is better to read every answer choice than to pick the first one that looks right without checking the others.

☑ ANSWER CHOICE FAMILIES

An answer choice family consists of two (in rare cases, three) answer choices that are very similar in construction and cannot all be true at the same time. If you see two answer choices that are direct opposites or parallels, one of them is usually the correct answer. For instance, if one answer choice says that quantity *x* increases and another either says that quantity *x* decreases (opposite) or says that quantity *y* increases (parallel), then those answer choices would fall into the same family. An answer choice that doesn't match the construction of the answer choice family is more likely to be incorrect. Most questions will not have answer choice families, but when they do appear, you should be prepared to recognize them.

☑ ELIMINATE ANSWERS

Eliminate answer choices as soon as you realize they are wrong, but make sure you consider all possibilities. If you are eliminating answer choices and realize that the last one you are left with is also wrong, don't panic. Start over and consider each choice again. There may be something you missed the first time that you will realize on the second pass.

☑ AVOID FACT TRAPS

Don't be distracted by an answer choice that is factually true but doesn't answer the question. You are looking for the choice that answers the question. Stay focused on what the question is asking for so you don't accidentally pick an answer that is true but incorrect. Always go back to the question and make sure the answer choice you've selected actually answers the question and is not merely a true statement.

☑ EXTREME STATEMENTS

In general, you should avoid answers that put forth extreme actions as standard practice or proclaim controversial ideas as established fact. An answer choice that states the "process should be used in certain situations, if…" is much more likely to be correct than one that states the "process should be discontinued completely." The first is a calm rational statement and doesn't even make a definitive, uncompromising stance, using a hedge word *if* to provide wiggle room, whereas the second choice is far more extreme.

⊘ Benchmark

As you read through the answer choices and you come across one that seems to answer the question well, mentally select that answer choice. This is not your final answer, but it's the one that will help you evaluate the other answer choices. The one that you selected is your benchmark or standard for judging each of the other answer choices. Every other answer choice must be compared to your benchmark. That choice is correct until proven otherwise by another answer choice beating it. If you find a better answer, then that one becomes your new benchmark. Once you've decided that no other choice answers the question as well as your benchmark, you have your final answer.

⊘ Predict the Answer

Before you even start looking at the answer choices, it is often best to try to predict the answer. When you come up with the answer on your own, it is easier to avoid distractions and traps because you will know exactly what to look for. The right answer choice is unlikely to be word-for-word what you came up with, but it should be a close match. Even if you are confident that you have the right answer, you should still take the time to read each option before moving on.

General Strategies

⊘ Tough Questions

If you are stumped on a problem or it appears too hard or too difficult, don't waste time. Move on! Remember though, if you can quickly check for obviously incorrect answer choices, your chances of guessing correctly are greatly improved. Before you completely give up, at least try to knock out a couple of possible answers. Eliminate what you can and then guess at the remaining answer choices before moving on.

⊘ Check Your Work

Since you will probably not know every term listed and the answer to every question, it is important that you get credit for the ones that you do know. Don't miss any questions through careless mistakes. If at all possible, try to take a second to look back over your answer selection and make sure you've selected the correct answer choice and haven't made a costly careless mistake (such as marking an answer choice that you didn't mean to mark). This quick double check should more than pay for itself in caught mistakes for the time it costs.

⊘ Pace Yourself

It's easy to be overwhelmed when you're looking at a page full of questions; your mind is confused and full of random thoughts, and the clock is ticking down faster than you would like. Calm down and maintain the pace that you have set for yourself. Especially as you get down to the last few minutes of the test, don't let the small numbers on the clock make you panic. As long as you are on track by monitoring your pace, you are guaranteed to have time for each question.

⊘ Don't Rush

It is very easy to make errors when you are in a hurry. Maintaining a fast pace in answering questions is pointless if it makes you miss questions that you would have gotten right otherwise. Test writers like to include distracting information and wrong answers that seem right. Taking a little extra time to avoid careless mistakes can make all the difference in your test score. Find a pace that allows you to be confident in the answers that you select.

✓ Keep Moving

Panicking will not help you pass the test, so do your best to stay calm and keep moving. Taking deep breaths and going through the answer elimination steps you practiced can help to break through a stress barrier and keep your pace.

Final Notes

The combination of a solid foundation of content knowledge and the confidence that comes from practicing your plan for applying that knowledge is the key to maximizing your performance on test day. As your foundation of content knowledge is built up and strengthened, you'll find that the strategies included in this chapter become more and more effective in helping you quickly sift through the distractions and traps of the test to isolate the correct answer.

Now that you're preparing to move forward into the test content chapters of this book, be sure to keep your goal in mind. As you read, think about how you will be able to apply this information on the test. If you've already seen sample questions for the test and you have an idea of the question format and style, try to come up with questions of your own that you can answer based on what you're reading. This will give you valuable practice applying your knowledge in the same ways you can expect to on test day.

Good luck and good studying!

Social Studies Skills and Thinking

Collecting Information and Organizing and Reporting Results

The first step of compiling data for useful implementation requires narrowing down on a **topic**. The student should first read background information to identify areas that are interesting or need further study and that the student does not have a strong opinion about. The research question should be identified, and the student should refer to general sources that can point to more specific information. When he or she begins to take notes, his or her information must be **organized** with a clear system to identify the source. Any information from outside sources must be acknowledged with **footnotes** or a **bibliography**. To gain more specific information about his or her topic, the student can then research bibliographies from general sources to narrow down on information pertinent to the topic at hand. He or she should draft a thesis statement that summarizes the main point of the research. This should lead to a working **outline** that incorporates all the ideas needed to support the main point in a logical order. A rough draft should incorporate the results of the research in the outlined order, with all citations clearly inserted. The paper should then be edited for clarity, style, flow, and content.

Formulating Research Questions or Hypotheses

Formulating research questions or hypotheses is the process of finding questions to answer that have not yet been asked. The first step in the process is reading **background information**. Knowing about a general topic and reading about how other people have addressed it helps identify areas that are well understood. Areas that are not as well understood may either be lightly addressed in the available literature or distinctly identified as a topic that is not well understood and deserves further study. Research questions or hypotheses may address such an unknown aspect, or they may focus on drawing parallels between similar, well-researched topics that have not been connected before. Students usually need practice in developing research questions that are of the appropriate scope so that they will find enough information to answer the question, yet not so much that they become overwhelmed. Hypotheses tend to be more specific than research questions.

Identifying Main Ideas in a Document

Main ideas in a paragraph are often found in the **topic sentence**, which is usually the first or second sentence in the paragraph. Every following sentence in the paragraph should relate to that initial information. Sometimes, the first or second sentence doesn't obviously set up the main idea. When that happens, each sentence in the paragraph should be read carefully to find the **common theme** between them all. This common theme is the main idea of the paragraph. Main ideas in an entire document can be found by analyzing the structure of the document. Frequently, the document begins with an introductory paragraph or abstract that will summarize the main ideas. Each paragraph often discusses one of the main ideas and contributes to the overall goal of the document. Some documents are divided up into chapters or sections, each of which discusses a main idea. The way that main ideas are described in a document (either in sentences, paragraphs, or chapters) depends on the length of the document.

Using Electronic Resources and Periodicals for Reference

Electronic resources are often the quickest, most convenient way to get background information on a topic. One of the particular strengths of **electronic resources** is that they can also provide primary-source multimedia video, audio, or other visual information on a topic that would not be accessible in print. Information available on the internet is not often carefully screened for accuracy or for bias, so choosing the **source** of electronic information is often very important. Electronic encyclopedias can provide excellent overview information, but publicly edited resources like Wikipedia are open to error, rapid change, incompleteness, or bias. Students should be made aware of the different types and reliabilities of electronic resources, and they should be taught how to distinguish between them. Electronic resources can often be too detailed and overwhelm students with irrelevant information. **Periodicals** provide current information on social science events, but they too must be screened for bias. Some amount of identifiable bias can actually be an important source of information, because it indicates prevailing culture and standards. Periodicals generally have tighter editorial standards than electronic resources, so completeness and overt errors are not usually as problematic. Periodicals can also provide primary-source information with interviews and photographs.

Using Encyclopedias, Bibliographies, or Almanacs for Social Science Research

Encyclopedias are ideal for getting background information on a topic. They provide an overview of the topic and link it to other concepts that can provide additional keywords, information, or subjects. They can help students narrow their topic by showing the subtopics within the overall topic and by relating it to other topics. **Encyclopedias** may sometimes prove to be more useful than the internet because they provide a clearly organized, concise overview of material. **Bibliographies** are bound collections of references to periodicals and books, organized by topic. Students can begin researching more efficiently after they identify a topic, look it up in a bibliography, and look up the references listed there. This provides a branching network of information a student can follow. A pitfall of bibliographies is that when in textbooks or other journal articles, the references in them are chosen to support the author's point of view and so may be limited in scope. **Almanacs** are volumes of facts published annually. They provide numerical information on just about every topic, and are organized by subject or geographic region. They are often helpful for supporting arguments made using other resources and do not provide any interpretation of their own.

Primary and Secondary Resources

Primary resources provide information about an event from the perspective of people who were present at the event. They might be letters, autobiographies, interviews, speeches, artworks, or anything created by people with first-hand experience. **Primary resources** are valuable because they provide not only facts about the event but also information about the surrounding circumstances; for example, a letter might provide commentary about how a political speech was received. The internet is a source of primary information, but care must be taken to evaluate the perspective of the website providing that information. Websites hosted by individuals or special-interest organizations are more likely to be biased than those hosted by public organizations, governments, educational institutions, or news associations. **Secondary resources** provide information about an event but were not written at the time the event occurred. They draw information from primary sources. Because secondary sources were written later, they have the added advantage of historical perspective, multiple points of view, or resultant outcomes. Newsmagazines that write about an event even a week after it occurred count as secondary sources. Secondary sources tend to analyze events more effectively or thoroughly than primary sources.

Review Video: Primary and Secondary Sources
Visit mometrix.com/academy and enter code: 383328

Organizing Information Chronologically and Analyzing the Sequence of Events

To organize information chronologically, each piece of information must be associated with a time or a date. Events are ordered according to the time or date at which they happened. In social sciences, chronological organization is the most straightforward way to arrange information, because it relies on a uniform, fixed scale—the passage of time. Information can also be organized based on any of the "who, what, when, where, why?" principles.

Analyzing the sequence of chronological events involves not only examining the event itself but the preceding and following events. This can put the event in question into perspective, showing how a certain thing might have happened based on preceding history. One large disadvantage of chronological organization is that it may not highlight important events clearly relative to less important events. Determining the relative importance of events depends more strongly on interpreting their relationships to neighboring events.

Recognizing Cause-and-Effect Relationships and Comparing Similarities and Differences

Cause-and-effect relationships are simply linkages between an event that happened (the **effect**) because of some other event (the **cause**). Effects are always chronologically ordered after causes. Effects can be found by asking why something happened or looking for information following words like *so, consequently, since, because, therefore, this led to, as a result,* and *thus*. Causes can also be found by asking what happened. **Comparing similarities and differences** involves mentally setting two concepts next to each other and then listing the ways they are the same and the ways they are different. The level of comparison varies by student level; for example, younger students may compare the physical characteristics of two animals while older students compare the themes of a book. Similarity/difference comparisons can be made by listing written descriptions in a point-by-point approach, or they can be done in several graphic ways. Venn diagrams are commonly used to organize information, showing non-overlapping clouds filled with information about the different characteristics of A and B, and the overlapping area shows ways in which A and B are the same. Idea maps using arrows and bubbles can also be developed to show these differences.

Distinguishing Between Fact and Opinion

Students easily recognize that **facts** are true statements that everyone agrees on, such as an object's name or a statement about a historical event. Students also recognize that **opinions** vary about matters of taste, such as preferences in food or music, that rely on people's interpretation of facts. Simple examples are easy to spot. **Fact-based passages** include certainty-grounded words like *is, did*, or *saw*. On the other hand, **passages containing opinions** often include words that indicate possibility rather than certainty, such as *would, should*, or *believe*. First-person verbs also indicate opinions, showing that one person is talking about his or her experience. Less clear are examples found in higher-level texts. For example, primary-source accounts of a Civil War battle might include facts ("*x* battle was fought today") and also opinions ("Union soldiers are not as brave as Confederate soldiers") that are not clearly written as such ("I believe Union soldiers..."). At the same time that students learn to interpret sources critically (Was the battle account written by a Southerner?), they should practice sifting fact from these types of opinion. Other examples where fact and opinion blend together are self-authored internet websites.

> **Review Video: Distinguishing Fact and Opinion**
> Visit mometrix.com/academy and enter code: 870899

Determining the Adequacy, Relevance, and Consistency of Information

Before information is sought, a list of **guiding questions** should be developed to help determine whether information found is adequate, relevant, and consistent. These questions should be based on the **research goals**, which should be laid out in an outline or concept map. For example, a student writing a report on Navajo social structure might begin with questions concerning the general lifestyle and location of Navajos and follow with questions about how Navajo society was organized. While researching his questions, he or she will come up with pieces of information. This information can be compared to his or her research questions to determine whether it is **relevant** to his or her report. Information from several sources should be compared to determine whether the information is **consistent**. Information that is **adequate** helps answer specific questions that are part of the research goals. Inadequate information for this particular student might be a statement such as "Navajos had a strong societal structure," because the student is probably seeking more specific information.

Drawing Conclusions and Making Generalizations About a Topic

Students reading about a topic will encounter different facts and opinions that contribute to their overall impression of the material. The student can critically examine the material by thinking about what facts have been included, how they have been presented, what they show, what they relate to outside the written material, and what the author's conclusion is. Students may agree or disagree with the author's conclusion, based on the student's interpretation of the facts the author presented. When working on a research project, a student's research questions will help him or her gather details that will enable him or her to **draw a conclusion** about the research material.

Generalizations are blanket statements that apply to a wide number of examples. They are similar to conclusions but do not have to summarize the information as completely as conclusions. Generalizations in reading material may be flagged by words such as *all, most, none, many, several, sometimes, often, never, overall*, or *in general*. Generalizations are often followed by supporting information consisting of a list of facts. Generalizations can refer to facts or the author's opinions, and they provide a valuable summary of the text overall.

Evaluating and Interpreting Maps

The **map legend** is an area that provides interpretation information such as the key, the scale, and how to interpret the map. The **key** is the area that defines symbols, abbreviations, and color schemes used on the map. Any feature identified on the map should be defined in the key. The **scale** is a feature of the map legend that tells how distance on the map relates to distance on the ground. It can either be presented mathematically in a ratio or visually with a line segment. For example, it could say that one inch on the map equals one foot on the ground, or it could show a line segment and tell how much distance on the map the line symbolizes. **Latitude** and **longitude** are often shown on maps to relate their area to the world. Latitude shows how far a location is north or south from Earth's equator, and longitude shows how far a location is east or west from Earth's prime meridian. Latitude runs from 90°N (North Pole) to 0° (equator) to 90°S (South Pole), and longitude runs 180°E (International Date Line) to 0° (prime meridian) to 180°W (International Date Line).

Review Video: Elements of a Map
Visit mometrix.com/academy and enter code: 437727

Popular Map Projections

- **Globe**: Earth's features are shown on a sphere. No distortion of distances, directions, or areas occurs.
- **Mercator**: Earth's features are projected onto a cylinder wrapped around a globe. This generates a rectangular map that is not distorted at the equator but is greatly distorted near the poles. Lines of latitude and longitude form a square grid.
- **Robinson**: Earth's features are projected onto an oval-looking map. Areas near the poles are truer to size than in the Mercator. Some distortion affects every point.
- **Orthographic**: Earth's features are shown on a circle, which is tangent to the globe at any point chosen by the mapmaker. This generates a circular, 3D-appearing map similar to how Earth is seen from space.
- **Conic maps**: This family of maps is drawn by projecting the globe's features onto a cone set onto the globe. Some distortion affects most points.
- **Polar maps**: The land around the poles has been projected onto a circle. This provides much less distortion of Antarctica and the land around the North Pole than other map types.

Cartographic Distortion and Its Influence on Map Projections

Cartographic distortion is the distortion caused by projecting a three-dimensional structure, in this case, Earth's surface, onto the two-dimensional surface of a map. Numerous map projections have been developed to minimize distortion, but the only way to eliminate distortion completely is to render Earth in three dimensions. Most map projections have minimal distortion in some location, usually the center, and the distortion becomes greater close to the edges of the map. Some map projections try to compromise and distribute the distortion more evenly across the map. Different categories of maps preserve, or do not distort, different features. Maps that preserve directions accurately are **azimuthal**, and maps that preserve shapes properly are **conformal**. Area-preserving maps are called **equal-area maps**, and maps that preserve distance are called **distance-preserving**. Maps that preserve the shortest routes are **gnomonic projections**.

Review Video: Map Projections
Visit mometrix.com/academy and enter code: 327303

Comparing Maps of the Same Place from Different Time Periods

Maps of the same place from different time periods can often be initially aligned by **geographic features**. Political and land-use boundaries are most likely to change between time periods, whereas locations of waterways and geologic features such as mountains are relatively constant. Once geographic features have been used to align maps, they can be compared side-by-side to examine the changing locations of human settlement, smaller waterways, etc. This kind of map interpretation, at the smallest scale, provides information about how small groups of humans **interact with their environment**. For example, such analysis might show that major cities began around ports and then moved inland as modes of transportation, like railroads and cars, became more common. Lands that were initially used for agriculture might become incorporated into a nearby city as the population grows. This kind of map analysis can also show the evolution of the **socio-economics** of an area, providing information about the relative importance of economic activities (manufacturing, agriculture, or trade) and even the commuting behavior of workers.

Natural, Political, and Cultural Features on Maps

Map legends will provide information about the types of natural, political, or cultural features on a map. Some maps show only one of these three features. **Natural features** such as waterways, wetlands, beaches, deserts, mountains, highlands, and plains can be compared between regions by type, number, distribution, or any other physical characteristic. **Political features** such as state and county divisions or roads and railroads can be compared numerically, but examining their geographic distribution may be more informative. This provides information on settlement density and population. In addition, road and railroad density may show regions of intense urbanization, agricultural regions, or industrial centers. **Cultural features** may include roads and railroads, but might also include historic areas, museums, archaeological digs, early settlements, and even campgrounds. Comparing and contrasting the number, distribution, and types of these features may provide information on the history of an area, the duration of settlement of an area, or the current use of the area (for example, many museums are found in current-day cultural centers).

Comparing Maps with Datasets or Texts

Maps can provide a great deal of information about an area by showing specific locations where certain types of settlement, land use, or population growth occurred. **Datasets** and **texts** can provide more specific information about events that might only otherwise be hypothesized from maps. This specific information may provide dates of significant events (for example, the date of a fire that gutted a downtown region, forcing suburban development) or important numerical data (e.g., population growth by year). Written datasets and texts enable map interpretation to become concrete and allow observed trends to be linked with specific causes ("Real estate prices rose in 2004, causing middle-class citizens to move northwest of the city"). Without specific information from additional sources, inferences drawn from maps cannot be put in **context** and interpreted in more than a vague way.

Evaluating and Interpreting Other Graphic Formats

The type of information being conveyed guides the choice of **format**. Textual information and numeric information must be displayed with different techniques. Text-only information may be most easily summarized in a diagram or a timeline. If the text includes numeric information, it may be converted into a chart that shows the size of groups, connects ideas in a table or graphic, or shows information in a hybridized format. Numeric information is often most helpfully presented in tables or graphs. When information will be referred to and looked up again and again, tables are often most helpful for the reader. When the trends in the numeric information are more important than the numbers themselves, graphs are often the best choice. Information that is linked to the land and has a spatial component is best conveyed using maps.

Interpreting Charts and Tables

Charts used in social science are a visual representation of data. They combine graphic and textual elements to convey information in a concise format. Often, **charts** divide the space up in blocks, which are filled with text and/or pictures to convey a point. Charts are often organized in tabular form, where blocks below a heading all have information in common. Charts also divide information into conceptual, non-numeric groups (for example, "favorite color"), which are then plotted against a numerical axis (e.g., "number of students"). Charts should be labeled in such a way that a reader can locate a point on the chart and then consult the surrounding axes or table headings to understand how it compares to other points. **Tables** are a type of chart that divides textual information into rows and columns. Each row and column represent a characteristic of the information. For example, a table might be used to convey demographic information. The first column would provide "year," and the second would provide "population." Reading across the rows, one could see that in the year 1966, the population of Middletown was 53,847. Tracking the columns would show how frequently the population was counted.

Interpret Graphs and Diagrams

Graphs are similar to charts, except that they graphically show numeric information on both axes. For example, a **graph** might show population through the years, with years on the *x* axis and population on the *y* axis. One advantage of graphs is that the population during the time in between censuses can be estimated by locating that point on the graph. Each axis should be labeled to allow the information to be interpreted correctly, and the graph should have an informative title.

Diagrams are usually drawings that show the progression of events. The drawings can be fairly schematic, as in a flow chart, or they can be quite detailed, as in a depiction of scenes from a battle. Diagrams usually have arrows connecting the events or boxes shown. Each event or box should be labeled to show what it represents. Diagrams are interpreted by following the progression along the arrows through all events.

Using Timelines in Social Science

Timelines are used to show the relationships between people, places, and events. They are ordered chronologically and usually are shown left-to-right or top-to-bottom. Each event on the **timeline** is associated with a date, which determines its location on the timeline. On electronic resources, timelines often contain hyperlinks associated with each event. Clicking on the event's hyperlink will open a page with more information about the event. **Cause-and-effect relationships** can be observed on timelines, which often show a key event and then resulting events following in close succession. These can be helpful for showing the order of events in time or the relationships between similar events. They help make the passage of time a concrete concept and show that large periods pass between some events, while other events cluster very closely.

Using Political Cartoons in Social Science Studies

Political cartoons are drawings that memorably convey an opinion. These opinions may be supportive or critical and may summarize a series of events or pose a fictional situation that summarizes an attitude. **Political cartoons** are, therefore, secondary sources of information that provide social and cultural context about events. Political cartoons may have captions that help describe the action or put it in context. They may also have dialogue, labels, or other recognizable cultural symbols. For example, Uncle Sam frequently appears in political cartoons to represent the United States government. Political cartoons frequently employ caricatures to call attention to a situation or a person. The nature of the caricature helps show the cartoonist's attitude toward the issue being portrayed. Every element of the cartoon is included to support the artist's point and should be considered in the cartoon's interpretation. When interpreting political cartoons, students should examine what issue is being discussed, what elements the artist chose to support his or her point, and what the message is. Considering who might agree or disagree with the cartoon is also helpful in determining the message of the cartoon.

Analyzing Artifacts

Artifacts, or everyday objects used by previous cultures, are useful for understanding life in those cultures. Students should first discover, or be provided with, a **description** of the item. This description should depict what time period the **artifact** was used in and what culture used it. From that description and/or from examination of the artifact, students should be able to discuss what the artifact is, what it is made of, its potential uses, and the people who likely used it. They should then be able to draw **conclusions** from all these pieces of evidence about life in that culture. For example, analysis of coins from an early American archaeological site might show that settlers brought coins with them, or that some classes of residents were wealthy, or that trade occurred with many different nations. The interpretation will vary depending on the circumstances surrounding the artifact. Students should consider these circumstances when drawing conclusions.

Early America Through the Founding of the New Nation

Age of Exploration

Obstacles to Exploration by Europe Before 1400

Before 1400, few Europeans knew anything about the world. When **Christopher Columbus** read of the exploits of the Italian Marco Polo, however, he was inspired to seek out new trade routes. Also, **Prince Henry** of Portugal established a navigation institute that encouraged sailors to explore. For a long time, extended sea voyages were restricted by a lack of navigational and seafaring technology; the inventions of the compass, astrolabe, and caravel remedied this situation. There was also a high cost associated with long travels (around 1400); however, new monarchs in France, England, Spain, and Portugal decided that they were willing to pay a high price to get a piece of the spice trade. Finally, the question of a motive for exploration was answered by the increasing fervor for missionary work, as well as the economic necessity of developing new trade routes.

Age of Exploration

The Age of Exploration is also called the **Age of Discovery**. It is generally considered to have begun in the early 15th century and continued into the 17th century. Major developments of the Age of Exploration included **technological advances** in navigation, mapmaking, and shipbuilding. These advances led to expanded European exploration of the rest of the world. **Explorers** set out from several European countries, including Portugal, Spain, France, and England, seeking new routes to Asia. These efforts led to the discovery of new lands, as well as **colonization** in India, Asia, Africa, and North America.

Review Video: Age of Exploration
Visit mometrix.com/academy and enter code: 612972

Role of Economics in the Age of Exploration

At the same time that the Renaissance was reinvigorating European cultural life, a desire to explore the world abroad was growing. Indeed, the ability to make long voyages was facilitated by the advances in **navigational technology** made around this time. The main reason for exploration, though, was **economic**. Europeans had first been introduced to eastern goods during the Crusades, and the exploits of Marco Polo in the 13th century had further whetted the western appetite for contact with distant lands. This increasing focus on exploration and trade caused a general shift in the balance of power in Europe. Landlocked countries, like Germany, found that they were excluded from participating in the lucrative new economy. On the other hand, those countries which bordered the **Atlantic** (England, France, Spain, and Portugal) were the most powerful players.

Major European Explorers

Vasco da Gama was the first European to sail around the Cape of Good Hope, on the southern tip of what is now South Africa. This made it possible to reach Asia by boat. **Balboa** explored Central America and was the first European to view the Pacific Ocean. **Magellan** is remembered as the first to circumnavigate the globe. **Cortes** was a powerful commander who subjugated the Aztecs in what is now Mexico; he used great brutality to achieve his ends. **Pizarro**, like Cortes, was a conquistador; he conquered the Incas in what is now Peru. **Amerigo Vespucci**, from whose name the word

America was derived, mapped the Atlantic coast of South America and was able to convince stubborn Europeans that these lands were not a part of India.

Joint-Stock Companies at the Time of the Age of Exploration

As exploration created new opportunities for amassing wealth, **Portugal** enjoyed special favor because of its excellent location and cordial relations with many of the Muslim nations of North Africa. The ruler of Portugal at this time was even known as Prince Henry "the Navigator" (1394-1460). In order to solidify trade arrangements, European rulers began to think about colonizing foreign lands. In order to fund these expensive trips, a new kind of business known as the **joint-stock company** was developed. In a joint-stock company, a group of merchants would combine their resources to pay for the passage of a vessel. These groups would later be influential in securing colonial charters for many of their agents. One of the most powerful examples was the **Muscovy Company of England**, which controlled almost all trade with Russia.

Mercantilism at the Time of the Age of Exploration

As foreign trade became the most important part of every nation's economy, the economic theory of **mercantilism** became popular. According to mercantilism, a nation should never import more than it exports. Of course, it is impossible for every country to achieve this goal at the same time, so European countries were in fierce competition at all times. The solution that most nations pursued was to establish **colonies**, because these could supply resources for export by the mother country without really being considered imports. This rush to colonize had disastrous consequences for the indigenous peoples of the Americas and Africa. Europeans often looted the Native Americans for anything of value, and their need for cheap labor to cultivate the land there spawned the **African slave trade**.

First European Explorers in America

Although **Christopher Columbus** frequently gets credit for "discovering" America in 1492 (even though people were already living on the continent), **Vikings** from Scandinavia actually arrived in about AD 1000. These explorers constructed no permanent settlements, however, and did not remain for long. It was not until economic expansion in Europe made exploration worthwhile that explorers returned. Columbus and the explorers who would come later were looking for the **Northwest Passage** that would take them directly to Asia and were annoyed by the new land that kept getting in the way. Columbus died believing that he had landed in some outpost of India (hence, calling the natives "Indians").

Review Video: Christopher Columbus
Visit mometrix.com/academy and enter code: 496598

English Interest in the New World

The English lagged somewhat behind other European nations in exploration of the New World. Finally, however, a combination of economic and social incentives convinced them to look west. For one thing, the **enclosure movement** in England had made land very scarce, and the practice of **primogeniture** meant that only the eldest son could inherit the land. For these reasons, many Englishmen moved to the New World for the promise of cheap land. England also had a large population at this time, so the government viewed the New World as a good place to send criminals and beggars. Another reason for the increase in interest in America was the **Protestant Reformation**. Many English Catholics and Protestants felt alienated by the new Church of England and wanted to find a place in which they could worship more freely.

Early European Colonization

Settling of North America by the English

The first English attempt to found a colony in the New World was made by Sir Humphrey Gilbert in **Newfoundland** in 1583 and was a complete failure. Sir Walter Raleigh would lead two more failed attempts at founding a colony on **Roanoke Island** in 1586 and 1588. The second of these colonies is known as the **Lost Colony**, because it disappeared without a trace while Raleigh was gone. Finally, the British were able to establish a permanent colony at **Jamestown**, Virginia in 1607. The settlers in Jamestown came for gold and to convert the Natives to Christianity. One of the important events of the early years of Jamestown was the issuing of the Virginia Charter, which declared that English settlers in the New World would be treated as Englishmen with full English rights.

Review Video: Founding of Jamestown
Visit mometrix.com/academy and enter code: 881040

Virginia Colony

Beginnings

The English colony of **Virginia**, which began at Jamestown, was at first plagued by a poor location and a scarcity of skilled laborers. Captain **John Smith** was elected leader in 1608, and he proved to be the strict leader the colony needed to survive. A large proportion of the settlers would die during the winter of 1609-10. What finally saved the Virginia colony was the wild popularity of **tobacco**. In 1619, the **House of Burgesses** met, becoming the first legislative body to be formed in the New World. King James I of England correctly predicted that this would only lead to trouble for his nation. Later that year, 20 African indentured servants arrived on an English privateer with a Dutch letter of marque; Virginia would become the first colony to legalize **slavery**, in 1660.

Review Video: The English Colony of Virginia
Visit mometrix.com/academy and enter code: 537399

Royal Colony

Virginia officially became a **Royal Colony** in 1624. This was in part because the Virginia Company (the joint-stock company that had previously administered affairs) had gone bankrupt, and partly because King James I wanted to exercise more control. After the English Civil War of the 1640s, many of the supporters of the king, known as **cavaliers**, settled in Virginia. During this period, the wealthy colonists began claiming the coastal land and pushing the poor people farther inland, where they were prey to Native American attacks and were underrepresented in the House of Burgesses. Frustrated, a group of settlers led by **Nathaniel Bacon** burned Jamestown to the ground. **Bacon's Rebellion**, as it came to be known, was thought of by some as a harbinger of things to come.

New Netherlands Colony

The Dutch East India Company hired the English explorer **Henry Hudson** to search for the Northwest Passage to Asia. Instead, he journeyed up the Hudson River and claimed the area now known as **New York** for the Dutch. The Dutch purchased **Manhattan Island** from the Lenape Native Americans for $24 and established a town called **New Amsterdam** there, an aristocratic town, in which everyone had to be a member of the Dutch Reform Church. Eventually, in 1664, this Dutch settlement would be overwhelmed by the British colonies surrounding it. King Charles II gave the area to his successor, James, Duke of York, who quickly gave the town and colony the name it bears today.

Beginnings of English Colonies of Maryland, the Carolinas, and Georgia

Maryland was established in 1634 as a **proprietary colony**, meaning it was exclusively owned by one person. The owner, Lord Baltimore, ran his colony like a feudal estate. Maryland prospered because of tobacco and became a haven for persecuted Catholics. **North Carolina** was originally settled by Virginians and quickly acquired a reputation as independent and democratic. Many English colonists avoided North Carolina because they felt it was overrun by pirates. **South Carolina**, meanwhile, was a proprietary colony established in 1670. South Carolina hosted a large number of religious groups. **Georgia**, meanwhile, was a proprietary colony established in 1733. Its namesake, George II, hoped that it would be a buffer zone between the colonists and the Native Americans and populated it almost exclusively with criminals and debtors.

Southern Colonies

Economic Life

In the early days of the Southern colonies, most people lived on **small farms**. Although they made up a tiny part of the population, the owners of the **coastal plantations** wielded enormous power. These aristocrats typically grew a single crop on their lands; in North Carolina, Virginia, and Maryland, **tobacco** was the cash crop, while the large growers in South Carolina and Georgia favored **rice** and **indigo**. Plantations, like the feudal manors of the past, were almost totally self-sufficient units, although the owners imported most of their luxury items from England. The Southern colonies had the closest ties with England, mainly because England provided the market for their tobacco; crops grown in the colonies were sold back in England by agents (known as factors).

Review Video: The Southern Colonies
Visit mometrix.com/academy and enter code: 703830

Social Life

The social lives of the Southern colonists were filled with dancing, card-playing, cotillions, hunts, and large community dinners. Southerners were considered to be very optimistic in temperament, in contrast to their more dour Northern counterparts. It was extremely difficult to move up in the **social hierarchy** in the South; the richer colonists generally took the best land and thus were able to maintain their position in the economy and in the government, as the poor had to move away from the towns to find farmland. Because farming was the only available occupation, there were not any venues for ambitious men to distinguish themselves. North Carolina was generally considered to be the state with the least **social stratification**.

Life Expectancy and Education

The average man in the Southern colonies could expect to live **35 years**. This was in part due to disease; stagnant water and unfamiliar heat helped the spread of many contagions throughout the population, and malaria was a constant danger. In response to the high mortality rate, families tended to have lots of children. Also, **education** was not a high priority in the colonies in those days. One problem was that the population was too scattered for a central public school to be possible. Wealthy plantation owners would hire a **tutor** for their children, who might later be sent off to the College of William & Mary or one of the new schools up North: Harvard, Yale, or Princeton. For the less affluent, however, it was more likely that any education would be received as an **apprentice** of an experienced craftsman.

Religious and Political Life

In all of the Southern colonies, the **Anglican Church** was supported by taxes. Anyone who wanted to enter politics would have to be a member of the Church, though the majority of the colonists were not. In general, the Southern colonies had the greatest degree of **religious toleration**. Politics during this period were largely controlled by the planter aristocracy. Each Southern colony had a **governor** (chosen by the colony's English sponsor), a **governor's council**, and an **assembly** to represent the people. During the 1700s, these assemblies took more and more power away from the governors. In order to run for office, a man had to be a member of the Anglican Church; many people, including Thomas Jefferson, would acquire membership in the Church and then never set foot inside it again.

Beginning of Slave Trade

After periods in which Native Americans or indentured servants from England were used as laborers, most of the labor in the Southern British North American colonies was performed by **African slaves**. These slaves were taken in wars between African chieftains and then sold to European traders. Oftentimes, the African leaders would trade slaves for guns in order to protect themselves from other slave traders. Several African states, most notably the Yoruba and the Dahomey, became wealthy from this trade. The journey from West Africa to the West Indies was dangerous and depressing, and many slaves died en route. Before they were sold into the American colonies, slaves first worked in the brutal heat of the sugar plantations of the British West Indies. Only about half would survive long enough to see America.

Legalization of Slavery

Between 1640 and 1660, the Southern colonies slowly evolved from a system of servitude to one of **slavery**. In 1661, Virginia became the first colony to legalize **chattel slavery for life**, and made it such that the children of slaves would be slaves as well. The number of slaves increased dramatically in the 1680s after the **Royal African Company** lost its monopoly and the industry was thrown open to anyone. Virginia established **slave codes** to keep revolts down: slaves could not be taught to read, could not gather together, could not have weapons, and could not leave the plantation without written permission. Naturally, slaves often rebelled against their treatment, but they were outnumbered and overpowered.

Early Resistance to Slavery

Many slaves resisted submission, and many died as a result. For any serious offense, a slave would be executed in front of his or her peers as a deterrent. From its inception, there was **resistance** to slavery. In 1688, the **Quakers** declared that slavery was inhuman and a violation of the Bible. Many felt that slavery degraded both master and slave. In order to justify the hateful institution, slave owners declared that black people were less than human, or that, as descendants of the Biblical figure Ham, they were ordered by God to serve white people. The hymn "Amazing Grace" was written by guilt-wracked former slave trader **John Newton**. Slaves could only become free by proving mulatto (half white) status or by buying their freedom (some masters would allow their slaves to work for pay on the weekends).

Puritanism and the Pilgrims in Massachusetts Colony

Puritans believed in the idea of predestination, meaning that God has already chosen which people will get into heaven. In order to suggest to others (and to themselves) that they were among the elect, **Puritans** were obsessed with maintaining proper decorum in public. Those Puritans who wanted to fully separate from the Church of England were known as **Pilgrims** (or Separatists). The Pilgrims originally went to Holland, but after determining that they would be unable to make a good life there, they got permission from the Virginia Company to settle in the northern part of the

Virginia colony in 1620. The **Plymouth Company** was commissioned, and the **Mayflower** set sail. Because of storms and poor navigation, however, they ended up in the area that would come to be known as Massachusetts. One of the early moves of the group was to agree to the **Mayflower Compact**, whereby all members of the group would be bound to the will of the majority.

Review Video: The Mayflower Compact
Visit mometrix.com/academy and enter code: 275859

Puritans

The Puritans established the colony of **Massachusetts Bay** in 1630. They hoped to purify the **Church of England** and then return to Europe with a new and improved religion. The Massachusetts Bay Puritans were more immediately successful than other fledgling colonies because they brought enough supplies, arrived in the springtime, and had good leadership (including **John Winthrop**). Puritans fished, cut timber for ships, and trapped fur. The local government was inextricably bound with the Church; only Church members were allowed to vote for the **General Court** (similar to the House of Burgesses), although everyone was required to pay taxes. The Puritans established a **Bible Commonwealth** that would last 50 years. During this time, Old Testament law was the law of the community.

Political and Social Life in the Early Massachusetts Colonies

The **Massachusetts Bay Puritans** were known for religious intolerance and a general suspicion of democracy. Even though they had left England because of religious persecution, they did not set up their colony as a safe haven for others. One of the people who was kicked out of the colony for blasphemy was **Roger Williams**, who went on to found a colony at **Providence**. Williams taught that the colonists should be fair to the Native Americans and that political leaders should stay out of religion. Roger Williams eventually founded the **Baptist Church**. The Puritans generally felt that the common people were incapable of governing themselves and should be looked after by their government. Also, many Puritans objected to democracy because they felt it was inefficient.

English Civil War and the New England Confederation

During the English Civil War, the Puritans tried to separate from the Church of England; they issued the **Body of Liberties**, which stated that the Massachusetts Bay was independent of England and was therefore no longer bound by English Civil Law, that there could be no arbitrary governors appointed to dissolve a local legislature, and that town meetings of qualified voters would be held to discuss local issues. Later, in 1643, a **New England Confederation** was formed, consisting of Massachusetts Bay, New Plymouth, Connecticut River Valley, and New Haven. The goals of this confederation were to protect the colonists from the French (in Canada) and the Native Americans, to safeguard their commercial interests from the Dutch in New Netherlands (later New York), and to return runaway slaves.

Dominion of New England

The impertinence of the **Massachusetts Bay colony** was a constant annoyance to **King Charles II** and he thus punished them by granting charters to rival colonies in Connecticut and Rhode Island and by creating the **Dominion of New England**. The purpose of this organization was to boost trade by enforcing the **Navigation Acts** of 1660 and 1663, which stated that all trade had to be done on English ships and had to pass through England before it could go anywhere else. The English, of course, made the colonists pay a tax on any exports that were not bound for England. The colonists loathed the Dominion government, not only because of its economic penalties but because it tried to promote the Anglican Church in America. A rebellion against the Dominion probably would have occurred if the **Glorious Revolution** in England had not ended it prematurely.

Review Video: The Massachusetts Bay Colony
Visit mometrix.com/academy and enter code: 407058

Land, Demography, Climate, Economics, and Slavery in Puritan Life

The **land** settled by the Puritans was rocky and bare, and it took tremendous labor to subsist off of its products. Massachusetts had an extremely homogenous **population**, mainly because there was little reason to stay there other than to be among people of the same faith. Non-Puritan immigrants usually moved south, where the soil was better and the population was more tolerant. Because agriculture was so tricky, a more diverse **economy** developed in New England than existed in the South. Puritans engaged in fishing and trapping, and there were a number of craftsmen in each town. There were **slaves** in New England, though not nearly as many as in the South. Furthermore, slaves in New England were more commonly used as household servants than hard laborers.

Social and Religious Life of the Puritans

There was more chance for **social mobility** in Massachusetts than in any other colony in America. This was mainly due to the diverse economy. As for religion, it dominated every area of an individual's life. The Puritan Church was known as the **Congregational Church**; at first, this was an exclusive group, but it gradually became easier to become a member. Indeed, by the mid-1600s, religious fervor seemed to be waning in Massachusetts. A group called the **Jeremiads** warned the people that they were in danger of lapsing into atheism, but many people did not mind. Around this time, ministers began to offer **half-way covenants**, which gave church members partial privileges.

Salem Witch Trials

During the 1690s in New England, there was still a strong belief in **Christian mysticism**. Many people were paranoid about spiritualists and mediums. This, combined with perhaps some local feuds, led to 19 women and one man being executed for **witchcraft** in 1692. Most likely, however, the accused individuals were only suffering from delusions caused by a kind of hallucinogenic bread mold (ergot). The witch trials only stopped when people in high places began being accused. The **Salem witch trials** tarnished the image of the clergy for a long time and further contributed to a general relaxation of religious fervor in this period.

Pennsylvania Colony, Quakers, and The Charter of Liberties

The Pennsylvania (literally "Penn's woods") colony was established by **William Penn** in 1681. Penn declared that the colony would provide religious and political freedom for all. The main religious group to settle in the area was the **Society of Friends** (Quakers). Quakers believed that every person could communicate with the divine, that the church should not be supported by tax dollars, and that all men are equal. The Quakers have always been pacifists, and they were the first group to oppose slavery. In Pennsylvania, voting rights were extended only to landholders or large taxpayers. The **Charter of Liberties** (1701) established a unicameral legislature working alongside a governor.

The Great Awakening

The Great Awakening was a religious revival in New England in the 1730s and 40s. It began in response to the growing secularism and was aided by the recent migrations into the cities, where it was easier for large crowds to form. **Jonathan Edwards** was one of the most famous preachers of this time. The **Great Awakening** was the first mass movement in America; it helped break down the divides between the various regions of the British colonies and led to the formation of some new Protestant denominations. Though the Revivalists did not directly advocate the abolition of slavery, they did suggest that there was divinity in all creation and that, therefore, black people were worthy of being converted to Christianity.

Bible Commonwealth and Political and Intellectual Life in New England

The New England colonies started out as **Bible Commonwealths**, where Biblical law was local law, and a man's standing in the church determined his political power. Over time, however, New England became more liberal, and politics came to be dominated by the **wealthy men** rather than by the church leaders. Life expectancy in the New England colonies became roughly what it is today. **Education** was valued greatly in New England, and the fact that most people lived close to a town made it possible for more people to receive inexpensive training. Puritans believed that ignorance of God's word could lead one to be tricked by the devil, and thus they made sure that all of their children learned to read.

Middle Colonies

Economic Life, Slavery, and Society

The **Middle Colonies** (New York, Pennsylvania, Delaware, East and West New Jersey) shared characteristics with both New England and the Southern colonies. The **economy** was diverse, though less so than in New England. Shipping and commerce would gradually become crucial in the port cities of Philadelphia and New York. There were plenty of **slaves** in the Middle Colonies, most of whom served as laborers on ships. The Dutch treated their slaves well; the English did not. People in these colonies tended to have a healthier lifestyle than their neighbors to the south, and therefore they tended to live longer. The diverse economy made **social mobility** possible, though large landowners were for the most part entrenched in positions of power.

Education, Religion, and Politics

Most education in the Middle Colonies was received as an **apprentice** to a successful craftsman. Often, local churches would maintain schools during the week. The two main religious organizations in this region were the **Anglican Church** and the **Dutch Reform Church**, often at each other's throat because they were competing for members and tax dollars. A typical government in the Middle Colonies had a **governor**, a governor's council, and a **representative assembly**. Men were only allowed to vote if they owned property. The Middle Colonies had the most diverse population, mainly because they had available land and promised religious freedom (at least in Pennsylvania).

Events Leading to and During the Revolutionary Period

Significance of the French and Indian Wars

The **British defeat of the Spanish Armada** in 1588 led to the decline of Spanish power in Europe. This, in turn, led the British and French into battle several times between 1689 and 1748. These wars were:

- King William's War, or the Nine Years War, 1689-1697. This war was fought largely in Flanders.
- The War of Spanish Succession, or Queen Anne's War, 1702-1713
- War of Austrian Succession, or King George's War, 1740-1748

The fourth and final war, the **French and Indian War** (1754-1763), was fought largely in the North American territory and resulted in the end of France's reign as a colonial power in North America. Although the French held many advantages, including more cooperative colonists and numerous Native American allies, the strong leadership of **William Pitt** eventually led the British to victory. Costs incurred during the wars eventually led to discontent in the colonies and helped spark the **American Revolution**.

Review Video: French and Indian Wars
Visit mometrix.com/academy and enter code: 502183

Navigation Acts

The Navigation Acts, enacted in 1651, were an attempt by Britain to dominate international trade. Aimed largely at the Dutch, the acts banned foreign ships from transporting goods to the British colonies and from transporting goods to Britain from elsewhere in Europe. While the restrictions on trade angered some colonists, these acts were helpful to other American colonists who, as members of the British Empire, were legally able to provide ships for Britain's growing trade interests and use the ships for their own trading ventures. By the time the French and Indian War had ended, one-third of British merchant ships were built in the American colonies. Many colonists amassed fortunes in the shipbuilding trade.

Triangular Trade

Triangular trade began in the colonies with ships setting off for **Africa**, carrying rum. In Africa, the rum was traded for gold or slaves. Ships then went from Africa to the **West Indies**, trading slaves for sugar, molasses, or money. To complete the triangle, the ships returned to the **colonies** with sugar or molasses to make more rum, as well as stores of gold and silver. This trade triangle violated the Molasses Act of 1733, which required the colonists to pay high duties to Britain on molasses acquired from French, Dutch, and Spanish colonies. The colonists ignored these duties, and the British government adopted a policy of salutary neglect by not enforcing them.

Review Video: The Triangular Trade
Visit mometrix.com/academy and enter code: 415470

Acts of British Parliament that Occurred After the French and Indian Wars

After the French and Indian Wars, the British Parliament passed four major acts:

1. The **Sugar Act**, 1764—this act not only required taxes to be collected on molasses brought into the colonies but gave British officials the right to search the homes of anyone suspected of violating it.
2. The **Stamp Act**, 1765—this act taxed printed materials such as newspapers and legal documents. Protests led the Stamp Act to be repealed in 1766, but the repeal also included the Declaratory Act, which stated that Parliament had the right to govern the colonies.
3. The **Quartering Act**, 1765—this act required colonists to provide accommodations and supplies for British troops. In addition, colonists were prohibited from settling west of the Appalachians until given permission by Britain.
4. The **Townshend Acts**, 1767—these acts taxed paper, paint, lead, and tea that came into the colonies. Colonists led boycotts in protest, and in Massachusetts leaders like Samuel and John Adams began to organize resistance against British rule.

Britain's Taxation of the American Colonies After the French and Indian War

The French and Indian War created circumstances for which the British desperately needed more revenue. These needs included:

- Paying off the war debt
- Defending the expanding empire
- Governing Britain's 33 far-flung colonies, including the American colonies

To meet these needs, the British passed additional laws, increasing revenues from the colonies. Because they had spent so much money to defend the American colonies, the British felt it was appropriate to collect considerably higher **taxes** from them. The colonists felt this was unfair, and many were led to protest the increasing taxes. Eventually, protest led to violence.

Effects of New Laws on British-Colonial Relations

While earlier revenue-generating acts such as the Navigation Acts brought money to the colonists, the new laws after 1763 required colonists to pay money back to **Britain**. The British felt this was fair since the colonists were British subjects and since they had incurred debt protecting the Colonies. The colonists felt it was not only unfair but illegal.

The development of **local government** in America had given the colonists a different view of the structure and role of government. This made it difficult for the British to understand the colonists' protests against what the British felt was a fair and reasonable solution to the mother country's financial problems.

Factors that Led to Increasing Discontent in the American Colonies

More and more colonists were born on American soil, decreasing any sense of kinship with the far-away British rulers. Their new environment had led to new ideas of government and a strong view of the colonies as a separate entity from Britain. Colonists were allowed to **self-govern** in domestic issues, but **Britain** controlled international issues. In fact, the American colonies were largely left to form their own local government bodies, giving them more freedom than any other colonial territory. This gave the colonists a sense of **independence**, which led them to resent control from Britain. Threats during the French and Indian War led the colonists to call for unification in order to protect themselves.

George Grenville and the Proclamation of 1763

George Grenville became the prime minister of Britain in 1763, and immediately abandoned the policy of "salutary neglect" that had been upheld by the former prime minister Robert Walpole. On the contrary, he asserted that the American colonists should have to pay for British military protection, even though the Americans claimed not to need it. According to the **Proclamation of 1763**, all American colonists were to stay east of the Appalachian Mountains. This policy was ostensibly created in order to protect the colonists in the wake of **Chief Pontiac's Rebellion** in 1763, in which Native Americans attacked colonists and were subsequently slaughtered by the British. Many colonists, however, felt that the Proclamation was a transparent attempt to maintain British control of the fur trade.

Sugar (Revenue) Act, Currency Act, and the Quartering Act

The Sugar (Revenue) Act of 1764 established a duty on basically any products that were not British in origin (e.g., molasses, indigo, and sugar). Unlike the Molasses Act, the **Sugar Act** was fully enforced. Most colonists resented this taxation, which they felt was used to fund the French and Indian War. The **Currency Act of 1764** forbade colonists from issuing paper money and stated that all taxes paid to England must be paid in gold and silver rather than paper. This act eliminated the worthless Continental Dollar. The **Quartering Act of 1765** required colonists to provide bedding and food to the regiments of British soldiers in America. This regulation increased paranoia amongst the colonists, who began to wonder exactly why the British soldiers were there in the first place.

STAMP ACT OF 1765

The Stamp Act of 1765 was levied without the consent of the colonists. It specified that a stamp must be applied to all legal documents (there was considerable debate over the definition of this phrase) indicating that a tax had been paid for the defense of the colonies. This act was extremely unpopular, perhaps most because its presence was so visible; its implementation generated loud cries of "**taxation without representation**." The British responded by claiming that the colonists had "virtual representation" by members of Parliament. The colonists continued to claim that they needed direct and actual representation, although many feared that even if they were to get it, they would probably lose most votes anyway.

STAMP ACT CONGRESS, THE SONS OF LIBERTY, AND THE DECLARATORY ACT

In 1765, the colonists created the Stamp Act Congress in New York in order to peacefully resolve the conflicts created by the Stamp Act. This group established the **Non-importation Agreements**, which amounted to a boycott of English products. At the same time, the **Sons of Liberty** in Boston were running amok: vandalizing British goods, tarring and feathering stamp collectors, and erecting so-called "liberty poles," from which collectors would be hung by their pants. In 1766, the new British prime minister **Rockingham** repealed the Stamp Act because the boycotts were damaging the British economy. In part to punish the colonists for their insubordination, in 1766 the British Parliament issued the **Declaratory Act**, which asserted that they had the right to legislate on behalf of the colonists at any time.

TOWNSHEND ACTS

The Townshend Acts, named after Charles "Champagne Charlie" Townshend, the prime minister of Britain from 1766-72, placed an indirect tax on household items coming into the colonies and tightened the custom duties. The Acts also called for stricter vice-admiralty courts and established the **Writs of Assistance**, which were essentially blank search warrants. The colonists' response to the Townshend Acts was twofold: a **pamphlet war** was waged by men like John Dickinson, James Otis, and Samuel Adams, and there were also more violent protests, as for instance the **Boston Massacre**, in which a mob in the Boston Commons was fired on by the British, perhaps accidentally. Colonists used the "Massacre" as a rallying cry, and the Townshend Acts were repealed (with the notable exception of the tax on tea).

LORD NORTH, THE GASPEE, THE COMMITTEES OF CORRESPONDENCE, AND JOHN WILKES

Lord North succeeded Townshend as British prime minister in 1772. In this year, the Sons of Liberty set fire to the **Gaspee**, a British revenue ship, off the coast of Rhode Island. The Sons of Liberty were driven to further violence by Massachusetts governor Tom Hutchinson's announcement that his salary would be paid by the British. The **Committees of Correspondence** were subsequently formed to organize the protest against the British and to keep colonists informed on British matters. At around this time, the British MP **John Wilkes** became a folk hero in the colonies because of his impassioned speeches in defense of liberty. Although Wilkes never spoke directly on behalf of the colonists, he was jailed for his speeches.

First Continental Congress

The First Continental Congress was held September 5, 1774, and was attended by a representative of every colony except Georgia. This Congress issued the **Suffolk Resolves**, stating that they would give Boston aid in the form of food and clothing, but would not take up arms on behalf of Boston. The **Continental Association**, an agreement not to buy or sell English goods, was formed. A conservative named Joseph Galloway advocated the creation of a **Council of All Colonies**, a legislative body which would share power with Parliament. The **Galloway Plan** was nixed by Massachusetts, however, because that colony refused to share power with any British authority. Massachusetts at this time was in a highly volatile state.

Coercive (Intolerable) Acts

The Coercive Acts, known as the **Intolerable Acts** in America, were issued in response to the Boston Tea Party and had several parts. The **Boston Port Act** closed the port down, supposedly until the destroyed tea was paid for, although this never happened. The **Massachusetts Government Act** put the colony under martial law. A military governor, Thomas Gage, was placed in charge of the colony. The **Administration of Justice Act** required that all judges, soldiers, and tax agents be English and that all crimes be tried in England. The **New Quartering Act** asserted that British soldiers were allowed to enter private homes and demand lodging. The **Quebec Act of 1774** declared that everything west of the Appalachians was Quebec; although this was basically done so that Britain could govern more effectively, it caused speculation among the colonists that the British were going to sell America to the French.

Thomas Gage and Paul Revere

Thomas Gage, the military governor of Massachusetts, was under increasing duress at the beginning of 1775 and asked the British government for either 20,000 more troops or a repeal of the Coercive Acts. Instead, Britain sent 2,000 troops, which **Gage** used to collect guns, gunpowder, and shot. On April 18 of 1775, the British troops sailed across Boston Harbor toward the large stockpile at Concord. **Paul Revere** then took his famous ride to warn the other colonists about the approach of the British. Although Revere was captured, his ride was finished by Samuel Prescott and William Dawes. On the way to Concord, in Lexington, shots were fired and 8 colonial militiamen were killed. The British then moved on to Concord, where the real fighting began.

Second Continental Congress

The Second Continental Congress was held May 10, 1775, in Philadelphia. **George Washington** became the commander of the Americans, mainly because it was felt that he would be able to bring the Southern colonies into the fold. This Congress also drew up the **Olive Branch petition**, a peace offering made to the King of England. The **Articles of Confederation** were drawn up here; their emphasis on states' rights proved to be a poor setup for organizing a comprehensive military strategy. This Congress created the **Committees of Safety**, a system for training community militias. This Congress created a bureaucracy for the purpose of organizing a navy and raising money. Finally, it was here that the colonists formally declared **independence**.

Review Video: The First and Second Continental Congress
Visit mometrix.com/academy and enter code: 835211

Reasons for Declaring Independence

At the time that the Declaration of Independence was issued, many colonists were opposed to complete separation from England. Many of them still considered themselves Englishmen and were afraid to be branded as traitors. They also realized that they were in uncharted waters; no revolt had ever been successful in winning independence. Finally, many colonists feared that even if they were successful in winning independence, the result would be chaos in America. The minds of many of these reluctant colonists were changed, however, by the **Battle of Bunker Hill**, which was won by the British. After this battle, King George II declared that the colonists were in a state of rebellion. Furthermore, the British labeled the members of the **Second Continental Congress** as traitors and ignored the **Olive Branch petition**. Confused colonists were further flamed by the British use of Hessian mercenary soldiers. The writings of **Thomas Paine** also converted many colonists to the revolutionary cause.

Declaration of Independence

The Declaration of Independence was proposed at the **Second Continental Congress** by Richard Henry Lee, and was composed by a committee of Franklin, Jefferson, John Adams, Robert Livingston, and Roger Sherman. The document has three parts: a **preamble** and reasons for separation; a **theory of government**; and a formal **declaration of war**. Jefferson attempted to have it include a condemnation of slavery, but was rebuffed. The Declaration had many aims: to enlist help from other British colonies; to create a cause for which to fight; to motivate reluctant colonists; to ensure that captured Americans would be treated as prisoners of war; and to establish an American theory of government. In fulfilling this last purpose, Jefferson borrowed heavily from Enlightenment thinkers like Montesquieu, Rousseau, and Locke, asserting famously that "all men are created equal."

Review Video: Declaration of Independence
Visit mometrix.com/academy and enter code: 256838

Significance

The issuing of the Declaration of Independence had effects both on the Revolutionary War and on world history at large. As far as its immediate effects, it changed the war in America from a war for liberty to a war for independence, by rhetorically **emancipating** America from Britain. It also opened a path for the **French Revolution** a few years later, one motivated by the principles expressed in the Declaration. Revolutions in South America, Africa, and Asia have also used the Declaration of Independence as inspiration. In the subsequent history of the United States, the document would be used by **abolitionists** as an argument against slavery and by **suffragists** as an argument for the right of women to vote.

Saratoga Campaign

The British military plan during the early stages of the Revolutionary War was known as the **Saratoga campaign** (or the German Plan). It called for a three-pronged attack aimed at capturing New York and thus separating the Northeast from the Southern colonies. This plan broke down because of the following reasons: One of the generals, Howe, was supposed to go up the Hudson River to Albany, but instead decided to go after Philadelphia. Another general, Burgoyne, was able to conquer Fort Ticonderoga, but then languished without supplies for months, and eventually had to surrender to colonial troops. The third general, St. Ledger, made considerable progress across New York from Lake Ontario but lost steam after a series of small battles.

Battle of Saratoga

The colonial General Gates defeated the British General Burgoyne at the **Battle of Saratoga** in 1777. This defeat confirmed the failure of the British Saratoga Campaign. More importantly, perhaps, it convinced the French that the Americans could win the war. The French then signed the **Treaty of Alliance** in 1778, which supplied the Americans with money, men, and ships. This treaty was in part negotiated by Benjamin Franklin. The French were not necessarily motivated by a spirit of goodwill towards the Americans; they hoped to gain back the territory they had lost in the French and Indian War. Moreover, the French believed that by aiding the Americans in the Revolutionary War they could position themselves to colonize parts of North America as yet unclaimed.

Southern Campaign in the Revolutionary War

The British military campaign in the **Southern colonies** was planned by Sir Henry Clinton and implemented by General Cornwallis in the years 1778 to 1781. Cornwallis quickly took **Savannah** and **Charleston** and then moved into the interior of South Carolina. Here and in North Carolina, a series of bloody battles (many of them against the great American general Nathaniel Greene) weakened Cornwallis and forced him to make a supply run to **Yorktown** on the Virginia coast. There, the British suffered a naval defeat at the hands of the French and then were routed by Washington-led troops. During their retreat, the British naval forces were further weakened by a violent storm, and Cornwallis was forced to **surrender** on October 17, 1781.

Legacy of the Revolutionary War

After the conclusion of the Revolutionary War, neither the Proclamation of 1763 nor the Quebec Act applied, and thus colonists could **move west** across the Appalachians. A few British loyalists lost their land. After the war, many states moved to separate the church and state; in Virginia, for instance, Thomas Jefferson wrote the **Virginia Statute of Religious Freedom**, creating total separation in that state. States also revised the **Criminal Codes**, in an effort to make the punishment more closely fit the crime. Finally, whereas in 1750 most citizens did not question the institution of slavery, by 1780 many states began to examine this policy. Vermont was the first state to **abolish slavery**. Meanwhile, Southern states argued that the war would not have been won without slave labor.

Review Video: The American Revolutionary War
Visit mometrix.com/academy and enter code: 935282

Development of the American Political System

Articles of Confederation

The Articles of Confederation were largely ineffective because they gave too much power to the states and too little to a central government. Many historians now say that the best thing about the **Articles** was that they showed the authors of the Constitution what to avoid. Part of the Articles was the **Land Ordinance of 1785**, a plan created by Jefferson for dividing the Western land into organized townships. The sale of land in these territories helped generate money for the new government. The **Northwest Ordinance of 1787** divided the land above the Ohio River into five territories, which would soon become states. This ordinance would become the model for how all future states would be formed.

Foreign Affairs

Both the Americans and the British violated the terms of the **Treaty of Paris**, which had ended the Revolutionary War in 1783. The British, for instance, never fully abandoned their lucrative fur trade in the Ohio Valley. Americans, on the other hand, never paid back their pre-war debts. Meanwhile, the Spanish (who controlled Louisiana and Florida) openly challenged American borders in the South, at times encouraging Native Americans to make war on the fledgling nation. Americans sought the right of deposit on the Mississippi; that is, the right to load material from a boat to a dock. The Spanish were not quick to grant this right. Meanwhile, American ships were forced to pay tribute to the Barbary states in order to trade in the Mediterranean.

Debt, Passing Legislation, Law Enforcement, the Court System, and Inflation and Depreciation

After the Revolutionary War, the United States found itself in a massive and troubling **debt**. Meanwhile, Congress was having great difficulty passing any **legislation** because in order to be made into law, a bill had to receive 9 of 13 votes, and there were often fewer than 10 representatives present. The government had no **chief executive** and thus law enforcement was left to the states. Another major problem was that the lack of a **central court system** made it hard to resolve disputes between citizens from different states, or between the states themselves. Congress did not have the power to **tax** the people directly, and could only request funds. Furthermore, although Congress could issue **currency**, it had no authority to keep the states from issuing currency of their own, so wild inflation and depreciation were common.

Competing Currencies and Legislative Troubles

Under the Articles of Confederation, Congress did not have the power to raise an **army** directly; it could only ask for troops from the states. The problems with this arrangement were amply demonstrated by **Shay's Rebellion** in Massachusetts in 1786 and 1787. This rebellion was in part a response to the economic uncertainty by competing currencies. Under the Articles, Congress did not have the power to regulate interstate or foreign commerce. Each state in the confederation had different tariffs and trade regulations, and no foreign countries would enter into trade agreements with a nation so disorganized. In short, the **Articles of Confederation** left America unable to maintain order at home, unable to gain respect abroad, and unable to improve its economy.

Philadelphia Convention of 1787

Although 55 delegates attended the **Philadelphia Convention of 1787**, only 39 signed the Constitution that emerged from this gathering. The attendees at the convention were exclusively rich men, but were all well-qualified to construct a new government. George Washington presided over the convention, and James Madison (the "father of the Constitution") served as secretary. The **representation** afforded to the people, as well as to states of different sizes, was a contentious issue throughout. Finally, in what is known as the **Great Compromise**, it was decided that the **lower house** (House of Representatives) would be chosen by the people, and the **upper house** (Senate) would be chosen by the state legislature. This convention also produced the **3/5 compromise**, whereby each slave was to be counted as 3/5 of a person. A 20-year moratorium was placed on the slave trade as well. Finally, it was decided at the convention that Congress should have control of commerce and tariffs.

Constitution

On September 17, 1787, the **Constitution** was presented to the people of the states. This document has three parts: a **preamble**, 7 **articles** outlining the powers and responsibilities of the 3 branches of government, and a section of **amendments**, the first ten of which are known as the **Bill of Rights**. The Constitution contains no bills of attainder, meaning that individuals cannot be denied life, liberty, and property without a trial. It does contain the concept of habeas corpus, meaning that arrested individuals must be charged with a crime within 72 hours. Federal judges are to be chosen for life, and there is an electoral college to select the president. In order to be in the House of Representatives, individuals had to be land-owning white males. The Constitution is famous for its system of **checks and balances** whereby the president can veto Congress, but Congress can override the veto with a 2/3 vote, and the courts can call the acts of either body "unconstitutional."

Ratification Process, Federalists, and Anti-Federalists

In order for the Constitution to take effect, it had to be **ratified** by ¾ of the states. The **Federalists** were those in favor of the Constitution. They were primarily wealthy men who lived along the coast and wanted the commercial protection afforded by a strong federal government. **Anti-Federalists**, on the other hand, were mainly small farmers and artisans who felt that the Constitution was not truly democratic and would erode the power both of the states and of individuals. The Anti-Federalists wanted a Constitution that allowed for annual elections, a standing army, and a Federal fortress. They also disapproved of the atheism of the document. Unfortunately for the Anti-Federalists, the superior organization of the Federalists helped the Constitution become ratified, despite the fact that most Americans were opposed to it.

Beginning of the Federalist Period and the Judiciary Act of 1789

After the ratification of the Constitution, **George Washington** was inaugurated as the first **president** in New York City. He immediately went outside the Constitution to form the first **Cabinet**: Thomas Jefferson, Secretary of State; Alexander Hamilton, Secretary of the Treasury; Henry Knox, Secretary of War; Edmund Randolph, Attorney General; and Samuel Osgood, Postmaster General. With the **Judiciary Act of 1789**, it was decided that there would be six justices and one chief justice on the Supreme Court. This act also established the federal court system and gave the Supreme Court original jurisdiction to issue writs of mandamus. The clause allowing the Supreme Court to issue writs of mandamus was later ruled unconstitutional in the case of ***Marbury v. Madison*** (1803), thereby establishing the doctrine of judicial review. **Judicial review** gives federal courts the authority to ensure state or national legislation does not violate the Constitution.

Hamilton's Funding and Economic Plan for the Financial System

The United States was born with $80 million in debt. **Alexander Hamilton**, however, was not terribly concerned by this; on the contrary, he encouraged **credit** as a means of financing the rapid capital improvements that would aid economic expansion. Hamilton introduced a **funding process**, whereby the government would buy back government bonds at full price in order to place money into the economy. Unfortunately, word of this plan leaked to some speculators, who bought the bonds at reduced rates and made huge profits. This led to accusations of a conspiracy. Another aspect of Hamilton's economic plan was for the federal government to **assume state debts**. This was done in part to tie state governments to the national government.

Custom Duties, Excise Taxes, and Federal Banks

In order to pay off the national debt, Hamilton promoted the **Revenue Act of 1789**, which was ostensibly a tax on imports, though it amounted to very little. Hamilton hoped to appease American industry with this measure without alienating foreign interests. The **Whiskey Tax**, instituted in 1791, was another attempt to generate revenue. This tax was wildly unpopular, however, and Washington was forced to call in several state militias to deal with various uprisings. At this time, Hamilton was also trying to establish a national bank, based upon the Bank of England. The **Bank of America** was established with $10 million in capital and aimed to repay foreign debts, provide a uniform national currency, aid in the collection of taxes, make loans, and act as a federal depository.

Foreign Diplomacy Under Washington

The United States stayed **neutral** during the wars of the French Revolution, even issuing a proclamation to that effect in 1793. Meanwhile, the British were constantly testing this neutrality: they did not leave their posts in the Northwest, they seized American ships and forced American sailors into service, and they frequently aided the Native Americans in their conflicts with the United States. This conflict eventually led to the **Jay Treaty** in 1794, which made the Spanish fear an Anglo-American alliance, causing them to become more willing to discuss American use of the

Mississippi River. **Pinckney's Treaty**, also known as the **Treaty of San Lorenzo** (1795), gave the United States free use of both the Mississippi and the city of New Orleans.

Jay Treaty

The Jay Treaty of 1794 aimed to calm the post-revolution conflicts between Britain and the United States. In it, the British promised to leave their forts in the Northwest and to pay for all the recent damages to ships. The British also allowed the US to form a limited commercial treaty with the British West Indies. The **Jay Treaty** asserted that the rivers and lakes of North America could be used by both Britain and the United States. However, the treaty made no provisions for any future seizures of American ships and made no mention of Native American attacks on the American frontier. The Southern states were annoyed that the treaty won no compensation for slaves freed during the Revolutionary War, and, moreover, stipulated that Southerners had to repay their pre-war debts. The controversy surrounding the Jay Treaty led to the formation of the first **political parties**.

Rise of the First Political Parties

Unlike a faction, which exists in order to achieve a single goal, a **political party** endures beyond the accomplishment of a specific goal. The first two political parties in the United States were the **Federalists** and the **Democratic-Republicans**. **Hamilton** is the primary figure associated with the Federalists, who were wealthy northeasterners in support of a strong central government and a loose interpretation of the Constitution. The Federalists advocated a strong president, the economic policies implemented by Hamilton, and a strong relationship with the British. The Democratic-Republicans, on the other hand, were associated with the so-called "common man" of the South and West. Led by **Jefferson** and **Madison**, they advocated a limited central government, a strict interpretation of the Constitution, a close relationship with France, and closely restricted government spending.

Washington's Farewell Address and Presidential Accomplishments

In 1796, Washington decided he was too tired to continue as president. In his famous **Farewell Address**, he implored the United States to avoid three things: permanent alliances, political factions, and sectionalism. Washington felt that the nation could only be successful if people placed the nation ahead of their own region. For his own part, Washington made some significant improvements during his presidency. He avoided war at a time when the nation was vulnerable. He also avoided political alliances and promoted the national government without alienating great numbers of people. Washington oversaw Hamilton's creation of the economic system and guided expansion to the west (as well as the creation of three new states: Vermont, Kentucky, and Tennessee).

Election of Adams and Conflict with the French

John Adams became the second president of the United States in the election of 1796; his opponent, **Thomas Jefferson**, became vice president because he received the second-most electoral votes. Adams was immediately confronted by the French, who were angry about the **Jay Treaty** and the broken **Treaty of Alliance of 1778**. After the French began destroying American ships, Adams sent American diplomats to meet with the French ambassador **Talleyrand**, who demanded tribute and then snubbed the Americans. There followed an undeclared naval war between 1798 and 1800, during which, the American military grew rapidly, warships were built, and the Department of the Navy was established. Finally, at the **Convention of 1800**, the Treaty of Alliance of 1778 was torn up and it was agreed in this new **Treaty of Mortefontaine** that the Americans would pay for damages done to their ships by the French, among a host of other clauses, including each country giving the other Most Favored Nation trade status.

Domestic Events Under Adams

The Alien and Sedition Acts were established in 1798, in part because of xenophobia arising from conflict with the French. The **Alien Act** increased the number of years before one could obtain citizenship, gave the president the power to deport anyone, and allowed the president to jail dangerous aliens during times of war. The **Sedition Act** made it a crime to libel or slander US officials or policies; many people believed this policy was a violation of First Amendment rights. The **Virginia and Kentucky Resolves**, promoted by Jefferson and Madison, stated that a contract exists between the state and national governments, but that the national government had exceeded its authority and broken the contract. This document advocated that states should have the power of nullification over national policies; only Virginia and Kentucky supported this policy, which had the potential to fatally undermine the Constitution.

Review Video: The Alien and Sedition Acts
Visit mometrix.com/academy and enter code: 633780

Expansion, Civil War, and Reconstruction

Major Events in Virginia and US History during the First Half of the Nineteenth Century

Federalist Period

The **Federalist period** had some remarkable successes and some bitter failures. It saw the establishment of the national bank and the Treasury system under Hamilton. The United States, amazingly, was able to pay off all of its debt during this period. The **Federalist administration** can also be credited with maintaining international neutrality, establishing the Pinckney Treaty, crushing the Whiskey Rebellion, and getting the British out of their northwest posts. On the other hand, over time, the Federalists became known as an elitist party, and the Alien and Sedition Acts were very unpopular. The Jay Treaty was seen as a diplomatic failure by most Americans, and in general, the Federalists were not able to maintain very cordial relations with Europe (especially France).

Election of 1800

In the election of 1800, the **Federalists** were represented by John Adams and C. C. Pinckney, and the **Democratic-Republicans** by Thomas Jefferson and Aaron Burr. The Federalists had been weakened both by the unpopularity of the Alien and Sedition Acts and the internal feud between Adams and Hamilton. They therefore focused their campaign on Jefferson, accusing him of being an atheist, of stealing money from the poor, and of having an affair with a slave. In the election, Jefferson finished with the same number of electoral votes as his supposed running mate, Burr, who surprisingly refused to concede. This situation led to the **12th amendment**, which states that a candidate must stipulate his desired office. **Jefferson** finally won the tie-breaking vote in the House of Representatives, sweeping the Federalists out of office.

Aaron Burr

After losing his challenge for the presidency in 1800, **Aaron Burr** was left out of the 1804 election and became embittered. He then lost a bid for the governorship of New York, in part because of the mudslinging of **Alexander Hamilton**. At this point, Burr began to toy with the idea of forming a new country in the West. Hamilton, hearing of this plan, informed Jefferson. Burr promptly challenged Hamilton to a **duel**, and in 1806 killed him at Weehawken, NJ. Burr headed west and planned to start a new country in Louisiana and the areas controlled by Spain. Jefferson formally charged Burr with treason, but, citing executive privilege, refused to attend the trial. Burr was eventually found not guilty, in part because he had only planned a new country, and in part because the US was unable to find any reliable witnesses.

The Marshall Court (1801-1835)

The Supreme Court led by **John Marshall** is credited with increasing the power of the national government over that of the states. This court also gave the judicial branch more power and prestige, notably in the case of **Marbury v. Madison** (1803). Marshall was known as an arch-Federalist and as a loose interpreter of the Constitution. In the case of **McCulloch v. Maryland** (1819), the court ruled that a national bank is allowed by the Constitution and that states cannot tax a federal agency. In the case of **Gibbons v. Ogden** (1824), the right of Congress to regulate interstate commerce was reaffirmed, and indeed federal regulation of just about anything was made possible. In **Fletcher v. Peck** (1810), the sanctity of contracts was asserted; this case also established the right of the Supreme Court to declare state laws unconstitutional.

Marbury v. Madison

Right before President **John Adams** left office after **Thomas Jefferson** won the presidency in the election of 1800, he passed the **Judiciary Act of 1801**. This act eliminated one seat on the Supreme Court, eliminated circuit duties for members of the Supreme Court, and created 16 federal circuit court judgeships. This allowed President John Adams to pack the federal court system with his fellow Federalists before Thomas Jefferson, a Democratic-Republican, took office. **William Marbury** was one of these individuals promised a position by John Adams. However, Adams's Secretary of State, **John Marshall**, did not have time to deliver Marbury's commission (which was the formal job offer for Marbury's position as Justice of the Peace for D.C.) before the Jefferson administration took over. The new Secretary of State, **James Madison**, refused to deliver Marbury's commission after he took office. This led to Marbury suing Madison for his commission, and the issue was brought before the Supreme Court in the case of ***Marbury v. Madison*** (1803).

Although Section XIII of the Judiciary Act of 1789 had a **Writ of Mandamus** which required Madison to honor the appointment, Chief Justice **John Marshall**, whom Adams appointed to the Supreme Court before leaving office, declared this section unconstitutional. This historic act established the doctrine of **judicial review**, which allows the Supreme Court to declare a legislative or executive act unconstitutional. Marshall thereby established an independent judiciary; he is quoted as saying, "The Constitution is the supreme Law of the Land, with the Supreme Court as the final interpreter."

Review Video: Marbury v. Madison
Visit mometrix.com/academy and enter code: 573964

Jeffersonian Republicans

After using his inauguration speech to try to pacify angry Federalists, Thomas Jefferson went on to introduce the "**spoils system**," replacing Federalist office-holders with **Republicans**. He also reversed many of the Federalist policies: the Alien Act was repealed, and the Sedition Act expired in 1801 (everyone arrested under its authority was pardoned and absolved and had their fines repaid). Jefferson also sought to reform the judiciary. The **Judiciary Act of 1801**, otherwise known as the **Circuit Court Act**, was passed by the Federalists in order to cement some of their judges in place; Jefferson in turn forced through the Judiciary Act of 1802, which effectively removed the judges by abolishing the new courts.

Foreign Policy Under the Jeffersonian Republicans

The most important event during the dominance of the Jeffersonian Republicans was the **War of 1812**, fought between France and Britain. In the United States, there was much speculation as to whether the young nation would side with the shark (Britain) or the tiger (France). In 1803, Jefferson had declared American ships neutral, an act which annoyed both sides. The British subsequently passed the **Orders-in-Council**, and the French the **Berlin and Milan Decrees**, all of which were designed to weaken American shipping in Europe. The US responded with the **Non-Importation Act of 1806**, though this was largely a failure. In 1807, an American ship called the **Chesapeake** was attacked by a British ship, leading Jefferson to issue the **Embargo Act of 1807**. This act forbade American ships from leaving for foreign ports; it was very unpopular and was repealed in 1809.

Madison and "Peaceful Coercion," and the Non-Intercourse Act of 1809

In the 1808 election, **James Madison** of the Democrat-Republicans easily defeated C. C. Pinckney. Madison continued Jefferson's policy of "**peaceful coercion**" with respect to France and Britain, but the lack of an organized American military made it difficult for him to get the attention of these major powers. In 1809, Madison convinced Congress to pass the **Non-Intercourse Act of 1809**, which forbade trade with Britain and France until they began treating American business fairly. When the British ambassador **David Erskine** vowed to improve the treatment of American businesses, Madison agreed to trade with England. However, Erskine's superior quickly overruled him, making Madison look ridiculous and souring Anglo-American relations further.

Yazoo Claims and John Randolph

In 1795, the corrupt Georgia legislature sold some land known as the **Yazoo Claims** for almost nothing to a group of northeastern speculators in exchange for a bribe. When a new group of legislators came into office in 1797, they revoked the land sales, infuriating the speculators. In 1802, the land claims were ceded to the national government and Jefferson decided to grant the speculators a cash settlement. **John Randolph**, however, was the chairman of the House committee responsible for paying this settlement, and he refused to make the payment, stating that the deal was "bathed in corruption." Though the Supreme Court eventually granted the settlements in the case **Fletcher v. Peck** (1810), Randolph was permanently alienated from Jefferson and went on to form a group called the **Tertium Quids**. This group was the ultra-conservative pro-states' rights contingent of the Democratic-Republicans.

Treaty of Ildefonso and the Louisiana Purchase

In an agreement between the French and Spanish known alternately as the **Treaty of Ildefonso** or the **Retrocession**, Napoleon Bonaparte acquired Louisiana. This, along with Spain's closing of New Orleans to American business, made Jefferson nervous, and he thus sent James Monroe to France in order to purchase New Orleans and West Florida. Bonaparte, himself made anxious by a rebellion in Haiti and a renewal of hostilities with the British, signed over 800,000 square miles to the US, making the **Louisiana Purchase** the largest land acquisition without bloodshed in human history. Napoleon hoped to curry favor with the United States to forestall a possible Anglo-American alliance.

Perception of the Louisiana Purchase and Acquisition of East and West Florida

The Louisiana Purchase was probably the high point of Jefferson's presidency; it was seen at home as a diplomatic victory that also avoided drawing the United States into conflict with the European powers. It destroyed the Federalist party. After the **Louisiana Purchase** was completed, explorers set out to discover just what had been bought; among these explorers were **Meriwether Lewis** and **William Clark**. Meanwhile, the United States began to make inroads into Spanish-controlled **West Florida**. In 1810, rebels attacked Baton Rouge and James Madison claimed that West Florida was now part of the US. Of course, the Spanish protested, but they were unable to reestablish themselves. In 1818, Andrew Jackson would lead a group of soldiers into **East Florida** under the pretense of taming the Seminoles. In 1819, the Spanish would reluctantly sign the **Treaty of Onis**, in which the US formally acquired East Florida for $5 million, which the Spanish promptly returned to pay off some of their debt to the US.

Macon's Bill No. 2

Madison replaced the Non-Intercourse Act of 1809 with **Macon's Bill No. 2**, which declared that America would be open to trade with any country. The bill also stipulated that if either Britain or France agreed to neutral trading rights with the US, the US would immediately cease trade with the other. France jumped at this opportunity, and the US cut diplomatic ties with Britain. The British, weakened by the American embargoes and by a bitter winter, rescinded the **Orders-in-council**, although the US had already declared war upon them. After the British Prime Minister was assassinated, the new foreign secretary, **Castlereagh**, tried to mend relations, but the US went to war anyway. The **War of 1812** was very unpopular, especially among Federalists in the Northeast.

Many Americans felt that England could not be beaten, that engaging in a war would damage US business, and that Napoleon was not a very savory ally.

War of 1812

Controversy

The conservative members of Madison's party, known as the **Tertium Quids**, opposed the **War of 1812** because they felt it would be too expensive, would result in the perpetuation of a standing army, would damage America economically, and would lead to the acquisition of Canada as a slave state. These critics were opposed in Congress by the **Warhawks**, so-called by the Federalists to imply that they were picking a fight. The Warhawks mainly represented the Southwest and the West, and included luminaries such as Henry Clay, John C. Calhoun, and Felix Grundy. They supported the war because they thought it would bolster foreign trade, would discourage the British from inciting Native Americans along the frontier, and could result in land gain. In selling the war to the American people, Madison stressed the British insult to American honor; he mentioned several stories about impressments of Americans into British military service.

Review Video: Overview of the War of 1812
Visit mometrix.com/academy and enter code: 507716

Review Video: Opinions about the War of 1812
Visit mometrix.com/academy and enter code: 274558

Events Leading Up to Combat

Despite a great deal of bloated rhetoric both for and against the war, the US fought against Britain for a few basic reasons, namely to gain more **land** and to destroy **alliances** between the British and Native Americans. Americans had become incensed when, following his defeat to the Americans at Tippecanoe Creek, **Chief Tecumseh** had fled north into British-controlled Canada. This provocation provided enough popular support to declare war. Unfortunately, the American military was both unprepared and overconfident. Most American military strategists thought it would be quite easy to take Canada, but the army had only 35,000 troops at the time. Moreover, the first Bank of the United States had just gone defunct, so there were scarce economic resources to support a war.

Major Battles

At the **Battle of Lake Erie** in September of 1813, the American Commander Perry secured Detroit for the US. At the **Battle of Lake Champlain**, the American General Thomas McDonough secured northern New York from British invasion. At the **Battle of the Thames**, the American General William Henry Harrison defeated a coalition of British and Native American forces; Tecumseh was killed. Andrew Jackson scored a decisive victory at the **Battle of Horseshoe Bend**. During this war, much of Washington, DC (including the White House) was torched. A crucial point of the war came when the US was able to successfully defend **Fort McHenry**, outside of Baltimore; this conflict inspired Francis Scott Key's composition of "The Star-Spangled Banner." At the **Battle of New Orleans**, Andrew Jackson used a rag-tag collection of soldiers and pirates to defeat the British navy.

Conclusion of the War

Throughout the War of 1812, there was loud opposition from the **Federalists** in the Northeast. At the **Hartford Convention**, they formally blamed Madison for the war and proposed changes to the Constitution whereby a 2/3 vote would be needed for declaring war and for admitting new states to the Union. The War of 1812 required several agreements to fully restore relations between the US and Britain. The **Treaty of Ghent** returned Anglo-American ties to their pre-war terms, and proposed that commissions be created to settle differences. The **Rush-Bagot Treaty of 1817** formally declared that there would be no naval race between the 2 countries. At the **Convention of 1818**, a line was drawn along the 49th parallel, dividing Canada from Louisiana, and it was declared that the 2 countries would jointly occupy Oregon. In the **Adams-Onis Treaty of 1819**, a western boundary for Louisiana was set, and the Spanish renounced their claims to Oregon.

SIGNIFICANCE

The War of 1812 did not really accomplish its supposed goal of establishing neutral trading rights for American ships. The exodus of Napoleon during the war made this a moot point. Nevertheless, from Madison's perspective, the war could only be seen as a major **success**. The United States lost no major territory, and scored enough victories to keep the British from making any extreme demands. More importantly, perhaps, Americans were overjoyed that the US was finally getting respect from the major European powers. **Nationalism** exploded in the US: people forgot the debacle of the failed national bank, and the economy boomed. Finally, the success of the War of 1812 effectively drove the final nail into the coffin of the **Federalist party**.

STRENGTHENING OF AMERICAN NATIONAL IDENTITY

The success of the War of 1812 and the prospering economy made Madison extremely popular. In the Northeast, with the implementation of the British factory system, and in the Southeast, with the invention of the cotton gin, manufacturing interests were booming. This sense of **national identity** was strengthened by the emergence of the United States' first generation of **post-colonial artists**. In literature, James Fenimore Cooper and Washington Irving (*The Legend of Sleepy Hollow*) were eminent. A uniquely American style of **architecture** developed, led by Jefferson, among others, emphasizing columns, symmetry, and classical proportions. The **Hudson River school** produced a group of painters influenced by the natural beauty of their region; among them was John James Audubon.

TRIUMPH OF NEO-FEDERALISM

In 1816, Madison declared that the government should increase the army, the national debt, and the banking interests, an agenda oddly reminiscent of Federalism. The **Second Bank of the United States** was shown to be necessary by the War of 1812, but it was poorly organized and came to be known as a "moneyed monster." The **Tariff of 1816** was established to protect fledgling industry; it was as popular in the Northeast as it was unpopular in the South. Much of the tariff money went to developing infrastructure; the new method of **paving** invented by John MacAdam enabled the creation of long thoroughfares, mostly in the North. It was even proposed in the so-called "Bonus Bill" that all of the surplus money from the new bank should go to the roads; Madison vetoed this measure to avoid further alienating the South.

"THE ERA OF GOOD FEELINGS" FROM 1817 TO 1825

In the election of 1816, the Democrat-Republican **James Monroe** defeated the last Federalist candidate, Rufus King, by a landslide. The Federalist opposition to the War of 1812 doomed the party to extinction. Monroe's early term was not without its problems, however. A mild depression caused by over-speculation on western lands led to the **Panic of 1819** and began a 20-year boom-bust cycle. These problems were exacerbated by the **Second Bank of the United States**; the Bank's pressure on the so-called "wildcat" banks to foreclose on properties, as well as the unwillingness of the Bank to loan money, made it very unpopular. The nationalism generated by the War of 1812 was damaged by these economic travails.

MONROE DOCTRINE

After a series of revolutions in Latin America, the United States was the first to recognize the **sovereignty** of the new countries. This was in part because the revolutionaries had used the United

States as inspiration; in part because the US preferred to have weak, independent nations nearby; and in part because the US wanted to maintain and expand its lucrative trade with Latin America. The British attempted to persuade the US to sign an agreement preventing foreign intervention in Latin America, but Monroe decided to maintain American independence and issue his own document. This document, known as the **Monroe Doctrine**, had as its two main principles *non-intervention* and *non-colonization*. Many considered it a "paper tiger," because it was really only as effective as the American ability to enforce it. Still, it seemed to encourage foreign nations to come to the bargaining table rather than test the American military.

Review Video: Monroe Doctrine
Visit mometrix.com/academy and enter code: 953021

Election of 1824 and Adams' Administration

All the major candidates in the 1824 election were **Democrat-Republicans**. Although Andrew Jackson received more electoral votes than **John Quincy Adams**, he did not win a majority, and Adams (with the help of Henry Clay) won the run-off in the House of Representatives. Adams was a fierce **nationalist** at a time when many in the country were sectionalist. Although his initiatives for a national university and public funding for the arts were well-meaning, Adams was still believed to be out of touch with the common man. He further alienated the middle and lower classes with the **Tariff of 1828**, known in the South as the "Tariff of Abominations." The South was already on shaky economic ground and the tariff became a scapegoat for its troubles. **John C. Calhoun** was an especially ardent Southern voice; he futilely proposed that states should have the ability to nullify federal regulations.

Review Video: John Quincy Adams as President
Visit mometrix.com/academy and enter code: 797549

1828

The election of 1828 is considered the first **modern campaign** in American politics. **Andrew Jackson** had the first campaign manager, Amos Kendall, and produced buttons, posters, and slogans to support his candidacy. These men—Jackson, Kendall, John C. Calhoun, and Martin van Buren—formed the beginning of the **Democratic party**. Meanwhile, the incumbent John Quincy Adams ran a very formal campaign, with little of the "flesh-pressing" of Jackson. Adams tried to discredit Jackson as an adulterer and bigamist because Jackson's wife had not been officially divorced at the time of their marriage. When his wife died during the campaign, however, the popular sentiment returned to Jackson, and he won the election by a considerable margin. Jackson's inauguration was an over-crowded, chaotic affair; the president suffered three cracked ribs during the festivities.

Jacksonian Democracy

The 1820s and 30s are known as the era of **Jacksonian democracy**, which was political rather than economic or social. Jackson was considered to be emblematic of the "common man." In the years after the conclusion of the War of 1812, it was generally considered that America was "safe for democracy," and thus **suffrage** was extended to poor people in many states. As more people became involved in politics, campaigning became more about image and perception than the issues. This change also ended the tradition known as "**King Caucus**," in which candidates were chosen by a small group of powerful men; now, candidates were to be selected by a series of primaries and nominating conventions. Furthermore, the members of the electoral college would be chosen by the voters rather than by the state legislature. The new system maintained the tradition of **patronage** (the spoils system), in which newly-elected officials would fill the government offices with their supporters.

Jackson as President

Andrew Jackson is often seen as a symbol of the rising power of the New West, or as an embodiment of the "rags to riches" fable. He spent much of his presidency trying to promote the idea of **nationalism** at a time when most of the country was ardently sectionalist. During his presidency, he dominated Congress, vetoing more legislation than all of the previous presidents combined. He was also famous for his so-called "**Kitchen Cabinet**," a group of close advisers without official positions. Many of these men later received formal appointments, including Secretary of State (Martin van Buren), Postmaster General (Amos Kendall), and Secretary of the Treasury (Roger B. Taney).

Review Video: Andrew Jackson's Presidency
Visit mometrix.com/academy and enter code: 667792

Review Video: American Nationalism
Visit mometrix.com/academy and enter code: 865693

Review Video: Andrew Jackson - Key Events and Major Issues
Visit mometrix.com/academy and enter code: 739251

Major Events of the Jackson Era

Raid into Florida and the Webster-Hayne Debate

One of the least successful events in Jackson's presidency was a **raid into Florida** in 1828, made to subdue the Seminoles. The raid did not go well, and even Jackson's Secretary of War, John C. Calhoun, referred to it as "idiotic." Another major event in Jackson's term was the **Webster-Hayne debate** of 1829-30, held to debate western expansion. The senators of the Northeast were opposed to western migration, mainly because they felt it would weaken manufacturing and create a new political rival. Senator **Robert Hayne** of South Carolina blasted the war record of the Northeast, in the hopes of allying the West and the South. **Daniel Webster** (MA) retorted that the US is not a collection of states but a union that happens to be divided into states; he asserted that if states could nullify federal measures, the only thing holding the Union together was a "rope of sand."

Maysville Road Veto and Native American Removal

In 1830, Jackson set a precedent by **vetoing the funding of a road** that was to be entirely within one state (Kentucky). Many believed that Jackson vetoed this bill to spite Henry Clay, but the move had some positive political consequences as well: the Southerners appreciated the idea that states should tend to their own business, and northerners liked it because the road would have given people easier access to the West. Jackson's attempts at **relocating Native Americans** were less successful. The passage of the **Indian Resettlement Act of 1830** was the first attempt by the national government to force migration. In the case of **Worcester v. Georgia** (1832), the Supreme Court ruled against those who sought to grab Native lands. John Marshall asserted that the **Cherokee nation** was sovereign, but a ward of the US. Despite Marshall's assertion of Native American rights, Jackson supported the slow and steady conquest of land in the South and West.

Tariff of 1832 and the Force Act of 1832

At a feast in celebration of Thomas Jefferson—a man noted for his nationalism—Andrew Jackson promoted the idea of the nation, saying, "Our Union, it must be preserved." John C. Calhoun responded with a speech in which he referred to "Our Union, next to our liberty most dear," indicating that the South was not going to back down. The milder **Tariff of 1832** was then offered by Jackson to appease the South and Calhoun; instead, Southern politicians declared it was not enough, and Calhoun resigned from Congress in order to organize the opposition to all tariffs.

Henry Clay, who realized that Jackson could easily overpower South Carolina, was further disturbed by the **Force Act of 1832**, which stated that the president had the right to use military force to keep a state in the Union. So, Clay proposed an even lower **Compromise Tariff of 1833**: the tariff would be lowered from 35% to 20-25% over the next ten years. Both sides agreed to this compromise.

Bank War of 1836

It had already been arranged that the **renewal of the Second Bank of America** would be discussed in 1836. It was common knowledge that Jackson hated the Bank, and thus Henry Clay and others tried to renew it ahead of time, in 1832. Jackson was then forced to assert his position: he declared that the bank was anti-West, anti-American, unconstitutional, and a "monopoly of money." The unpopularity of Clay's attempt to renew the Bank was one of the main reasons that he was crushed by Jackson in the 1832 election. After making sure that the Bank would not be renewed, Jackson sought to mend fences with the Northeast by avidly promoting the Union. This was Jackson's genius as a politician; he always was careful to get what he wanted without fully alienating any faction.

Election of 1836 and the Van Buren Presidency

When Jackson decided not to pursue a third term as president, his vice president **Martin Van Buren** ran and won over a group of challengers including the Whig candidate William Henry Harrison. Van Buren's presidency was marked by frequent border disputes with Canada. Also, Van Buren suffered through the **Panic of 1837**; like in 1819, this was caused by over-speculation in the West. In the 1836 "Specie Circular," Jackson had declared that all land bought from the government must be paid for in gold coins. Because gold was hard to come by, many people lost their property. Further economic problems were created by overspending on infrastructure in many states. One of the results of Van Buren's handling of the situation was that it became acceptable for the president to influence the amount of money in circulation. In 1840, a listless Van Buren was defeated by **Harrison**, who promptly died after a month as president. **John Tyler** became the next president.

Review Video: Martin Van Buren's Presidency
Visit mometrix.com/academy and enter code: 787203

Tyler Presidency

John Tyler, a Virginia aristocrat, was the first vice president to take over in mid-term. Oddly, even though he was the Whig candidate, he opposed almost all of the Whig agenda. Henry Clay hoped to dominate Tyler, but his attempts to create a third national bank and to improve infrastructure in the West were both vetoed by Tyler. Tyler's presidency was also fraught with conflict with the British; he endured the **Lumberjacks' War of 1842** and the **Hunters' Lodges skirmishes** in 1838, both of which were minor conflicts along the Canadian border. There was also the incident of the ***Caroline***, an American ship sunk by the British for allegedly smuggling supplies to Canadian rebels. In the **Webster-Ashburton Treaty of 1842**, fugitives were exchanged, the border of Maine was set at the St. John River, and it was established that the British could no longer search American ships.

Expansion and Manifest Destiny

The phrase "**manifest destiny**," meaning the inevitability and righteousness of the American expansion westward, was coined by the editor **John O'Sullivan**. This idea was lent further credence by the work of Horace Greeley, the journalist responsible for the admonition, "Go west, young man!" Besides this mythology, however, there were some sound reasons why the United States expanded westward. For one thing, there was cheap and fertile land in the West, and the more that was claimed by the Americans, the less which could be claimed by the British. Americans also had an eye toward claiming the western ports to begin trading with Asia. Finally, many Americans felt that they would only be benefiting the world by spreading their ideals of liberty and democracy across as much land as possible.

Review Video: Manifest Destiny
Visit mometrix.com/academy and enter code: 957409

Texas' Role in US Expansion

In 1821, **Mexico** received its independence from Spain. Mexico sold Texan lands to Americans, yet these people were still required to live under Mexican civil law (for one thing, people had to convert to Catholicism). In 1832, however, **Santa Anna** led a coup in Mexico and decided to crack down on the Texans. This led to the **Texas Revolution of 1836**, in which Texan General William Travis' men were massacred by the forces of Santa Anna at the **Alamo**, in which both Davy Crockett and Jim Bowie were killed. After suffering some other defeats, the Texans, led by Sam Houston, finally defeated Santa Anna at the **Battle of San Jacinto** in 1836, and he was forced below the Rio Grande. Nevertheless, Texas was not made part of the US, mainly because the issue of slavery was so contentious at the time.

US Expansion Including Salt Lake City, Oregon, and California

The territory of **Oregon** became more important to the US government as fur-trapping became a lucrative industry. Oregon was also known to contain rich farmland. As for **California**, its natural bounty had been described by whalers since the 1820s. In the 1840s, whole families (including the ill-fated Donner party) began to migrate there. Around this time the **Church of Jesus Christ of Latter-day Saints**, otherwise known as the Mormon Church, was founded by Joseph Smith. Among the beliefs espoused by the Mormons were polygamy, communalism, and the abolition of slavery. After Smith's death, the Mormons were led by Brigham Young and settled in what is now **Salt Lake City**. Meanwhile, in 1848 gold was discovered in a California stream, generating still more excitement over the economic potential of the West.

Presidency of James K. Polk

The election of 1844 brought to the forefront a number of critical issues; the economy was still hurting from the Panic of 1837, there was growing support for abolitionism and the issue of manifest destiny was gaining steam. Somewhat surprisingly, the bland North Carolinian **James K. Polk** defeated Henry Clay and succeeded John Tyler as president. He instituted the **Walker Tariff**, which lowered the rate at which foreign goods were taxed from 35% to 25%. He also reinstated the **Independent Sub-Treasury system** in 1846. Mainly, however, Polk's presidency is associated with westward expansion; **Texas** was brought into the Union as a slave state in December of 1845. Polk also spent considerable time trying to gain possession of Oregon.

Mexican War

Causes

The immediate causes of the **Mexican War** were the American annexation of Texas, disputes over the southern border of Texas, and the large amount of money owed to the United States by Mexico. Moreover, it was well known that the Mexicans held the US in contempt, considering them greedy land-grabbers. **Polk** sent an emissary to buy Texas, California, and some Mexican territory for $30 million; he was refused. **Zachary Taylor** then led an American expedition into a disputed area of Texas where some of them were killed. Polk was able to use these deaths as a rationale for war, despite considerable opposition in Congress. Overall, the Democrats supported the war, while the Whigs, led in part by Abraham Lincoln, were opposed.

Major Battles and Conclusion of War

The United States scored major victories over Mexico at **Buena Vista**, where they were led by Zachary Taylor, and **Vera Cruz**, where they were led by Winfield Scott. The American effort in New Mexico was led by Stephen Kearney and in California by John C. Fremont. The **Treaty of Guadalupe-Hidalgo** was signed in 1848 after Polk sent an emissary with cash in an effort to persuade Santa Anna to stop the war. Under the terms of the treaty, the US got California, the rest of Texas, and all of the Mexican territory between Louisiana and California (including what would become Utah and Nevada). In exchange, the US erased a good deal of Mexico's debts. Controversy immediately erupted over whether the new territories would be allowed to have slaves; some abolitionists wanted to cancel the treaty, while some Southern Democrats wanted to claim the entirety of Mexico.

Road to Civil War

There was immense controversy surrounding the **slavery policy** in the new American territories after the war with Mexico: Polk wanted to simply extend the line of the **Missouri Compromise** out to the Pacific, while abolitionists offered the **Wilmot Proviso**, which declared that none of the territories should have slaves. The Southern states felt slavery should be allowed, and a more moderate view was offered by Stephen Douglas, who declared that the people of the new states should decide whether they wanted slavery or not. In the election of 1848, the war-hero **Zachary Taylor** (Whig) defeated Lewis Cass (Democrat) and the former president Martin Van Buren (Free Soil party, a collection of abolitionist interests).

Review Video: Missouri Compromise
Visit mometrix.com/academy and enter code: 848091

Era of Bonanzas

Between the years 1848 and 1858, the miners known as the "**forty-niners**" dug about $555 million out of the Western soil. In particular, the **Comstock Lode** of Virginia City, Nevada was famous for producing vast amounts of gold and silver. After buffalo were largely eradicated from the Great Plains, there was a "cattleman's bonanza," aided by the invention of barbed wire. The **Cattleman's Association** was a union of cattle dealers joined together to preserve the integrity of the industry, to stop cross-breeding, and to stop cattle thievery. This era marked the end of the open range, mainly because of horrible droughts and bad winters, range wars between the cowboys and sheep farmers, the railroads, and barbed wire.

Civil War and Reconstruction Eras

Gold Rush and the Compromise of 1850

After **Zachary Taylor** won the election of 1848, he immediately had to deal with the issue of slavery in the new western territories. This issue was magnified by the California gold rush. Taylor declared that all of the lands would be free, enraging the Southerners. Soon after, however, Taylor died of food poisoning and was succeeded by Vice-president **Millard Fillmore**. In order to solve the problem of slavery in the West, Henry Clay proposed the so-called **Compromise of 1850**: California would be a free state, while New Mexico would be allowed to decide for itself; there would be no more slave trading in the District of Columbia; there would be tighter laws regarding fugitive slaves; and Texas would receive $10 million for its lost territories. Fillmore readily signed this agreement, but problems with it arose immediately. One of which was that the **Underground Railroad** of **Harriet Tubman** was already making it very difficult to catch fugitive slaves.

ELECTION OF 1852 AND THE GROWING CRISIS OF SLAVERY

In the election of 1852, Democrat **Franklin Pierce** easily defeated the Whig Winfield Scott who was hurt by his association with the abolitionist William H. Seward. At this time, despite the growing crisis of slavery, there were some positive changes in the US. One was that the introduction of **California** as a free state permanently upset the sectional balance. Immigration into the Northeastern cities was bringing a wealth of new ideas. The Northern states resisted the fugitive slave laws by passing initiatives in support of personal liberties and by aiding the Underground Railroad. Harriet Beecher Stowe enraged the South with her novel *Uncle Tom's Cabin* (1852). In 1857, Hinton R. Helper published "The Impending Crisis of the South," an essay that suggested the South was becoming a slave to the North because of its reactionary view on slavery.

TRANSCONTINENTAL RAILROAD, OSTEND MANIFESTO, AND KANSAS-NEBRASKA ACT

The construction of the **Transcontinental Railroad** was begun in 1853 for the purpose of transporting easterners to California. With the **Gadsden Purchase**, the US had purchased some New Mexican lands so the train could avoid the mountains. With the **Ostend Manifesto** in 1854, the US attempted to purchase Cuba from Spain for $120 million; Spain refused, and though the US threatened to take the island by force, they never did (in part because it was believed that the South wanted to make it a slave state). The **Kansas-Nebraska Act** (1854), authored by Stephen Douglas, divided the Nebraska territory into two parts (Kansas and Nebraska) and declared that slavery would be determined by popular sovereignty in those territories. This act drove northerners to the liberal side and caused the creation of the **Republican party**. The opposing factions engaged in violence to try to win the popular vote. Though Kansas worded its constitution in an attempt to have slaves, the document fell apart upon review by Congress, and Kansas entered as a free state.

SUMNER-BROOKS INCIDENT, ELECTION OF 1856, AND THE DRED SCOTT CASE

In 1856, Senator **Charles Sumner** (MA) gave an impassioned speech on the "Crime against Kansas," in which he blamed the South for the violence. One of the men whom he singled out for blame was the uncle of Senator **Preston Brooks** (SC); Brooks beat Sumner with his walking stick, and was glorified in the South. In the election of 1856, **James Buchanan** (Democrat) defeated several candidates, including Millard Fillmore (American party; some Southern states had threatened to secede should Fillmore prevail). Next came the **Dred Scott** case. Scott was a slave taken to a free state by his owner and then transported back to a slave state. Abolitionists said he should be a free man. The Supreme Court, however, ruled that slaves are property and can be transported across state lines without being changed. This decision effectively rendered the Kansas-Nebraska Act, the Missouri Compromise, and the whole idea of popular sovereignty being unconstitutional.

ABRAHAM LINCOLN

Abraham Lincoln, the 16th President of the United States, is best known for leading the country through the Civil War. **Lincoln** began his political career in 1832 at the age 23 when he ran for the Illinois General Assembly. He lost that election but on his second attempt two years later, he was elected. In 1846, Lincoln was elected to a single term in the US House of Representatives. After serving his two-year term, he returned to Springfield to practice law. In the presidential race of **1860**, Lincoln defeated Stephen Douglas, John Breckinridge, and John Bell to become the 16th President of the United States. By February of 1861, seven states had seceded from the Union and formed the Confederate States of America.

BEGINNING OF THE CIVIL WAR

On **April 12, 1861**, **Confederate** forces fired on Union troops at **Fort Sumter**, effectively beginning the Civil War. Lincoln took several immediate actions to quell the rebellion: expanding his war powers, imposing a blockade on Confederate shipping ports, disbursing funds without the approval of Congress, and suspending habeas corpus to allow the arrest and imprisonment of thousands of suspected Confederate sympathizers without trials.

Gettysburg Address

The **Gettysburg Address** was a speech that **President Abraham Lincoln** delivered in **Gettysburg, Pennsylvania**, during the Civil War. The speech was given to dedicate a national cemetery on the grounds of the Battle of Gettysburg. President Lincoln's speech was a comment on the ideals of democracy: liberty and freedom for all. He felt that these ideals were being threatened by the Civil War. He reminded the country that it was founded on the precept that all men are created equal and that the country fought hard to have a government of the people, by the people, and for the people. He wanted the citizens to join together to preserve the ideals of democracy.

Emancipation Proclamation

In January of **1863**, more than a year and a half into the Civil War, Lincoln signed a presidential proclamation declaring that **all slaves** in the states still in rebellion against the Union were thereby **freed**. Over the course of the next several years, all states were encouraged or coerced into prohibiting human slavery as a practice.

Abraham Lincoln vs Jefferson Davis

Abraham Lincoln

Abraham Lincoln's primary goal as President of the United States was to preserve the Union. In **his first inaugural speech in 1861**, Lincoln made it clear that, although he was known to disagree with slavery, he had no intention of interfering with the practice of slavery in the areas in which it already existed. He even agreed to the laws requiring the return of fugitive slaves to their owners. He believed that unless the federal government violated specific wording of the Constitution, the southern states would have no reason to secede. In both the **Gettysburg Address** and **his 1865 inaugural speech**, the president reiterated his desire to see the states once again become united under one government. Lincoln believed that government was meant to serve the citizens and wanted to support states' rights. However, he was also firm in the belief that the Constitution provided legal, peaceful means for states to amend the government if they were discontented. He was adamant that it was unconstitutional for a state to leave the Union and that he would do whatever was necessary to keep the Union intact.

Jefferson Davis

Jefferson Davis was the first and only president of the **Confederate States of America**. His **inaugural address in 1861** outlined the justification for **secession** of the southern states and his plan for the new Confederacy. Davis claimed that, because the Constitution established that the authority of the government existed only through the consent of the people, the people reserved the right to alter or abolish the government at any time. He also described the Confederacy as an alliance of individual states that would allow each state to decide how its government would run. He expressed hope that the United States and the Confederate States could learn to coexist and continue to benefit economically from one another. He also stated that the Confederacy had no interest, under any circumstance, in reuniting with the North. Davis expressed a desire for peace in his address, but he promised that the South would be ready to engage militarily if provoked by the Union.

Lincoln and Davis on Slavery

Although Davis never mentioned slavery in his speech, the sentiment that slavery should **continue** in the South was shared by **both presidents** in **1861**. Lincoln was not a supporter of slavery, but to preserve the Union, he would not interfere with the institution. However, by the time Lincoln gave his **1865 inaugural address**, he openly **denounced slavery** and claimed that the Civil War was God's punishment for the endurance of slavery past the time when it should have been abolished.

LINCOLN-DOUGLAS DEBATES AND JOHN BROWN'S RAID

During the campaign to become senator of Illinois in 1858, **Abraham Lincoln** and **Stephen Douglas** eloquently debated the issue of slavery. In the so-called **Freeport Doctrine**, Lincoln questioned whether the people of a territory could vote against slavery. The Supreme Court would say no, but Lincoln wondered whether the people should not have the final say. Douglas essentially agreed, stating that the people of the territory should decide. Douglas won the election, though his stance on slavery irritated Southerners. In 1859, the abolitionist **John Brown** led a raid on a federal arsenal at Harper's Ferry, Virginia. Brown's group was only able to take a fire station, and Brown himself was captured and executed by a battalion led by **Robert E. Lee**. Brown became a martyr to the North.

ELECTION OF 1860 AND SECESSION OF THE SOUTH

In the election of 1860, **Abraham Lincoln** defeated three other challengers. Lincoln's platform was anti-slavery, though he vowed to leave it intact where it already existed. He also promised full rights to immigrants, the completion of a Pacific Railroad, free homesteads, and a protective tariff. After the election, South Carolina **seceded**, followed by the rest of the Deep South (Mississippi, Alabama, Georgia, Louisiana, Florida, and Texas). These states established the **Confederate States of America**, with its capital in Montgomery, Alabama. The president of the CSA was **Jefferson Davis**. Outgoing US President Buchanan claimed that he had no constitutional authority to stop the secession, but upon entering office, Lincoln attempted to maintain control of all Southern forts. This led to the firing on **Ft. Sumter** (SC) by the Confederates. As Lincoln called for aid, the Upper South (Virginia, Arkansas, North Carolina, and Tennessee) seceded as well, and the CSA made Richmond, Virginia its new capital.

COMPROMISES TO SAVE THE UNION

The US government made a number of compromises in an attempt to preserve the Union after Lincoln's election. The **Crittenden Compromise** extended the line of the Missouri Compromise and promised federal protection of slavery south of that line. The **House of Representatives Compromise** offered an extension of the Missouri Compromise and a Constitutional amendment to protect slavery. The **Virginia Peace Convention** produced an offer to extend the line of the Missouri Compromise and establish that slavery can never be outlawed except by the permission of the owner. Finally, Congress offered $300 for each slave. The South said that this was not enough money, and the North was appalled by the offer, regardless.

CIVIL WAR

The Civil War was fought for a number of reasons, but the most important of these was the controversy regarding **slavery**. The issue of slavery touched on moral, economic, and political themes. Also, the differing geography of the North and South had caused the latter to develop an **economy** that they felt could only survive through slavery. The Civil War also sprang from the ongoing debate over **states' rights**; many in the South felt that states should have the power to nullify federal regulations and believed that the North had too much representation in Congress (and, indeed, the North had received much more federal aid for infrastructure). Finally, there was a general difference in **culture** between the North and South; the North was more of a dynamic and democratic society, while the South was more of a static oligarchy.

> **Review Video: Overview of the American Civil War**
> Visit mometrix.com/academy and enter code: 239557

Advantages of the North

The **Northern side** in the Civil War contained 22 states with 22 million people. The North also contained most of the US' coal, iron, and copper, as well as 92% of the industry. The Union side had more than twice as much railroad track as the Confederacy and a vastly larger navy. Most importantly, perhaps, the Union had a huge advantage in **troops**. Most of the Northern troops were either volunteers or had been conscripted (starting in 1863). It was permissible to pay someone to take your space in the military. The North generally had between 2 and 3 times as many troops as the South during the war. The South was really only able to survive for so long because it fought a very defensive war.

Advantages and Disadvantages of the Confederacy

The **Confederate States of America** was comprised of 11 states with only 9 million people. When the war began, the South had no organized army or navy. At first, the troops were strictly volunteers, but eventually the CSA established a draft to bolster the ranks. The Confederacy did have some advantages, however. One was that they were fighting on their own soil and thus they already had interior lines of defense as well as knowledge of the terrain. On the whole, the Confederate commanders were more experienced and talented. Finally, the Confederacy had a psychological advantage over the North: they were fighting for a **tangible reason** (namely, to preserve their lives and property), while the North had to motivate its troops with notions of "preserving the Union."

Military Strategies of the North and South

The North began the Civil War by trying to **blockade** the Southern coast and seal off the border states; they hoped to end the war quickly by preventing supplies from reaching the Confederacy. The North also wanted to divide the South into two parts by seizing control of the Mississippi River. This plan would later be adjusted, and **Sherman's March** would try to divide the South into a northern and southern half. The Confederacy, meanwhile, knew that its best chance for success was to fight **defensively** (the South did not want any Northern territory). They also knew that they would need help from European powers. The South hoped to outlast the North's will to fight, to capture Washington, DC, and to receive Maryland into the Confederacy.

> **Review Video: American Civil War: North vs. South Overview**
> Visit mometrix.com/academy and enter code: 370788

Major Battles

First Bull Run, Shiloh, and Second Bull Run

The **First Battle of Bull Run** was fought in Manassas, VA in July of 1861. The North believed that an easy victory here would allow them to quickly take Richmond. Washingtonians even picnicked around the battlefield, anticipating a pleasant spectacle. It was not to be, however: led by Stonewall Jackson (who actually earned that nickname at this battle), the South won a shocking victory. As a result, the South became somewhat overconfident, and the North realized it was in for a long war. At the **Battle of Shiloh** (TN) in April of 1862, Ulysses S. Grant led the Union to its first major victory. At the **Second Battle of Bull Run** in August of 1862, Stonewall Jackson again defeated a Northern army, this time with the help of Robert E. Lee.

Antietam

At the **Battle of Antietam** (MD) in September of 1862, the Confederate General Robert E. Lee went on the offensive, hoping to bring Maryland into the Confederacy; sever the channels between Washington, DC and the North; and attract the recognition of the European powers. This was the bloodiest battle of the Civil War and ended in a draw. It was after this battle that Lincoln issued his famous **Emancipation Proclamation**. This document freed the slaves in any area that was taken by the Union, or in areas from which slaves could enter the Union. It did not, however, free slaves in the Border States, because Lincoln wanted to maintain loyalty to the Union in these areas. The aims of the Emancipation Proclamation were three: to keep the British from assisting the South, to motivate the Northern troops, and to effect a positive moral change.

Review Video: Emancipation Proclamation
Visit mometrix.com/academy and enter code: 181778

Fredericksburg, Chancellorsville, and Gettysburg

At the **Battle of Fredericksburg** (VA) in December of 1862, Robert E. Lee successfully repelled the attacks of the Union General Burnside. At the **Battle of Chancellorsville** (VA) in May of 1863, Lee scored his greatest victory of the war; it was during this battle, however, that the Confederate General Stonewall Jackson was mortally wounded by his own troops. At the **Battle of Gettysburg** (PA) in July of 1863, the Confederacy troops led by Lee suffered a damaging defeat. Lee had hoped to take some pressure off the South with a successful surge into the North, but instead got caught in an unfavorable tactical position and endured massive casualties. Most historians believe the Union victory at Gettysburg was the turning point in the war.

Vicksburg, Atlanta, and Sherman's March

The Union General mounted a siege against the crucial Confederate city of **Vicksburg** (MS) in July of 1863. When the Confederates had finally been starved into surrender, the Union had total control of the Mississippi River. Then, between July and October of 1864, the major Southern rail hub of **Atlanta** was conquered and burned by Union troops under General William Sherman. This victory guaranteed that Lincoln would be reelected in the election of 1864. It also marked the beginning of **Sherman's March to the Sea**, a campaign of devastation mounted by the Union in late 1864 and early 1865. Sherman's troops melted Southern rails and destroyed Southern crops and factories, creating a swath of chaos that stretched from Atlanta to Savannah.

Homestead Act of 1862 and the Transcontinental Railroad

The US government tried many different ways to improve conditions for farmers in the West. Under the **Homestead Act of 1862**, farmers were sold 160 acres for $10, with the proviso that they had to improve the land within 5 years. Between the years 1865 and 1900, only one in six farms began this way. The **Timber Culture Act of 1873** gave more land to farmers, with the proviso that they had to plant some trees on that land.

One thing that helped to populate the West was the completion of the **Transcontinental Railroad** in 1869. The Union Pacific met the Central Pacific railway at Promontory Point, Utah. In 1889, the US government opened Oklahoma for settlement, and by 1893 it was completely settled.

Impact of the Civil War across America

The Civil War impacted various people in America in remarkable ways. The people most affected were likely African Americans, who were at the center of the divide between the North and the South. Many African Americans directly fought in the war on both sides. Those in the Southern states were ultimately freed as a result of the Emancipation Proclamation of 1863. Soldiers in the war saw brutal warfare and faced physical and psychological repercussions of combat. It has long been said about the Civil War that soldiers often knew or were related to the very people they were fighting. This was especially so in states that hosted battles or lied on the borders between Southern and Northern states, such as Virginia and Tennessee. Others affected included women and children who were, in some cases, located fairly near the fights and played roles as suppliers, medics, and activists, leading to some precursors to the women's rights movement. In the reconstruction, economic, political, legal, and emotional fallout had to be dealt with, leading to many decades of repair following the war.

Lincoln's Reconstruction Plan

According to Lincoln, the relation between the North and the South after the completion of the Civil War would include "malice for none, charity for all." He imagined that the President would lead the **Reconstruction** effort, and, in 1863, he vowed that once 10% of the 1860 voters in a Southern state pledged loyalty to the Union, they could draft a new state constitution and receive "executive recognition." Lincoln was unsure whether black people should be gradually emancipated or relocated, but he knew they should be free. As for his own **Republican party**, Lincoln asserted that it should become a national party and that it should include freed black people, who would receive the right to vote.

Congress' Reconstruction Plan

With the **Wade-Davis Bill of 1864**, Congress outlined their plan for the rehabilitation of the South after the Civil War. Unlike Lincoln, who had only asked for a 10% (of 1860 voters) loyalty nucleus, Congress wanted a majority before admitting Southern states back into the **Union**. Participants in the state constitutional conventions would be required to sign an "ironclad oath" pledging eternal loyalty to the Union. Ex-Confederate officials would not be allowed to vote or hold office. Slavery, of course, would be **abolished**. Finally, the Confederate debt would be repudiated, and those who loaned money to the Confederacy would be unable to get it back. Lincoln **vetoed** this bill, mainly because he wanted the abolition of slavery to be an amendment rather than a law.

Second Industrial Revolution

The Second Industrial Revolution was possible in the United States because of the abundance of raw materials and the laissez-faire economic policies of the government. In the space between the years 1860 and 1914, industry grew to about twelve times its original size. This rapid progress was made possible by the rapid growth of the **American railway system**. The railroads were subsidized by the federal government. Around this time, Samuel Morse developed his **telegraph code**, enabling almost instantaneous communication across vast distances. Jay Gould and James J. Hill were among those who made immense fortunes as railroad managers. Cornelius Vanderbilt and his son William were both railroad magnates with a reputation for ignoring the plight of their workers.

Review Video: Second Industrial Revolution
Visit mometrix.com/academy and enter code: 608455

Review Video: The American Railroad System
Visit mometrix.com/academy and enter code: 843913

Hampton Roads Peace Conference, Last Battles of Civil War, and Assassination of Lincoln

At the Hampton Roads Peace Conference in February of 1865, **Lincoln** and Secretary of State **Seward** met with the vice president of the CSA, **Alexander Stephens**. Lincoln made a stern offer: reunion of the states, emancipation of the slaves, and immediate disbanding of the Confederate army. The Confederates, however, were not yet ready to return to the Union. The Northern General US Grant then led troops toward the CSA capital at Richmond. Finally, at **Appomattox** (VA) in April of 1865, Lee surrendered to Grant. Soon after, the Confederate President **Jefferson Davis** would be caught and jailed. Finally, on April 14, 1865, Lincoln was fatally wounded by two shots from the gun of **John Wilkes Booth** in Ford's Theater in Washington.

Presidential Reconstruction Plan Under Andrew Johnson

Andrew Johnson, a Jacksonian Democrat from Tennessee, became president after the assassination of Lincoln. Though a Southerner, he believed the yeoman farmers of the South had been tricked into war by "cotton snobs." Johnson's plan for reconstruction called for **amnesty** to be granted to all ex-Confederates except for high-ranking officials and wealthy cotton planters, who would be allowed to apply for special pardons. Johnson also called for a **provisional Unionist governor** to be appointed in each Southern state; this leader would hold a constitutional convention at which it would be necessary to disavow secession, repudiate the CSA debt, and accept the 13th amendment. This plan was largely a failure, however, because it infringed on the powers of Congress, was seen as too lenient on the South, threatened the Republicans by giving too much power to Southern Democrats, and ignored freed black people, who were repressed in the South by the so-called **Black Codes**.

Labor Organizations After the Civil War

National Labor Union and Noble and Holy Orders of the Knights of Labor

At the end of the Civil War, only about 2% of all US workers were **unionized**; many believed joining a union was an admission that one would never move up. Over time, though, people began to realize that the consolidation of business interests (trusts) had to be met by a consolidation of labor. In 1866, the **National Labor Union** was founded by William H. Sylvis; this idealistic organization advocated an 8-hour workday but disbanded after backing the loser in the 1872 election. In 1869, Uriah Stephens founded the **Noble and Holy Orders of the Knights of Labor**; this group excluded doctors, lawyers, and bankers and supported the end of sexism, the 8-hour workday, paper money, income tax, and the prohibition of alcohol.

Haymarket Square and American Federation of Labor

In 1886, the **Knights of Labor** gathered in **Haymarket Square** in Chicago to protest an attack against another union. During the protest, a bomb was thrown and several people were killed; 7 members of the union were arrested, and some were executed. This incident linked labor unions with violence in the popular imagination. At the same time, less idealistic labor unions like the American Railway Union (led by Eugene V. Debs), the United Mineworkers, and the Molly McGuires were making great inroads in working communities. The **American Federation of Labor** was an alliance of many unions formed in 1881. This group sought a shorter workday, better working conditions, and workman's compensation; they were also not afraid to strike. The AFL frequently engaged in collective bargaining, in which a strike was threatened in order to bring management to the negotiation table.

Opposition to Organized Labor

The general public **opposed** labor unions because they disliked the idea of closed shops (those places in which one had to be a union member to work) and because they had a reputation for violence. Unions were also fiercely competitive with one another, and there was some animosity between the unions for skilled and unskilled workers. Unions were always at a disadvantage in their dealings with management, in part because management could hire lobbyists (to promote anti-union legislation in Washington) and lawyers and could bribe politicians. Owners often had blacklists of union troublemakers who would not be hired and plenty of "yellow-dog" workers who had signed contracts pledging never to join a union. Owners often hired spies to obtain information among workers, and, in the event of a strike, they could always hire "scabs" to cross the picket lines. It was not unheard of for managers to hire thugs to cause trouble among strikers and perpetuate the rowdy reputation of the unions.

Agricultural Problems During Populism

In the years following the Civil War, the US heartland suffered from an **overabundance** of wheat and rice; these surpluses, coupled with the advances in transportation and communication, drove prices down. Farmers were forced into high debt which they could never repay, leading to **deflation** and a scarcity of currency. Since many farmers didn't own the land that they worked, the banks often had to **foreclose** when farmers were unable to pay their debts. Farmers blamed their problems on a number of different factors. They blamed the railroads, which usually gave discount rates to bigger shippers. They blamed the banks, which loaned money to the rich but were unforgiving of farmers' economic plight. They also blamed the tax system, claiming that it was easy for businesses to hide their assets and impossible for farmers to do so. Additionally, they blamed the tariff, which discouraged other countries from buying US goods.

Early Farm Organization During Populism

The **Patron of Husbandry (Grange)** was founded in 1867 by Oliver Kelley to establish cooperatives, in which individuals bought goods directly from the wholesale distributor. His group was also responsible for the **Granger Laws**, which attacked railroad and grain elevator interests. The Grange had basically disappeared by 1875. The **National Farmer's Alliance and Industrial Union** pursued a number of different initiatives: more national banks, cooperatives, a federal storage system for non-perishable items, more currency, free coinage of silver, reduction of tariffs, direct election of senators, an 8-hour workday, government control of railroads and telegraphs, and one term for the president. This group's success led to the formation of the **Populist Party** in 1890. This party aimed to speak for the farmers and included all of the farmers' unions as well as some labor unions, the Greenbackers, and the Prohibitionists. The party suffered from internal divisions from its inception.

Radical Republican Reconstruction Plan

By 1867, Johnson's Reconstruction plan had largely failed. His unwillingness to change drove many moderate congressmen to become radicals. Radical Republicans came up with their own Reconstruction plan. First, a "Joint Committee of 15" went south to explore the damage done by the war; while there, they discovered the "Black Codes" repressing freed slaves. With the **Civil Rights Act of 1866**, they provided basic rights for ex-slaves (not including the right to vote). The **14th amendment** then gave black people citizenship and said that state governments could not deny anyone life, liberty, and property without due process. This amendment disqualified ex-Confederates from holding public office and declared that states could lose representation if they infringed on the rights of black people. With the **Congressional Reconstruction Act** (Military

Reconstruction Act) of 1867, the South was divided into 5 districts and placed under martial law; Congress forced this bill through, and eventually all of the Southern states capitulated.

> **Review Video: The Reconstruction Era**
> Visit mometrix.com/academy and enter code: 790561

Tenure of Office Act and the Supreme Court's Activity

The Tenure of Office Act of 1867 established that in order to fire any Cabinet member, the president had to get the approval of the Senate. Though essentially unconstitutional, this act almost ended the presidency of Johnson when he tried to dismiss **Edwin Stanton**, his Secretary of War. Johnson was charged with a crime, **impeached** by the House of Representatives, and missed being impeached by the Senate by one vote. The Supreme Court, though generally quiet during this period, made a couple of significant rulings. In **ex parte Milligan** (1866), the Supreme Court asserted that it is unconstitutional for military rule to continue after regular courts have been reinstated. In **ex parte McCardle** (1868), a similar case, the Supreme Court was too afraid of Congressional radicals to make a ruling.

Radical Republican Reconstruction Governments in the South

Carpetbaggers were Northerners who, under the guise of reinvesting in the Southern economy, took advantage of the situation by acquiring positions in local governments and raising taxes. **Scalawags** were white Republican Southerners who took similar economic advantage. During the rule of the Reconstruction governments, black people were allowed to hold some public offices, though not if they were freed slaves; the black Senator **Hiram Revels** (MS) served in Jefferson Davis' old seat. Black people had very few economic rights and had no land. **Thaddeus Stevens** declared that black people should receive "40 acres and a mule," but nobody was willing to take this land from its present owners. **Sharecropping** became basically another form of slavery. In short, the Reconstruction governments were corrupt, spent too much, levied too many taxes, and took advantage of newly freed slaves. Still, these governments established state constitutions, built roads and schools, and made education compulsory.

Election of 1868 and the Grant Administration

After the Civil War, the US was consumed by **materialism**. The election of 1868 pitted **Ulysses S. Grant** (Republican) against Horatio Seymour (Democrat). Grant was a war hero, and Seymour spent much of the campaign defending himself from allegations that he aided the Confederacy. The Democrats proposed that states should decide for themselves the question of black suffrage, and they wanted to give amnesty to former Confederates. Republicans had much more success with their campaign, blaming the Democrats for the war (a strategy known as "waving the bloody shirt"), and Grant won handily. Grant's presidency would not be as easy as his campaign, however. He had no political experience and was unused to compromise. He frequently fought with his Cabinet, though Secretary of State Hamilton Fish was able to convince him to sign the **Treaty of Washington** (1871), in which Britain compensated the US for aiding the Confederate navy.

Graft and Corruption Under Grant

Crédit Mobilier Scandal, Schuylar Colfax, and Fisk-Gould Scandal

The Grant administration was so corrupt that the president himself had to apologize. One of the most famous fiascos of the era was the **Crédit Mobilier scandal**: the Union Pacific gave a contract to the Crédit Mobilier of America construction company after the federal government secretly loaned Crédit Mobilier of America money for their bid. Then, Vice President **Schuyler Colfax** was caught accepting a bribe in return for ceasing the investigation. In the **Fisk-Gould scandal**, Jim Fisk and Jay Gould convinced Grant to keep government gold out of the New York Stock Exchange, because they hoped to corner the market. Grant became angry with the men and dumped $4 million worth of gold onto the market. September 24, 1869, is known as **Black Friday** on Wall Street; this was the day that Grant's gold flood caused the price of gold to drop so rapidly that the entire market crashed. Gould was able to survive this catastrophe; Fisk was not.

Tammany Hall, Congressional Salary Grab, and Whiskey Ring Scandal

William Marcy "Boss" Tweed was the political boss of New York City. He ran the **Tammany Hall** political machine, a group that fixed elections by recruiting voters with food and jobs. Another instance of corruption under Grant was the **Congressional salary grab**: Congress voted to give themselves a 50% raise, set retroactively by two years. The public was outraged by this avarice, and so, though they kept the pay raise, Congress gave up the back pay. In the **Whiskey ring scandal**, some tax agents who were supposed to be taxing barrels of whiskey were found to have been accepting bribes; this scandal went up as high as Secretary of the Treasury Benjamin Bristow. When historians look at this period and try to figure out why there was so much corruption, they generally decide that it was a carryover from the brutality of the war, combined with the naiveté of the president.

Opposition to Grant and Corruption Under Grant

Thomas Nast was one of the first famous political cartoonists; he made his name satirizing corrupt politicians like Boss Tweed. Grant established the **Civil Service Commission** in 1871, an organization whose mission was to study corruption and make recommendations to the president. Grant paid little attention to this group, however, and it died a quiet death in 1875. During Grant's first term, a group of upper-class Republicans, calling themselves the **Mugwumps**, began to call for a civil service based only on merit. At the same time, the **Liberal Republicans**, another splinter group of the Republican party, spoke out against the graft in civil service, the use of paper money, and the Republican Reconstruction policy. This group supported a lower tariff and better treatment for farmers.

Industrial Era Scandals and Innovations

The infamous **Credit Mobilier scandal** occurred during Grant's presidency in 1872 and involved the Union Pacific Railroad. A more egregious crime was perpetrated on the stockholders of the Erie Railroad; the owners were trying to avoid being bought out by Vanderbilt, and thus they printed up a huge amount of new stock, making it impossible for Vanderbilt to get a majority interest but also vastly diminishing the value of each share. During this era, the following **innovations** and inventors accelerated industry: sleeper cars (George Pullman), air brakes for trains (George Westinghouse), time zones, double tracking (so that two trains could run on the same line), and the standardization of the distance from one rail to another.

Review Video: Industrialization
Visit mometrix.com/academy and enter code: 893924

Election of 1872 and Final Collapse of Grant

In the election of 1872, **Grant** won a second term (over Liberal Republican Horace Greeley) because of his enduring status as a war hero, and because the worst scandals of his administration had yet to be exposed. Quickly, though, Grant's administration fell apart. Five Cabinet members would be found guilty of **corruption**. Then came the **Panic of 1873**. This was the result of three factors: the withdrawal of European investment (Europeans were funneling their money into the Franco-Prussian War), the stock market crash caused by the Fisk-Gould scandal, and the inflexibility of the banks caused by heavy investment in non-liquid assets. As a result of these factors, **Jay Cooke and**

Co., one of the largest banks in the US, collapsed, taking several other banks with it. Eighty-nine railroads soon went under, and then the iron and steel mills had no business. By 1875, half a million Americans were unemployed, and farmers were beginning to lose their land to foreclosure.

Ku Klux Klan and Amnesty Act of 1872

In the 1870s, Southern white people, as members of the Conservatives or Redeemers, began to regain control of the local governments; they sought to do away with "Negro rule." The **Ku Klux Klan** was founded in 1867 by former Confederate General Nathan Bedford Forrest and other ex-Confederates. Though founded as a social club, this group quickly got out of hand, causing the passage of the **Ku Klux Klan and Force Acts** (1870-1), unsuccessful attempts to subdue the Klan by allowing for black militias. The **Amnesty Act of 1872** extended the right to vote to many more ex-Confederates. Gradually, the North began to lose interest in the South for the following reasons: they were disgusted by the corrupt governments, they were frustrated by the persistent racism, and they had agreed to remain distant in exchange for a higher tariff.

Solutions to the Panic of 1873

By 1873, **currency deflation** was a major problem in the US. There were a number of supporters of cheap money, and they encouraged the US government to issue $26 million in greenbacks to stimulate the economy; this plan failed. There was another group of hard-money advocates who suggested using a gold standard, so the government made a compromise called the **Specie Resumption Act of 1875**. This act increased the number of national banks in the South and West, allowed national banks to issue as many notes as they wanted (up to a $300 million limit), and named a "day of redemption," on which all greenbacks could be exchanged for gold coins. The day of redemption never came to pass, however, which seemed to be a victory for the cheap money supporters. Instead, it became evident that the promise of gold exchange caused the public to treat greenbacks as if they were "good as gold." By 1879, the economy was back on track and the Republicans had acquired the reputation as the party in favor of business.

Subordination of Western Native Americans Until 1874

The Native Americans who roamed the Great Plains were known as fierce hunters, and there were a few bloody encounters between settlers heading west and the natives. In 1851, the US established the **Concentration policy**, which encouraged Native Americans to live close to one another. This strategy was untenable, however, and the period from 1860-90 was marked by frequent conflict. In the **Sioux Wars** of 1865-7, the Sioux were led by **Red Cloud**; they fought and lost to American troops after their sacred hunting ground was mined. For a while, the US tried to group tribes on reservations in Oklahoma and the Black Hills; from 1869-74, Generals Sherman and Sheridan engaged in a **War of Extermination** to kill those who refused to move.

Subordination of the Western Native Americans from 1875-1887

According to **Grant's Peace Program**, each Native American tribe would be put under the control of different religious groups. In 1875, miners were allowed back into the Black Hills, prompting the **Sioux War** of 1875-6, during which Sitting Bull defeated Custer at the **Battle of Little Big Horn**. Around this time, Chief Joseph attempted to lead his Nez Perce tribe to Canada; this mission failed and the Nez Perce were sent to Oklahoma. The Apache leader Geronimo was defeated in Arizona in 1887. At the **Battle of Wounded Knee**, the US army massacred 300, mostly women and children. Native Americans were doomed by their inferior weapons; by the destruction by white people of their food supply, the buffalo; and by railroads which made it easier for white people to encroach on their hunting grounds.

ELECTION OF 1876 AND NATIONAL SELF-EVALUATION

The election of 1876, won by **Rutherford B. Hayes** (Republican) over Samuel J. Tilden (Democrat), coincided with the **US centennial**, so people were compelled to consider the history of the country thus far. When Americans of 1876 looked back, they had some reason to be pleased: they had survived a Civil War intact and had witnessed the end of slavery. They also had developed a strong national government. On the other hand, many Americans were disillusioned at this time by the scandals of the Grant administration. There had also been violent and disheartening struggles between black militiamen and the Ku Klux Klan in the South. Finally, many in the country were still reeling from Custer's bloody defeat at the Battle of Little Big Horn.

ELECTION OF 1876 AND COMPROMISE OF 1877

In 1876, **Rutherford B. Hayes** (Republican) defeated Samuel Tilden (Democrat) after an electoral commission composed mostly of Republicans ruled that certain votes by carpetbag governments should have gone to him. As part of the ensuing **Compromise of 1877**, the South was given federal money for improvements to infrastructure, a Southerner was placed in Hayes' Cabinet, and the Union troops propping up the carpetbag governments were removed. This election established the tradition of the "**Solid South**": it was assumed that every year the majority of Southerners would vote for the Democratic candidate.

HAYES PRESIDENCY

HIGHLIGHTS

Foolishly, **Rutherford B. Hayes** made himself a lame-duck president by announcing soon after taking office that he would not seek a second term. Hayes' wife was nicknamed "Lemonade Lucy," because she would not allow any alcohol in the White House. Hayes tried to restore the power of the presidency after the debacle of Grant, but he was weakened by intense struggles over his Cabinet confirmations. One thing Hayes can be credited with is making a gallant attempt to destroy the **spoils system**. He replaced the Collector of the Customs House after discovering the corruption of that body, and he appointed Carl Schurz Secretary of the Interior on the basis of merit. In turn, Schurz established a merit system in his department, creating an entrance exam for potential employees.

LOW-POINTS

One of the failures of the Hayes administration was its handling of the **Great Rail Strike of 1877**. When over two-thirds of the rail lines were shut down by strikes, Hayes sent in federal troops, and there was considerable bloodshed. This set a bad precedent for how strikes would be handled in the future. Hayes vetoed an attempt by western labor unions to restrict Chinese immigration, saying that this would be a violation of the **Burlingame Treaty**. One of the main issues in the Hayes years was monetary policy. Farmers, who were often in debt, wanted a soft currency not backed by anything; they were willing to settle for a silver standard. In **Hepburn v. Griswold** (1869), the Supreme Court had ruled that there could not be paper money without a gold standard; in the **Legal Tender cases of 1871**, however, the Court reversed itself. The bickering over these conflicting rulings plagued the Hayes administration.

HAYES VS. GREENBACKERS AND THE SILVERITES

After the **Specie Resumption Act of 1875**, Hayes worked to minimize the effects of the oncoming "day of redemption," in which paper money could be exchanged for gold coins. He began a policy of contraction, wherein the government gradually took in paper money and issued gold, and he funded attempts to mine more gold. The **Greenbackers** were those who wanted Hayes to postpone the day of redemption; he did not, and it ultimately proved anticlimactic, as people assumed their paper money was "good as gold" and didn't bother to redeem it. Hayes also had to deal with the **Silverites**. In 1873, the government had enraged silver prospectors by announcing that it would no longer make coins out of silver. In answer to their fury, Hayes pushed through the **Bland-Allison Act**, which established that a minimum of $2 million of silver had to be purchased and coined by the government every month.

Competition and Disorder in the Industrial Era

The late 19th century was marked by intense competition between the railroads. Railroads offered secret illegal refunds to big customers, and in areas where they had no competition, they charged exorbitant prices. After the 1870s, various states tried to tame the railroads; one such instance of this kind of regulation was the **Granger Laws**. Farmers often felt that they were charged more than others. In **Munn v. Illinois** (1877), the Supreme Court asserted that the state governments had the right to regulate the railroads. In Wabash, St. Louis, and **Pacific Railroad Co. v. Illinois** (1886), the Supreme Court reversed its former opinion and declared that only the federal government could regulate the railroads. Finally, with the **Interstate Commerce Act of 1887**, the federal government forbade discriminatory practices like refunds and price-fixing; unfortunately, these laws were rarely enforced.

Great Strike of 1877, the Homestead Strike, and the Pullman Strike

The Great Strike of 1877 occurred in West Virginia when state police and militiamen were sent to break up a railway strike and joined it instead. President Hayes sent in the army, and at least 100 people were killed breaking up the strike. This debacle set a bad precedent for future strikes. In the **Homestead (PA) Strike** of July 1892, a group of soldiers called by Henry Clay Frick (temporarily in charge of one of Carnegie's steel mills) brutally broke up a strike. In 1894, a group of **Pullman railcar employees** began a strike, supported by the American Railway Union of Eugene V. Debs. All rail workers then went on strike out of sympathy for the Pullman workers. The rail owners got an injunction, claiming that the rail workers were interfering with interstate trade and therefore violating the **Sherman Anti-trust Act**. This did not end the strike, and thus President Grover Cleveland had to send in the army under the false premise that the strike was holding up the US mail.

Election of 1880

In the election of 1880, the **Republican party** was beset by internal squabbling between the stalwarts and half-breeds over the issue of patronage. This led to a chaotic nominating convention in which a campaign manager, **James A. Garfield**, became the candidate. Garfield won a narrow victory over the Democrat Winfield Scott Hancock, a war hero with no political experience. Garfield was a charismatic figure whose administration began with a successful compromise among Republicans; unfortunately, he was shot and killed in 1881. Garfield was succeeded by his vice-president, **Chester A. Arthur**. The major event of his presidency was the **Civil Service Act of 1883**, which established a commission to create competitive examinations for potential government employees. Arthur also helped create the modern US navy.

New South in the 1880s

In the 1880s, the old Southern plantations began to break up, in part because the high taxes imposed by the new governments made them unprofitable. The land was mainly worked by tenant farmers and sharecroppers: **tenant farmers** worked and paid rent on someone else's land, while **sharecroppers** worked the whole plantation and got a share of the crop. Tenant farmers were mostly poor white people, while sharecroppers were mostly freed black people. There was considerable diversification in agriculture around this time, brought on not only by innovation (cotton picker, tractor), but by the **Morrill Land Grant Act**, which gave grants for the creation of agricultural colleges. Clarence Birdseye's development of the refrigerated railroad car spurred farming as well. Also, as the road and rail infrastructure improved in the South, so did Southern industry.

Other Reforms During the Civil War and Reconstruction Eras

Contributions of Women to American Society

For nearly a century of America's history, women were mostly viewed as insignificant or delicate and had no place or desire for roles outside of the home. When the Civil War began, women were able to break out of their traditional gender roles in mighty ways. Many women raised money for war efforts, served in militias and industry, supplied food for troops, or worked as nurses behind combat lines. Many women worked with the Underground Railroad to aid runaway slaves and campaigned for women's suffrage. Through their efforts, many slaves were able to escape to freedom and Wyoming first allowed women to vote in 1869. However, women would have to continue lobbying for the national right to vote for decades to come.

Abolitionist Movement

The abolitionist movement of the 19th century was a social movement to end slavery and emancipate slaves. Slavery was an integral part of the American South. Most abolitionists were Northerners. They considered slavery a moral disease that threatened the Union. Abolitionists worked through political channels to free slaves and end the system of slavery. Some worked to help escaped slaves on the Underground Railroad. The turning point for the movement came in 1860 when Abraham Lincoln, who opposed the spread of slavery, became president of the United States.

American Prison Reform

Zebulon Brockway and Dorothea Dix are two of the most prominent figures in the history of American prison reform. Brockway worked at or ran numerous prisons over his lifetime and was an advocate for prison education and training inmates with vocational skills. He also introduced the idea of parole. After spending many years visiting prisons, Dorothea could not bear the sights she had witnessed. It was not uncommon for men, women, and children to be grouped together in the same prison, and those that were sick were not provided with adequate medical care. She took particular note of the wretched state of those with mental illnesses, as they were chronically abused and mistreated. Through her efforts, mental asylums were established to better care for those with mental illnesses, and many states developed an independent system to better deal with children.

Care for Individuals with Disabilities

Much of the reform movements for the care of disabled individuals began towards the end of World War I. With so many injured and disabled veterans returning home from the war, the Fess-Smith Civilian Vocational Rehabilitation Act was passed in 1920 to try to meet the large spike in needs for the disabled. The Social Security Act, which was passed by President Franklin D. Roosevelt in 1935, included grants for state assistance programs for the blind and disabled children; however, this did not amend the discrimination still felt by disabled individuals as they were extremely less likely to be hired for employment. In response, the American Federation of the Physically Handicapped is formed in 1938 by Paul Strachan, as America's first cross-disability political organization. It lobbied extensively for fair employment for the disabled, including a National Employ the Physically Handicapped Week.

Attitudes Toward Education in the Early 19th Century

Horace Mann, among others, felt that schools could help children become better citizens, keep them away from crime, prevent poverty, and help American society become more unified. His

Common School Journal brought his ideas of the importance of education into the public consciousness and proposed his suggestions for an improved American education system. Increased literacy led to increased awareness of current events, Western expansion, and other major developments of the time period. Public interest and participation in the arts and literature also increased. By the end of the 19th century, all children had access to a **free public elementary education**.

Labor Reform

Rapid industrialization in the late 19th century revolutionized how the workforce operated. The mass migration of workers to factories brought great economic gain, but it also brought hazardous working conditions and unfair labor practices. The labor movement desired fair working hours and wages for the quickly growing labor force. Unions, such as the National Labor Union and the Knights of Labor, arose in the midst of these struggles to fight for the rights of workers across the nation. It was not until 1886, that Samuel Gompers founded the American Federation of Labor for skilled workers that ultimately established the union and labor movement as a force with real power to act as an agent of change. Safer working conditions began steadily increasing throughout different industries and work hours began decreasing towards the standard eight-hour workday we have today.

Early Leaders in the Women's Rights Movement

The women's rights movement began in the 1840s, with leaders including Elizabeth Cady Stanton, Sojourner Truth, Ernestine Rose, and Lucretia Mott. In 1869, Elizabeth Cady Stanton and Susan B. Anthony formed the **National Woman Suffrage Association**, fighting for women's right to vote.

In 1848, in Seneca Falls, the first women's rights convention was held, with about 300 attendees. The two-day **Seneca Falls Convention** discussed the rights of women to vote (suffrage) as well as equal treatment in careers, legal proceedings, etc. The convention produced a "Declaration of Sentiments," which outlined a plan for women to attain the rights they deserved. **Frederick Douglass** supported the women's rights movement, as well as the abolition movement. In fact, women's rights and abolition movements often went hand-in-hand during this time period.

Review Video: The Women's Rights Movement in America
Visit mometrix.com/academy and enter code: 987734

Temperance Movement of the 19th Century

The temperance movement of the 19th century was a social movement, led mostly by women, to discourage the consumption of alcohol. As the movement gained ground in the mid-1800s, it changed from a purely social movement advocating moderation in the consumption of alcohol to a political movement that was successful in getting the government to regulate the sale of alcohol. The 18th Amendment to the Constitution established Prohibition, which made alcohol illegal in this country. Through this lens, the temperance movement of the 19th century was very successful in achieving its goals and had a significant impact on life in the United States. (The 18th Amendment was repealed by the 21st Amendment in 1933 and is the only constitutional amendment to have been repealed.)

W.E.B. Du Bois's Work as Civil Rights Activist

Du Bois was the foremost intellectual and political activist for African-Americans in the 20th century's first half and was called "The Father of Pan-Africanism." He and educator Booker T. Washington collaborated on ideas for solutions to political disenfranchisement and segregation, and on organizing the "Negro Exhibition" showing black contributions to American society at

Paris's 1900 Exposition Universelle. In 1905 he cofounded the Niagara Movement, championing free speech, voting, leadership, and antiracist ideals. Cofounder William Trotter felt whites should be excluded. Du Bois disagreed and cofounded the National Association for the Advancement of Colored People (NAACP) in 1909 where races could unite for civil rights. He left his faculty position at Atlanta University and became NAACP's publications director in 1910, publishing Harlem Renaissance writers Langston Hughes and Jean Toomer. Becoming more radical as NAACP became more institutionalized, Du Bois suggested black separatism as an economic policy in the 1930s and returned to teaching at Atlanta University. He corresponded with NAACP member Albert Einstein, who called racism "America's worst disease" in 1946.

Frederick Douglass's Work as a Civil Rights Activist

Frederick Douglass was an American activist who worked on various fronts of advocacy for civic rights. Douglass was born as a slave and was separated from both of his parents at an early age. His mother was a slave and his father was an unknown white man. Early in his adulthood, he successfully escaped from slavery by boarding a train to the North. He became a powerful orator and writer and played a key role in progress toward civil rights for African Americans.

Industrialization, Emergence of Modern America, and World Conflicts

Growth of the Nation between the Reconstruction and Early-Twentieth Century

GILDED AGE

CHARACTERISTICS

The period in American history between Reconstruction and the Progressive Era is commonly known as the **Gilded Age**. During this period, the US seemed to be simultaneously abandoning the ideals of the past and failing to anticipate the future; this was in large part due to the confusion of a horrendous Civil War and massive immigration, industrialization, and urbanization. During this period, many Americans sought refuge in **community organizations** like the Moose Lodge, the Elks Club, and the Masonic Lodge. The politicians of the Gilded Age tended to avoid the major issues of **social injustice and inequality**, instead focusing on minor issues like public v. parochial schools, and the blue laws (laws restricting commercial activity on Sunday).

Review Video: The Gilded Age: An Overview
Visit mometrix.com/academy and enter code: 684770

POLITICS

Although the **Republicans** dominated the executive branch during the Gilded Age, Congress was evenly divided. The Republican party was composed mainly of people from the Northeast and Midwest. Black people typically were Republicans (that is, when they were allowed into the political process). In general, the Republicans supported high tariffs and sound money. One of the main internal disputes in the Republican party was between the **stalwarts**, who supported the spoils system, and the **half-breeds**, who did not. As for the **Democrats**, they were largely based in the South or in the big cities of the North. The Democrats and Republicans butted heads over ethnic, religious, and cultural issues, but they tended to avoid larger economic and social issues. Extremely talented individuals were more likely to go into business than politics during this era. Another trend of the Gilded Age was the domination of the president by Congress.

AMERICAN LABOR IN THE GILDED AGE

As the US emerged from the Civil War, one of the main economic problems was that most workers were **unskilled**. In general, working conditions were horrendous and wages were low. There was little homogeneity in the labor force, either, making it difficult for workers to switch jobs. **Immigrants** were usually willing to take more dangerous jobs than natives; during the 1880s, more than 5 million immigrants entered the US. In 1882, the **Chinese Exclusion Act** put a 10-year moratorium on Chinese immigration. In 1885, the **Foran Act** prohibited American businessmen from traveling to China to recruit workers. Both of these acts were open violations of the **Burlingame Treaty of 1868**, which had provided for open Chinese immigration.

SOCIAL CRITICS AND DISSENTERS IN THE GILDED AGE

In his book *Dynamic Sociology*, **Lester Frank Ward** railed against the Social Darwinism espoused by the upper class; he declared that humans were more than mere animals. In *Progress and Poverty*, **Henry George** asserted that poverty was the result of poor legislation rather than any inherent weakness in the poor. **Edward Bellamy** promoted socialism in his novel *Looking Back* (1888); in it, a man of the year 2000 describes how America was turned into a utopian society through the abolition of corporations. Also, at this time, **Thorstein Veblen** exposed the phenomenon of "conspicuous consumption" in his *Theory of the Leisure Class*. All of these critics were disgusted by the hypocrisy of the **robber barons**; these magnates claimed to support laissez-faire government, yet they wanted high tariffs to protect their businesses.

Laissez-Faire Conservatism and the Gospel of Wealth

The so-called "**Gilded Age**" of American history, which ran roughly from 1880 to 1900, only looked prosperous from a distance. Many at this time believed that wealth justified itself and that God showed his favor in people by making them rich. Many business leaders did not trust politicians because they did not feel that they had had to fight their way to the top. Businessmen believed that the role of the government was to protect property and trade through tariffs. **William Graham Sumner** wrote the essay "What the Social Classes Owe Each Other," in which he declared that corporations shouldn't demand high tariff rates, but the government shouldn't respond to requests to clean up the slums. There was a general sense that the poor were responsible for their plight. Around this time, the popular imagination was inspired by the rags-to-riches fables of **Horatio Alger**.

Industrialism in the Gilded Age

The first and second industrial revolutions both started in England in the late-1700s- and mid-1800s, respectively. Following the Civil War, some of the advances in technology spread to America and sparked the **American Industrial Revolution**, introducing new technologies such as improved steel production, railroads, the lightbulb, and the telephone. Factory jobs became available and instigated the rise of larger cities that were untenable before some of these advancements. Despite the rise in new technologies and new types of jobs, poverty was rampant in many parts of the country. Those who took on factory jobs also frequently saw **poor working conditions**, such as dangerous situations, long hours, and low wages. On the other hand, those who had success in the industrial period had newfound time for **leisure**, leading to an emergence of leisure activities, such as theater, sports, and amusement parks. Over time, wages slightly increased and more people had time and money to participate in leisure activities, shaping an early culture of entertainment in America.

Redeemers

The "Redeemers" sought to prevent black people from voting and to return power to the "natural leaders." In response, the **Populist party** was formed; it was an uneasy alliance of black people and poor white people. Southern Democrats tried to exploit the tension within the Populist party. In order to keep black people from voting, Democrats subjected voters to literacy tests, property tests, criminal background checks, residency requirements, and the so-called **Grandfather Clause**, which stated that individuals could not vote unless their ancestors had voted before January 1, 1867. These restrictions, known collectively as the **Mississippi Plan**, were upheld by the Supreme Court, which ruled in **Williams v. Mississippi** (1898) that they were legal because they never explicitly stated that black people could not vote.

Black Southerners and Segregation

Most Southern Democrats supported **segregation**, or the separation of the races. Although the **Civil Rights Act of 1875** had outlawed segregated restaurants and hotels, among other things, the Supreme Court ruled in 1883 that this act violated the 14th amendment because only states, and not individuals, could be forbidden from segregation. The **Jim Crow laws** were those rules that segregated black people and white people. Although de facto (by custom) segregation had existed in the North for years, the South began to implement segregation de jure (by law). In **Plessy v. Ferguson** (1896), the Supreme Court ruled that accommodations should be "separate but equal." In **Cummings v. Board of Education** (1898), the Supreme Court allowed public schools to be segregated.

Booker T. Washington and W.E.B. DuBois

Booker T. Washington was an ex-slave who founded the Tuskegee Institute in 1881; he felt that black people should establish economic independence before worrying about political rights. In his **Atlanta Exposition speech**, he declared that black people needed to humble themselves to white people. Professor **W.E.B. DuBois** attacked Washington's speech as a compromise; DuBois believed black people should take everything they were due. In 1914, both Washington and DuBois met with Marcus Garvey, who believed that black people should return to Africa and establish a separate country (interestingly, most of Garvey's financial support came from the KKK). At around this time, Paul Laurence Dunbar was achieving renown as the "poet laureate of the Negro race," and Charles Waddell Chestnut was admired as a popular black novelist.

Election of 1884

In 1884, the incumbent Arthur was passed over by his party in favor of Secretary of State James G. Blaine. This proved to be a bad move, as the **Democratic** candidate, **Grover Cleveland**, was able to win the support of conservative Republicans (Mugwumps) and claim a narrow victory. The highlights of the Cleveland administration include the further reform of civil service and the government's successful stand against ex-Union soldiers who were protesting for large pensions. Cleveland reluctantly signed the **Interstate Commerce Act**, and he was correct in predicting that it would not be enforced. Cleveland also spent a great deal of time on tariffs: he attempted to reduce the overall duty with the **Mongrel Tariff** and the **Mills Bill of 1888**, neither of which were very successful.

Solutions to the "Indian Problem"

The US government constructed several policies in an attempt to solve the so-called "**Indian Problem**." The **Dawes (Severalty) Act of 1887** asserted that Natives needed to be assimilated into American society; tribes were moved onto "allotments of severalty" (reservations), which they supposedly owned, although they had no control of the land. The **Indian Reorganization (Howard-Wheeler) Act of 1934** encouraged a return to tribal life and offered Natives money for college. In 1953, with the so-called "**termination policy**," Natives became the responsibility of the states rather than the federal government. In 1970, the new strategy was "self-determination without termination": Natives were allowed to move where they choose and were promised money (which they did not receive).

Election of 1888

In 1888, the Republican **Benjamin Harrison** narrowly upset the incumbent Cleveland, despite having less of the popular vote. Harrison did not accomplish much civil service reform and spent a great deal of time managing insubordination in Congress. Harrison's Republican agenda promoted the **Federal Election Bill**, which was a response to the Mississippi Plan designed to protect the voting rights of freedmen. The **Silver Purchase Bill** was favored by the west but lacked the votes to get through. In the **Compromise of 1890**, the Western Republicans got the silver purchase (Sherman Silver Purchase Act), Southern Democrats got the defeat of the Federal Election Bill, and the Northern Republicans got a higher tariff (McKinley Tariff of 1890). Harrison's administration became known for giving money away for virtually any reason: pensions were excessive, the silver purchase cost federal money, and all of the income tax taken during the Civil War was given back to the people.

Election of 1892 and the Panic of 1893

Grover Cleveland (Dem) defeated Benjamin Harrison (Rep) in the election of 1892 primarily because of his financial conservatism, his promise to change the tariff, and Harrison's weakened state following the epidemic of strikes in 1892. Then came the **Panic of 1893**, caused by labor troubles, over-speculation in the railroads, and an agricultural depression. First, the Philadelphia and Reading Railroads collapsed, then the stock markets collapsed, then the banks folded, draining the gold reserves, then the other railroads folded, and finally the factories were forced to close. Cleveland believed that the cause of this Panic was the **Sherman Silver Purchase Act**, so he repealed it. This plan did absolutely nothing financially, and it split the Democratic party politically.

Panic of 1893 and Domestic Affairs Under Cleveland

After the Panic of 1893, a group known as the **Silverite school** declared that the economic problems could be solved if the US would begin coining silver again. Cleveland, however, ignored this advice and elected to buy gold with the profits from the sale of government bonds. This strategy was somewhat successful. It was during the **Panic of 1893** that the suggestion to battle economic depression by employing people on public works was first made. One of Cleveland's major policy moves in his second term was the **Wilson-Gorman Tariff of 1894**. This lowered the tariff rate and established trade with Latin America. It also established a small income tax on wealthy individuals, though this income tax would be repealed in the **Supreme Court case Pollock v. Farmer's Loan and Trust** (1895). Cleveland's last term was diminished by ineffective enforcement of the **Sherman Anti-trust Act** and the **Interstate Commerce Act**.

J.P. Morgan and Banker Control

The **Panic of 1893** was brought on by the collapse of the **Philadelphia and Reading Railroads**; soon after, 192 railroads failed. In a panic, railroad magnates turned to bankers, especially the "Railroad Doctor," **J.P. Morgan**. Morgan insisted that all of the business' records be opened to him. His usual strategy was to encourage old investors to reinvest; to sell more, "watered-down" stock; and to place either himself or one of his associates on the Board of Directors. In this way, Morgan was able to create a set of "interlocking directories," conglomerations of businesses in which he had an interest. He created many large companies this way, among them General Electric, Western Union, and Equitable.

Andrew Carnegie and Steel

The potential for making money in **steel** was made possible by the development of the **Bessemer process**, whereby iron ore was converted into wrought iron and then had its impurities removed with cold air. **Andrew Carnegie**, an immigrant from Scotland who rose to the top of the Pennsylvania Railroad, was one of the first to make his fortune in steel. He was not especially knowledgeable about steel, but he was the first manager to make a point of **vertical integration**; that is, control of every step of the production process. Carnegie bought out most of his competitors, until he was eventually bought out by J.P. Morgan. Carnegie and his fellows believed in a sort of "gospel of wealth," the idea that they had risen to the top through a process like natural selection. They also believed in using their money for the community.

Review Video: Andrew Carnegie and the Steel Industry
Visit mometrix.com/academy and enter code: 696753

John D. Rockefeller and the Trust

John D. Rockefeller came from a working-class background but gradually rose to become the owner of the wildly profitable **Standard Oil company**. Rockefeller was known for spying on his competitors and intimidating his employees. In 1870, Standard allied itself with 40 other companies; when this alliance began, the group controlled 10% of the market, but by 1881 they controlled almost 95%. In 1882, Standard Oil created a **trust**: alliance members gave their stock to Standard in exchange for trust certificates. The federal government began to get suspicious of these powerful trusts, and in 1890 the **Sherman Anti-trust Act** was passed. This act forbade trusts, but it was worded so vaguely that it was ineffective. In the case of **US v. E.C. Knight Co.** (1895), the Supreme Court ruled that the Knight sugar refinery was not a monopoly because it didn't hurt interstate trade; businesses saw this ruling as a call to monopolize.

Republican Ascendancy in the Election of 1896

The Republicans had been successful in the Congressional elections of 1894, and they nominated **William McKinley** for president in 1896. McKinley was in favor of high tariffs and the gold standard. He was opposed by William Jennings Bryan of the Democrats. McKinley had a wealth of political experience and money, and the Democrats were blamed by many for the economic depression under Cleveland; McKinley won fairly easily. This election marked a 36-year period of domination by the **Republicans**. It also spelled the end of the Populist party. Around this time, gold was found in the Yukon, lending credence to the Republican belief in the gold standard.

Imperialism

During the Period of Withdrawal (Civil War to 1880s)

In the period after the Civil War, the US for the most part withdrew from **foreign affairs**. The Secretaries of State in this period, however, were very aggressive: **Seward** interfered in Korean politics, tried to assert influence in the Caribbean, and famously purchased Alaska from Russia in 1867 for $7.2 million. **Hamilton Fish** tried and failed to annex Santo Domingo. Aside from these instances, though, the US kept its distance. For the most part, this was because it was preoccupied with its own problems. There was also a common belief that invading and colonizing other countries would be a violation of the US **Declaration of Independence**. Many were remembering Washington's farewell address, in which he advised the US to avoid military entanglements, and others were wary of violating the **Monroe Doctrine**.

During the New Manifest Destiny (1880s to 1920s)

In the 1880s, the US began to take a stronger interest in **foreign affairs**. This was in part due to humanitarian concern; the US felt it could improve the standard of living around the world. There was also, of course, an economic motive; manufacturers wanted to find a new source of raw materials, as well as a new market for their products. Missionaries began to travel abroad in this period, trying to convert foreigners to Christianity. There were also military reasons for the increased activity abroad; the US decided it would be a good idea to acquire naval bases in the Pacific, and a group known as the **Jingoists** openly looked for a military conflict. Theodore Roosevelt and Henry Cabot Lodge were both Jingoists.

Bering Sea, Pan-American Union, and Samoan Islands Conflict

The "**Seal Battle**" was fought in the Bering Sea between British Canada and the US mainly over boundary lines. In 1893, the two sides met and established mutual boundaries between Alaska and Canada. In 1889, the first meeting of the **Pan-American Union** was held in Washington, DC. In 1878, the US had established a naval base at Pago Pago. Both the British and Germans demanded access to the base. In 1889, the US allowed both the British and Germans to jointly occupy the base. In 1899, the **Samoan islands** were divided up among the US and the European powers.

Conflict with Italy, Baltimore Incident, Boundary Disputes in South America, and Hawaii

Between the years 1889 and 1891, the US came into conflict with **Italy** after members of the **Sicilian Black Hand**, a terrorist group, were lynched without just cause in New Orleans. The US also sparred with Chile after 2 sailors from the ***USS Baltimore*** died during a bar fight in Valparaiso, Chile. At around this time, a boundary dispute erupted between **British Guiana** and **Venezuela** after gold was discovered in the vaguely defined border region. Britain was ready to send troops into South America, but the US dissuaded them from doing so, citing the Monroe Doctrine. Meanwhile, all throughout the 19th century, the US had been closing in on a conquest of **Hawaii**. After New England missionaries stumbled upon the islands, the US had gotten the natives to sign trade treaties with various US companies. In the 1890s, the US army, led by pineapple magnate Sanford Dole, ousted the native leadership. Hawaii was annexed by the US in 1898.

Review Video: An Overview of American Imperialism
Visit mometrix.com/academy and enter code: 629170

Emerging Role of the United States in World Affairs

Spanish-American War

Causes

The **Spanish-American War** centered around **Cuba**. There had already been several revolts against the Spanish leadership on that island, and the **Wilson-Gorman Tariff** had damaged the Cuban economy. In 1896, the Spanish sent General Valeriano Weyler to establish a reconcentration camp, where the dissenting Cubans could be weeded out. Many in the United States pushed the government to intervene in Cuba; businessmen were worried about their crops, Christians and humanitarians were worried about the Cuban people, and imperialists saw a good chance to seize the island. The two final causes of the war were the **DeLome letter**, in which the Spanish minister to the US insulted President McKinley, and the explosion of the ***USS Maine*** in Havana Harbor. Although the Spanish still claim to not have caused this explosion, the US nevertheless declared war on April 25, 1898.

Overview

The Spanish-American War only lasted between six and eight weeks before the US claimed victory. The first phase of it was fought in the Philippines and the second in Cuba. In Cuba, the United States scored a crucial victory when a rag-tag group of soldiers known as the **Roughriders** (Theodore Roosevelt among them) took Kettle Hill and secured Santiago. Although the **Teller Amendment of 1898** had promised independence to Cuba after the war, the **Platt Amendment**, which was inserted into the Cuban Constitution in 1901, made Cuba a protectorate of the US. The US control of **Guantanamo Bay** dates back to this amendment. In 1934, Cuba received its independence. The Spanish-American War formally ended with the signing of the **Treaty of Paris** in 1898. The US received Guam, the Philippines, Puerto Rico, Cuba, and Wake Island. The US also paid the Spanish $20 million because Manila had supposedly surrendered after the end of the war, making it an invalid wartime concession.

Debate over the Philippines and the Filipino War

In the years 1898 and 1899, the question of what to do about the **Philippines** was hotly debated in the US. **Imperialists** (including Henry Cabot Lodge and Theodore Roosevelt), wanted to make the group of islands into a state, argued against **Anti-imperialists** (e.g., Andrew Carnegie, Mark Twain) who felt that the US would be drawn into Asian conflicts. Some politicians, like William Jennings

Bryan, voted for the Treaty of Paris and the acquisition of the Philippines because they felt it would be a disaster that would discourage further imperialism. In 1899, the Filipino leader **Aguinaldo** led the people against US forces. This uprising was only crushed after much cruelty. Later, the **Tydings-McDuffie Act of 1934** promised independence to the Philippines within 10 years but they did not receive it until 1946. Some relevant Supreme Court rulings from this period were in the **Insular Cases of 1901**: the Court asserted that citizens of US territories do not have the same rights as citizens of the continental US.

John Hay's Defense of China

From 1898 to 1905, **John Hay** was the Secretary of State. One of his great achievements was establishing the **Open Door Policy** with respect to China. China had just been defeated by Japan and was in the process of being carved up by the European powers into various spheres of economic influence. Hay asserted that each nation should allow equal access for all nations and should respect the rights of the Chinese. Somewhat surprisingly, Europe agreed to this policy of goodwill. The Open Door Policy did not, however, keep China from being exploited by foreign traders. In the **Boxer Rebellion of 1900**, the Chinese rose up against foreigners and were promptly routed by an international coalition (including the US).

Election of 1900 and Theodore Roosevelt

In the election of 1900, **McKinley** and Theodore Roosevelt of the Republicans defeated William Jennings Bryan of the Democrats. McKinley was then assassinated on September 6, 1901, and **Roosevelt** took over. Roosevelt is known as a follower of the African proverb, "Speak softly and carry a big stick." He was known for having very little respect for the system of checks and balances. If the Constitution were too rigid on an issue for his tastes, he ignored it; if Congress acted up, he would subdue them with a mixture of compromise and coercion. Roosevelt displayed his blunt skill in diplomacy in the **Alaska Panhandle dispute of 1903** (in which he decided which islands the US would get, and which would belong to the British) and in the **Morocco Dispute of 1905**, in which he (along with Britain and France) dissuaded Germany from trying to take the North African country.

Panama Canal

Beginnings Under Roosevelt

The Spanish-American War had demonstrated that the US needed a **Latin American canal** in order to become a major naval power. At that time, however, their hands were tied by the **Clayton-Bulwer Treaty of 1850**, which had stated that neither the US nor Britain would build a canal in Latin America without the other. Fortunately for the US, the British were distracted by the Boer War in South Africa and thus were willing to sign the **Hay-Pauncefote Treaty** in 1901, allowing the US to go it alone. Many in the US, including Roosevelt, wanted to build the canal in Nicaragua because it has a number of lakes that could be connected, and because it is mostly flat. Others lobbied for Panama, pointing out that a French contractor had already started work on a canal there and that Panama was narrower than Nicaragua.

Organization Required to Build

In 1902, the United States struck a deal with a Panamanian builder for the control of the canal project. The US then needed to acquire the land. Panama at this time was owned by Colombia; the Colombians rejected the first offer made by the US, leading Roosevelt to call them "blackmailers." Then, in 1903, a rebellion broke out in Panama; Roosevelt recognized the new, independent country after less than a day of fighting. Fifteen days later, the US purchased the **Panama Canal Zone** from the new foreign minister for $10 million initially and $250,000 per year. Many observers were embarrassed by the deal the United States had won from a fledgling country. Nevertheless, Roosevelt then hired engineer John Stephens to finish the job.

Building and Opening

Once Roosevelt finally secured the building supplies and the land to construct the Panama Canal, the brutal and dangerous work began. In order to prevent malaria, the US paved streets, drained swamps, and built houses so that the workers would not have to sleep in tents. Nevertheless, the workdays were long, and the pay was low. In the end, the canal cost about $400 million; it was finished in 1913 but did not open until the next year. Roosevelt's visit to Panama made him the first president to leave the US during his term. In 1920, a guilty Democratic Congress gave Colombia $25 million. At present, about 12,000 ships go through the canal every year, and it takes about 8 hours to get from one end to the other.

Roosevelt and the 2nd Venezuelan Crisis

In 1902, many Latin American countries were deep in debt to Europe and were not making any moves to repay their debts. Enraged, European countries began to use military force. At first, Roosevelt supported this policy, but he gradually changed his mind, in part because the American public was opposed to it. When Germany, therefore, sent ships to Santo Domingo in 1904, Roosevelt announced the **Roosevelt Corollary** to the Monroe Doctrine. This document stated that nations may not use force to collect debts. Roosevelt asserted that the US would peaceably arbitrate these disputes before Europe could get violent; he felt these interventions would help Latin America and prevent European recolonization. The US developed a reputation as "the policeman of the Caribbean."

Roosevelt Republicans and Roosevelt as a "Trustbuster"

For Roosevelt Republicans, the principles of good **domestic policy** could be summed up as the "3 Cs": control of the corporations, consumer protection, and the conservation of natural resources. Roosevelt had made his name as a member of the **Roughriders** in the Spanish-American War. Interestingly, his presidency was a result of his unpopularity in his own party: his fellow Republicans had nominated him as vice president because this was felt to be a weak position. They were of course quite displeased when McKinley was assassinated, and Roosevelt became president. Roosevelt quickly became famous for his attacks on the trusts. He went after the **Northern Securities Company**, run by, among others, J. P. Morgan and John D. Rockefeller. Morgan attempted to bribe Attorney General Philip Knox to halt the investigation; Knox promptly reported this to Roosevelt. In all, 44 **anti-trust cases** were heard during Roosevelt's presidency.

Roosevelt's Square Deal

Roosevelt's Square Deal was a domestic agenda designed to help the working class and diminish the power of the corporations. The **Elkins Act** made railroad rebates illegal, making it difficult for preferential treatment to be given to corporations. Roosevelt formed the **Department of Commerce and Labor** to help workers. One telling episode was the **Anthracite Coal Strike** in 1902. When the owner of the mines asked Roosevelt for an injunction forcing the employees back to work, Roosevelt instead sent troops in to mine the coal for the government! The owner and the labor leader then met at the White House to settle their differences. This was the first time both sides in a strike had accepted an executive commission, and the first time the president had threatened to seize property. It was also the first time a president had sided with a labor union.

Election of 1904

In the election of 1904, Roosevelt used the **Square Deal** as his platform and was able to defeat the Democrat Judge Alton B. Parker. As part of the Square Deal, Roosevelt mandated an **open shop**

policy; workers would be free to join a union without being obliged to do so. A case in which Roosevelt's government did not benefit workers was the **Danbury Hatters' Strike**. During this dispute, the workers organized a general boycott of Danbury Hats. The management argued that this boycott violated the **Sherman Anti-trust Act** and the **Interstate Commerce Act**, and the Supreme Court agreed. Many workers blamed Roosevelt for this decision.

Roosevelt's Reforms

The **Hepburn Act of 1906** gave the ICC the authority to set shipping prices in the event that a shipper complained about the rates. This act also allowed the government to regulate pipelines and express and sleeping car companies. The **Pure Food and Drug Act of 1906** established the Food and Drug Administration to regulate what had become a very corrupt industry. The **Meat Inspection Act of 1906** was inspired by Upton Sinclair's novel *The Jungle*, which exposed the corruption of the meatpacking industry. It established tougher regulation of meat handlers. Not all of Roosevelt's legislation passed, however. He was unable to pass laws against child labor, establish a national worker's compensation, or restrict the power of the **National Association of Manufacturers** to gain injunctions against strikers.

Roosevelt's New Programs and the Old Guard Republicans

Many Old Guard Republicans disagreed with Theodore Roosevelt on the issue of resource conservation. The **Newlands Reclamation Act of 1902** tried to reclaim the wilderness through the construction of dams. Roosevelt believed that the United States only had about a quarter of its original trees; this act set aside land in the Grand Canyon, Yosemite, and Yellowstone for the preservation of forests. Roosevelt also had to endure the **Panic of 1907**, which was caused by too much supply, a decrease in demand, and a short money supply resulting from a lack of gold. The **Aldrich-Vreeland Act of 1908** authorized national banks to issue emergency currency. Over time, it seemed that Roosevelt had become more radical. The **Employers Liability Act of 1906**, for instance, had provided for workman's compensation but was struck down by the courts. Roosevelt promptly went after the courts.

Second Hague Disarmament Conference, Treaty of Portsmouth, Japanese Laborers, and Great White Fleet

At the Second Hague Disarmament Conference in 1907, a number of nations gathered to reaffirm the **Hague Conference rules** of humane warfare and agreed upon how the collection of debts should be pursued. After the **Russo-Japanese War**, Roosevelt rather reluctantly agreed to mediate between the two countries. The result was the **Treaty of Portsmouth**, in which the Japanese lost some land (though not as much as the Russians felt was appropriate). For this, Roosevelt received the 1906 **Nobel Peace Prize**. After the Russo-Japanese War, many **Japanese workers** came to the US; Roosevelt had to intervene and prevent them from being discriminated against. Finally, Roosevelt promoted the **US Navy** by painting a number of ships white and parading them past the Asian coast.

Review Video: The Treaty of Portsmouth
Visit mometrix.com/academy and enter code: 566070

Progressive Movement

Demographic Trends and Working Class

The **Progressive Movement** was marked by advances in rights for workers, women, and minorities. As the 20th century began, it seemed as if the rich were getting richer and the poor were becoming more numerous. Per capita income and population had both increased dramatically, but wealth seemed to be concentrated in a smaller and smaller group. Between one-third and one-half of all factory workers lived in poverty and management showed no concern for these workers in the form of unemployment or worker's compensation. Many of the wealthy magnates felt the poor were that way because of their sinfulness and thus had no desire to provide aid. At the same time, many in the middle class feared that the lower class would revolt, although they didn't want to cause trouble themselves.

Labor Unions, Immigrants, and Black People

By 1914 the **American Federation of Labor** had 2 million members, although most Americans still did not trust labor unions. Meanwhile, immigrants had withstood several challenges to their legitimacy. The **Immigration Restriction League** had tried many times to require immigrants to pass a literacy test. For their part, immigrants were annoyed that they had to go to school, they hated Prohibition, and they hated the settlement houses into which they were often forced by the government. Black people were one group that would not receive much help during the Progressive era. In 1905, W. E. B. DuBois had spearheaded the Niagara Movement, which led to the formation of the **National Association for the Advancement of Colored People**. In 1911 the **National Urban League** was formed to help black people move into the cities.

Effects on Women and Farmers

During the early part of the 20th century, women aggressively pursued more rights. **Sarah Platt Decker** led the **General Federation of Women's Clubs**, a group that worked hard to improve working conditions for women and children. The **International Ladies' Garment Workers Union** was also popular; it received a great deal of publicity after 146 women died in a fire at the Triangle Shirt factory. **Jane Addams** supported Prohibition, as did the Women's Christian Temperance Union and the Anti-Saloon League. **Carrie A. Nation** became famous for attacking saloons with an ax. For their part, farmers were doing much better in the early years of the 20th century than in years past; those who were still struggling joined with the Progressives.

Social Critics and State Reforms

Eugene V. Debs was a prominent Socialist leader during the Progressive era. The **Industrial Workers of the World**, established in 1905 by "Big Bill" Haywood and known as the "Wobblies," was a radical and militant labor union that appealed to unskilled workers. There were some interesting state and local experiments in this period. In Galveston, Texas, the city switched to a commission system in which the heads of various departments were elected. In Staunton, Virginia, the office of the mayor was done away with in favor of a managing council. **Robert LaFollette's** many reforms in Wisconsin led Roosevelt to refer to this state as the "laboratory of democracy." LaFollette tied the university system, the railroads, and the banks to the state government. Governor Woodrow Wilson of New Jersey planned to use corporate taxes to pay for public education.

National Reforms

The **16th amendment** (1913) allowed for an income tax. The **17th amendment** (1913) provided for the direct election of US senators. The **18th amendment** (1919) prohibited alcohol. The **19th amendment** (1920) gave women the right to vote. In the case of **Muller v. Oregon** (1908), the Supreme Court upheld Oregon's 10-hour workday for women. In **Hammer v. Dagenhart** (1918), the Supreme Court declared the Keating-Owen Act of 1916 was unconstitutional. This act had prohibited interstate shipping of goods made in factories that employed children. The Court declared that the regulation of factories was the concern of the states. In response to this decision, many states passed acts banning child labor. The first **minimum wage** (25¢) was established in

Massachusetts in 1912. New York established the first lasting workman's compensation rules in 1910. In 1896, Utah had become the first state to limit the workday to ten hours.

SUMMARY

It is important to note that Progressivism is not synonymous with Socialism; **Progressives** wanted to change the system, while **Socialists** wanted to destroy it altogether. Progressives believed that the government should regulate all business. Moreover, the Progressives wanted to take government out of the hands of the rich and put it into the hands of the common people. Often, Progressives had difficulty getting organized. This problem had been the death knell of the Populists; the Progressives were able to succeed in spite of their turmoil because they had great leaders: Roosevelt, Taft, and Wilson. The Progressive philosophy was started by a small minority of liberal intellectuals, including William James and Henry Adams. Among the authors who wrote on Progressive themes were Jacob Riis (*How the Other Half Lives*), Frank Norris (*The Octopus*, on railroad corruption), and Upton Sinclair (*The Jungle*, on corruption in the meatpacking industry).

THEODORE ROOSEVELT'S LEGACY AND THE ELECTION OF 1908

Theodore Roosevelt, like Andrew Jackson, was truly a public servant. Most of his domestic policies really seemed aimed at improving the lot of the common American. During his administration, Roosevelt greatly enlarged the powers of the president. He created the national parks system and gave the Progressive Movement some respectability. In the 1908 election, Roosevelt chose **William Howard Taft** to become his successor. Roosevelt felt confident that Taft would carry on the mission of the Progressives. Taft ran against William Jennings Bryan of the Democrats, a veteran leader who favored a lower tariff and limited injunctions against strikers. Taft won the election, primarily because of his association with Roosevelt.

TAFT PRESIDENCY

FOREIGN POLICY OF TAFT (1909-13)

Roosevelt was succeeded in the White House by **William Howard Taft**, who became known for "**dollar diplomacy**"; the United States would loan money to Latin American countries so that these countries could pay off their European debts. The US would also dabble a bit in Latin American politics, trying to influence the governments for the benefit of American business. The Taft administration also wanted to encourage trade with China and therefore helped prop up some American banking interests there. Taft is also known for his association with the creation of the **World Court**. The US, Britain, and France tried to establish an international judiciary. This idea enraged former president Roosevelt; he preferred settling differences on the battlefield.

TARIFFS AND THE PAYNE-ALDRICH ACT

Taft was a very cautious president. His administration saw the deepening of the gradual split between Progressive and Old Guard Republicans. Though Roosevelt had promoted him as a Progressive, Taft slowly began to act more like a member of the **Old Guard**. These tensions came to a head over the tariff in 1909. The Old Guard wanted to keep the tariff as it was, while Progressives fought for reductions. After the House and Senate came up with conflicting tariff bills, Taft was able to engineer a compromise; the **Payne-Aldrich Act of 1909** brought the tariff down to 40.8%. This act also contained a corporate tax and the promise of an income tax in the future.

SPLIT BETWEEN TAFT AND ROOSEVELT

In the Congressional elections of 1910, the radical Progressives (known as the **insurgents**) were able, with the help of the Democrats, to diminish the power of the Old Guard Republicans in the House. Meanwhile, President Taft drifted closer and closer to the side of the Old Guard. In 1909, Secretary of the Interior **Richard Bollinger** leased national land to corporations, incurring the wrath of forester Gifford Pinchot, who asked for a Senate investigation. Bollinger was forced to resign to take the heat off of Taft. In the Congressional election of 1910, former President Roosevelt announced a mixture of Progressive and Liberal ideas called the **New Nationalism program** and was labeled a Marxist. Then, finally, Taft destroyed a merger between US Steel and Tennessee Coal and Iron that Roosevelt had supported, infuriating the former president.

1912 Election and the Legacy of Taft

At the Republican convention before the election of 1912, the incumbent **Taft** was nominated even though **Theodore Roosevelt** had won most of the primaries. Enraged, Roosevelt left the Republicans and formed the **Progressive (Bull-Moose) party**. Roosevelt ran on his platform of **New Nationalism**: voting rights for women and a ban on child labor were among the initiatives. As an interesting side note, while campaigning in Wisconsin, Roosevelt was shot in the torso during a speech but managed to finish the speech in spite of the injury. Ultimately, the election came down to a contest between Roosevelt and **Woodrow Wilson** of the Democrats. These two candidates had similar views on a number of issues, but while Roosevelt was willing to allow some trusts, Wilson wanted to eliminate trusts across the board. Wilson ended up winning a rather comfortable victory. As the Taft presidency came to a close, most observers saw his greatest accomplishments as the "rule of reason," in which the judiciary was allowed to pick which trusts to bust; the **Mann-Elkins Act**, which brought the telephone and telegraph industries under the control of the federal government; and the creation of the **Department of Labor**.

Wilson Presidency

Tariff Reform and the Federal Reserve Act

Woodrow Wilson appointed **William Jennings Bryant** as his Secretary of State; Bryant became known for his policy of "cooling off," wherein volatile situations would be ignored until all parties had a chance to reconsider their positions. One of Wilson's first major acts as president was to push through the **Underwood-Simmons Tariff of 1913**. This reduces the duty rate to 27% and drastically reduced the tariff on a thousand other items. It also included a slightly greater income tax. Another important economic move was the **Federal Reserve Act of 1913**. This set up a national banking system to be overseen by a Federal Reserve Board. The Federal Reserve system would become the first effective national banking system since the Second Bank of the United States and would be one of the great legacies of Wilson's term. It gave the government a ready means to adjust the amount of currency in circulation.

Effects on Trusts

When Wilson entered office, he declared that there was no such thing as a good trust. With the **Federal Trade Commission Act of 1914**, a bipartisan committee of 5 was created to investigate trusts and issue reports to the government and to the public. The creation of the FTC slowed the growth of monopolies. Peeved by the ineffectiveness of the Sherman Anti-trust Act, Wilson supported the passage of the **Clayton Anti-trust Act of 1914**. This prohibited businesses from selling at reduced prices to favored customers if this price discrimination helped create a monopoly. It also prevented so-called "tying contracts," which forbade a purchaser from buying or selling the products of a competitor. The act also outlawed large interlocking directories; formally allowed the existence of labor unions and farm organizations, as well as strikes and boycotts; and declared that no injunctions could be issued unless property was at stake.

Accomplishments of Wilson's New Freedom Agenda

The **Smith-Lever Act of 1914** brought public education into rural areas. The **Smith-Hughes Act of 1917** allocated money for vocational training and home economics courses. The **Federal Farm Loan Act of 1916** divided the US into 12 agricultural districts and established federal farm loan banks with low interest rates. The **Adamson Act of 1916** asserted that railway workers should be paid for a 10-hour day, though they should only be required to work 8 hours. During Wilson's presidency, **Lewis Brandeis** became the first Jewish member of the Supreme Court. In general, then, Wilson believed in regulating business and improving social welfare. He did not, however, see anything wrong with segregation.

Wilson's Moral Diplomacy

Along with his Secretary of State William Jennings Bryant, Woodrow Wilson promoted the view that nations should treat one another ethically. For instance, the **Panama Canal Tolls Act of 1912** had made it so that the US did not have to pay tolls to use the canal, unlike every other nation; Wilson did away with this measure. Wilson's actions in the **Dominican Republic** were more dubious. The Dominican Republic had been in deep debt early in the 20th century, and the Roosevelt administration had been glad to help in exchange for keeping some troops in the country. When in 1916 the Dominican Republic asked the US to leave, Wilson refused and sent in the Marines. It was only in 1940 that the Dominican Republic was no longer considered a US protectorate. A similar scenario occurred in **Haiti**: the US offered to help the tiny nation but was unwilling to leave when asked (mainly because of economic interest).

US and Mexican Revolution

Mexicans traditionally resented the US for its seizure of Texas and the Southwest. When the US-friendly leader **Porfirio Diaz** was overthrown in 1910 and eventually replaced by the murderous dictator **Victoriano Huerto**, the US sent weapons to his opponents. Then, in April 1914, two American soldiers of the *USS Tampico* were jailed in Mexico, and the US did not receive an apology upon their release. This angered the US, and they, in turn, seized a German ship that was believed to be unloading war materials to Mexico. The only thing that kept the US out of a more serious conflict was the **ABC Mediation**: Argentina, Brazil, and Chile met and convinced Huerto to retire. Still, **Pancho Villa**, a challenger for control of Mexico, continued to antagonize the US; he killed several Americans and was unsuccessfully pursued by American forces.

World War I

America's Role in the Build-Up to War

There had been relative peace in Europe since the end of the Napoleonic Wars in 1815. Many even felt that the age of great wars was over. In 1910, the US had become involved in the **Pan-American Union**, which was organized to settle differences with diplomacy rather than violence. At the **First Hague Conference** in 1899, 26 nations agreed on the principles of mediation, the humane rules of war, and the creation of a permanent court of arbitration. At the **Second Hague Conference** in 1907, 44 nations reaffirmed the old agreements and declared that the payment of debts could not be forced through war. Unfortunately, there would be no Third Hague Conference; it was canceled due to World War I.

Causes

The rise in **nationalism** at the beginning of the 20th century helped contribute to the possibility of war. There was also some conflict between the **imperialist** (France, Britain, and the US) and the **non-imperialist** (Germany, Italy) nations. Many large nations were seeking economic expansion outside of their own borders, and the competition for foreign markets was intense. There was also a complex system of entangling alliances; many countries were involved in several different alliances at the same time. The spark for World War I, though, was the assassination of **Archduke Franz Ferdinand**, heir to the throne of Austria-Hungary, in April of 1914 by a Serbian nationalist. When Emperor Franz Joseph declared war on Serbia, it set off a chain reaction that involved virtually every nation in Europe.

US Attempts at Neutrality

For a while, the US tried to remain **impartial** in World War I, not least because it was making a great deal of money producing supplies for both sides. Among the general public, there was general support for Britain and France, but many German and Irish immigrants supported the Central powers. There were a small group of American citizens who flew missions for the French, known as the Lafayette Escadrille. Gradually, the US government became angry with both sides, even as it tried to maintain trade with both sides. The British blockade of neutral Scandinavia annoyed the US, as did the German's flouting of the rules of war with their aggressive U-boats. In 1915, the British ship ***Lusitania*** was sunk off the coast of Ireland, killing 128 Americans. This convinced many Americans that neutrality could not be maintained.

Increasing American Involvement

During the early years of WWI, the tide of **nationalism** was rising in the US. Many people felt it would be impossible for America to remain neutral; even Theodore Roosevelt decried conscientious objectors. Nevertheless, many **pacifists** objected to any involvement. William Jennings Bryant resigned as Secretary of State after the sinking of the *Lusitania*, advising the US to stay off of British ships, to stop selling weapons to both sides, and to not side so unthinkingly with the British. At around this time, Roosevelt began recruiting and training men as part of the **Plattsburg Experiment**. Finally, Wilson increased the number of troops in both the Army and the Navy with the **National Defense Act of 1916**. Wilson also set into motion a campaign to build more ships.

Election of 1916 and Entrance into WWI

In the election of 1916, **Wilson** narrowly defeated the Republican Charles Evans Hughes. Wilson ran on a **peace platform**. Soon after, however, diplomatic relations were broken off with the Central powers and submarine warfare began. The American entrance to WWI was accelerated by the "**Zimmermann Note**," in which the German minister to Mexico encouraged that country to attack the United States. In 1917, merchant vessels were ordered by Wilson to arm themselves. Among the reasons the US sided with the Allies was the fact that American business was more deeply connected with these countries than with the Central powers. Also, the US had traditionally had stronger ties with Britain and France.

Wilson's War Agenda

On April 2, 1917, Wilson addressed the nation on the subject of World War I. He declared that the conduct of the German U-boats was "a war against humanity itself," and that, if managed successfully, WWI would be "a war to make the world safe for democracy." Four days later, a **declaration of wa**r was passed. The **Selective Service Act of 1917** registered and drafted millions of American men for military service; about 4.7 million Americans served in the war. The American war effort was mainly paid for with borrowed money, though an increased income tax and the sale of war bonds contributed. Wilson also mobilized American industry; the **War Industries Board**, headed by Bernard Baruch, strove to cut waste and create new industries to aid the war effort. The **National War Labor Board**, headed by ex-President Taft, tried to streamline the labor force to aid the war effort.

Contributions of the American Public and Public Opinion of the War

The **18th amendment** to the Constitution, otherwise known as the **Volstead Act**, outlawed alcohol in 1920. This amendment was purported to conserve food, though it was really an attempt to influence public morality. Through the **Food Administration**, Wilson encouraged people to plant "victory gardens," and to skip meat one day a week. The war was also supported through the **Espionage and Sedition Acts of 1917-8**, which made it illegal to say negative things about the war or to interfere with the sale of war bonds. In **Schenck v. US** (1919), the arrest of the Socialist leader Charles Schenck for criticizing the war was upheld by the Supreme Court, which asserted that First Amendment rights were only exercisable when they did not present a clear and present danger to the nation. In **Abrams v. US** (1919), a Russian immigrant critical of the US actions in Russia was also declared to be a clear and present danger.

Perception of Americans Soldiers

The situation for the Allies was desperate after Russia left the war under the **Brest-Litovsk Treaty of 1917**. The US began to convoy British and French ships in an attempt to prevent U-boat attacks. The American soldiers in Europe were referred to as Doughboys, Yanks, and Devil Dogs. Some of the American heroes in the war were **Alvin York** ("Sergeant York"), who reportedly killed 20 and captured 132; **J.J. Pershing**, who led the American Expeditionary Force; and **Eddie Rickenbacker**, a pilot credited with 22 kills. Americans were praised for their efforts at Cantigny, at Reims, and in the Argonne Forest campaign, where there were over 128,000 American casualties.

Wilson's Fourteen Points Program

Wilson issued his Fourteen Points program supposedly to try to create a quick and lasting peace. Also, however, Wilson hoped to draw the Russians back into the war, to inspire the war-weary Allies, and to demoralize the enemy nations by appealing to the dissenting contingents. Some of the changes called for in the **Fourteen Points** were open diplomacy, freedom of the seas, no tariffs, reduced land artilleries, right of self-determination for all people, temporary international control of colonies (not imperialism), and the creation of the **League of Nations**. Wilson's proposal encouraged the Slavic peoples in Germany and Austria-Hungary to resist the war. Its success in defusing the German war effort allowed Wilson to insist that he would only negotiate with a ruler of the people's choice; **Kaiser Wilhelm** was forced to abdicate the throne.

Armistice of WWI and the Treaty of Versailles

On November 11, 1918, the Germans agreed to an **armistice** provided that Wilson's Fourteen Points be used as a treaty. Overall, between 9 and 10 million people died in the war, including 320,000 Americans. In the **Treaty of Versailles** (1919), the **League of Nations** was created to handle international disputes. A number of new countries, such as Poland and Czechoslovakia, were created by this treaty; also, Germany was disarmed and forced to pay war reparations. Later, the Treaty of Versailles would come to be seen as an uneasy mixture of vengeance and conciliation. It also relied too much on the good faith of the signers. Wilson recognized many problems with the treaty, but he felt the League of Nations would be able to correct them in the future.

US and the League of Nations

The League of Nations had five permanent members: Japan, Britain, Italy, France, and the US. Germany and Russia were not included. The League would have a **General Assembly** and a **Court of International Justice**. It would try to use economic sanctions and, if necessary, force to guarantee the territorial integrity and political independence of every nation. The problems the League developed in practice were many: it was almost impossible to set into motion, because a unanimous vote was required for action; it created a number of artificial and unsuccessful countries (Sudetenland, for example); it had no power to regulate economics; it excluded two major nations (Russia and Germany); and it had no power to force a nation to disarm.

Review Video: WWI Overview
Visit mometrix.com/academy and enter code: 659767

US Response to the Treaty of Versailles and the League of Nations

The US Senate rejected both the Treaty of Versailles and the League of Nations. Republicans, including Henry Cabot Lodge, created the "**Round Robin Manifesto**" guaranteeing that the Treaty would not be approved; some felt that the Republicans were hurt that none of their members had been invited to the table in Versailles. Other politicians were simply angry that the Kaiser had not been killed. Wilson attempted to take the matter of the treaty directly to the American people, but he suffered a stroke in 1919 and both the Treaty and the League were rejected by Congress. Lodge issued the **Lodge Reservations**, a rebuttal to Wilson's Fourteen Points, in which he declared that it was an infringement on Congress' power for Wilson to assert that the US military would be used to protect other nations. In the national climate of isolationism and disillusionment that followed the war, it was perhaps inevitable that the US would never sign the Treaty or join the League.

Eugenics Movement

In the late 19th and early 20th century, the idea of selective breeding became a relatively common notion in Europe. **Eugenics** refers to a set of ideas about breeding, including both promoting the breeding of only the best specimens of humans and the sterilization of undesirable people. The movement started in Britain and spread across Europe and to the United States. This movement had various modes of implementation, including preventing certain populations from breeding, such as inter-racial couples, those with mental or physical disabilities, criminals, and even impoverished peoples. These ideas eventually went on to influence the Nazis and led to some of the atrocities of the holocaust, but they were also surprisingly popular abroad. Notably, the state of Virginia was permitted by the Supreme Court to force sterilization of individuals with intellectual disabilities and criminals. The **Virginia Sterilization Act of 1924** allowed for forced sterilization to take place until as late as 1979, sterilizing over 7,000 individuals on the basis of race, disability, or criminality. The eugenics movement was heavily tied to "scientific racism," which came out of Darwinism, Mendelian genetics, and poor social conditions of urbanization. Eugenicists had a vested interest in producing means of sterilization, contraception, and abortion methods.

Key Events During the 1920s and 1930s

1920s

Election of 1920 and the Background to the 1920s

The election of 1920 was known as the "solemn referendum." In it, Republican **Warren G. Harding** (who had voted against the League of Nations) defeated Democrat James Cox (who had Franklin Roosevelt as his running mate). Harding's election was in part due to his opposition to the League, but also it was due to his being a radical departure from Wilson. As the 1920s began, Americans felt disillusioned; few people felt that WWI would be the end of war, and massive immigration had left the US scrambling for an identity. There was also hostility lingering from the war: anti-radical, anti-immigration, anti-black, and anti-urban groups had broad followings. The general negativity at the beginning of the decade was not helped by the post-war **recession** and a massive outbreak of **influenza** that killed half a million people.

Immigration and Labor Issues at the Beginning of the 1920s

The radical **International Workers of the World** was defunct by 1920, but many people still feared the influx of new ideas (including communism) and immigrants to the US. Indeed, immigrants became the scapegoat for many of the nation's problems. With the **Immigration Restriction Act of 1921**, only a certain quota of immigrants would be allowed into the country. The **National Origins Act of 1924** restricted immigration even further and stipulated that no Japanese would be allowed into the US. Basically, Americans only wanted Nordics to be able to enter the country. Anti-communist sentiment flared up for the first time during this period; **A. Mitchell Palmer**, the attorney general under Wilson, encouraged citizens to "rouse the Reds."

Race Relations in the Early 1920s

In July 1919, there were violent **race riots** because of competition for jobs; in Chicago, a black swimmer crossed into the wrong area of Lake Michigan, sparking another riot. At around this time, the **KKK** increased in popularity in part because of D.W. Griffith's movie "Birth of a Nation," which depicted the Old South as a paradise led by the Klan. The KKK was led by Hiram Evans and had between 4 and 5 million members; it was anti-black, anti-immigration, anti-Jewish, anti-Catholic, and anti-alcohol. Membership in the Klan declined slightly in the wake of some lynchings and as the economy improved. Nevertheless, many black people sought refuge in the big cities, as part of the **Great Black Migration**. Also, at this time, the **Harlem Renaissance** was reinvigorating black culture; this movement included Langston Hughes, Countee Cullen, Duke Ellington, Paul Robeson, and Louis Armstrong. Many black people subscribed to the beliefs of Marcus Garvey, who thought black people should return to Africa.

Provincialism v. Modernity

At the beginning of the 1920s, the American population was evenly divided between city-dwellers and country-dwellers. While the cities were booming in the post-war period, **farmers** found themselves in economic trouble because of their surpluses. At around this time, many writers, including Ernest Hemingway, F. Scott Fitzgerald, and the members of the **Ashcan School,** sharply criticized the growing materialism of the **urbanites**. In 1920, the "noble experiment" of **Prohibition** began; it was constantly undermined by corrupt government and organized crime, and the government lost the money it had made on the taxation of alcohol. Another incident that brought the differences between Americans into sharp relief was the **Scopes Monkey Trial** in Dayton, Tennessee (1925). In this trial, Clarence Darrow successfully defended a science teacher who had taught the students Darwin's theory of natural selection.

Review Video: 1920's
Visit mometrix.com/academy and enter code: 124996

Harding Presidency

When Warren G. Harding came into office, he promised a "return to normalcy." He almost immediately passed the **Esch-Cummins Act of 1920**, which allowed for virtual trusts in the railroad industry. Harding raised tariffs and was known for having a strong Cabinet, which included **Herbert Hoover** as Secretary of Commerce. Harding's administration was also known for a large number of scandals. It was discovered at one point that Attorney General Harry Daugherty was selling pardons, parole, and liquor; his successor, Jesse Smith, was later found to be doing exactly the same thing. In the **Forbes Scandal**, the head of the Veterans Bureau was found to have embezzled $250 million from the organization. In the **Teapot Dome Scandal**, the Secretary of the Interior was discovered to have sold government oil reserves to private interests. Near the end of his term, Harding had a stroke and was succeeded by **Calvin Coolidge**.

Coolidge Presidency and the Election of 1924

Calvin Coolidge won the election of 1924 by distancing himself from the scandals of the Harding administration. He is famous for saying, "The business of America is business," and his administration embodied that credo. He allowed the return of **trusts** (now known as "mergers"), and he made major efforts to protect American business abroad. When struggling farmers looked to the government for help, Coolidge responded by vetoing the **McNary-Haugan Bill**, which would have established a minimum price for agricultural products. The **Clayton Anti-Trust Act** was totally ignored during the Coolidge presidency.

Election of 1928 and Hoover's Agricultural Program

The election of 1928 pitted **Herbert Hoover** of the Republicans against **Alfred E. Smith** of the Democrats. Hoover, who had served as Secretary of Commerce under Harding, was associated with rural voters, Prohibition, and Protestantism and earned a solid victory over Smith after a dirty campaign. Hoover immediately put into action his "self-help" program for agriculture. With the **Agricultural Marketing Act,** he established cooperatives. He also established the **Federal Farm Board** to loan money to farmers and the Grain and Cotton Stabilization Corporation to buy surpluses. Hoover passed the **Hawley-Smoot Tariff of 1930**, which allowed the president to adjust the tariff at his own discretion; Hoover set it at the highest peacetime rate in American history.

Causes of the Great Depression

The Great Depression was the result of a number of converging factors. For one thing, there was an agricultural depression in the 1920s brought on by tremendous post-war surpluses. The automobile and housing industries both experienced diminished demand in the 20s. One major problem was that wealth was so unevenly distributed: one-third of the nation's wealth was controlled by 5% of the population. There was not much in the way of international trade, in part because of Hoover's high tariff. Overproduction on assembly lines led to factory surpluses and unemployment. Finally, there was persistent unsound speculation in the stock markets. By 1929, many stocks were considered to be overvalued and thus no one was buying them. This caused the catastrophic market crashes of **Black Thursday** and **Black Tuesday** (October 24 and 29, 1929), in which 40% of the market value (about $30 billion) was lost.

Hoover and the Great Depression

Hoover's first strategy for combating the Great Depression was to balance the budget, reduce federal spending, keep the US on the gold standard, and just wait it out. Later, he developed some **work-relief programs**, employing people on public work projects. The **Hoover Dam** was one of those projects. Hoover also created the **Reconstruction Finance Group**, which loaned money directly to state and local governments as well as to railroads and banks. Hoover's aid projects were unprecedented; still, he resisted giving direct aid to the people in the form of welfare. World War I veterans descended on Washington in 1932 when they were told that their pensions would not be paid until 1945. These so-called "**Bonus Marchers**" eventually had to be dispersed with force, leading many citizens to believe that the country was descending into anarchy. The **20th amendment**, known as the anti-Hoover amendment, actually brought the date of the next inauguration forward.

Review Video: Causes of the Great Depression
Visit mometrix.com/academy and enter code: 635912

Franklin Delano Roosevelt and the New Deal

Franklin D. Roosevelt was elected president in the election of 1932. He was determined to preserve the US government and tried to calm the general public with his folksy "**Fireside Chats**." As the governor of New York, Roosevelt had been able to experiment with social welfare programs. He was a pragmatist and a follower of the **Keynesian school of economics** which insisted that the government had to spend money in order to get out of the Depression. Unlike Hoover, then, Roosevelt supported massive government spending and little volunteerism; he wanted the government to regulate agriculture and industry and also for it to take an interest in the daily economic decisions of the people.

In the early days of his term, FDR promoted the **3 Rs**: relief, recovery, and reform. He announced a bank holiday for five days to stop the drain on the cash flow. The **Emergency Banking Act** authorized the **Reconstruction Finance Group** to buy bank stocks in order to finance repair. The **Glass-Steagall Act** made it illegal for banks to loan money to people for the purpose of playing the market and established the **Federal Deposit Insurance Corporation** to protect banks. The **Economy Act** cut $400 million from veterans' payments and $100 million from government salaries. Roosevelt had the gold standard and prohibition repealed. The **Federal Emergency Relief Administration** was established to provide $3 billion in direct relief to people.

The **Civil Works Administration**, headed by Harry Hopkins, was established to give people work. The **Civilian Conservation Corps** was a civilian army that built things such as the Blue Ridge Parkway. Other organizations created to **employ** people were the Public Works Administration, the Works Progress Administration, the Tennessee Valley Authority (responsible for the construction of 21 dams), the National Youth Administration (gave work to high school students), and the Rural Electrification Administration. The **National Industrial Recovery Act** tried to encourage fair competition and create scarcity to drive prices up. It established a minimum wage, a maximum number of weekly hours, and the right of labor to organize. In **Schechter Poultry v. US** (1935), the Supreme Court would rule that the NIRA should have been made up of laws instead of codes, because there were too many loopholes.

As part of his **New Deal program** to help the US recover from the Great Depression, FDR established the **First Agricultural Adjustment Administration**. This agency provided farmers with loans to help them with mortgage payments and paid them not to plant or sell agricultural products. The formation of the **AAA** was economically successful but was one of the least popular measures in the New Deal; it would later be declared unconstitutional in Butler v. US (1936). The **Federal Securities Act** stated that the securities dealers must disclose the prices of stocks and bonds. The **Wagner Act of 1935** made it illegal for employers to have blacklists of unionized workers. The **Federal Housing Administration** was established to provide lower interest rates for people willing to repair or purchase a house. The **US Housing Authority** was created to loan money to state and local governments for the construction of low-cost housing.

Resistance to FDR's New Deal

Father Coughlin was a priest who became famous for his radio broadcasts; he blamed the banks and an "international Jewish conspiracy" for the Depression. **Dr. Francis E. Townsend** was a famous advocate for senior citizens who advocated a national sales tax. **Alf Landon** ran against FDR in the 1936 presidential election and was defeated soundly because of his ties to big business. In the **"Court Packing" controversy** of 1937, FDR tried to overcome Supreme Court resistance to the New Deal by increasing the number of justices on the Court from 9 to 15. This attempt was unsuccessful, but Roosevelt was able to fill Court vacancies with New Deal supporters. A final bit of resistance to the New Deal occurred during the so-called "**Roosevelt Recession**" of 1937-8, in which the economy seemed to be making much less progress than before. Many historians attribute this recession to the fact that New Deal programs were getting much less use in this era.

Life of Black Americans and the Great Depression

In the **Scottsboro (AL) case of 1932**, 9 young black men were accused of raping 2 white women. Although the evidence was scant, all 9 of the men were convicted. In **Powell v. Alabama**, the Supreme Court would rule that the men had not been given a fair trial because they had not had adequate representation. At around this time, the white **Harold Ickes** was the head of the NAACP. He worked hard to get New Deal jobs for black people, Thurgood Marshall among them. **Eleanor Roosevelt** also was an advocate for black people in this period. She came into open conflict with the

Daughters of the American Revolution after this group denied Marian Anderson, a black opera singer, the right to sing at Constitution Hall. In general, the New Deal helped many black people obtain leadership positions that otherwise would have been closed to them. The Roosevelt administration was the first to show any real concern for black people, so most black people became life-long Democrats.

Latin American Foreign Policy from 1920 to 1945

The US had tremendous financial investments in **Latin America** and most of the government's policy there was aimed at securing these investments. In 1921, the US paid $21 million to **Colombia**, in part for stealing the land for the Panama Canal and in part to keep them from seizing US oil investments. At this time, the US also had bad relations with **Mexico** until the election of President Calles, a pro-American politician. During the Hoover administration, the US tried to promote "good neighborism" with respect to Mexico and the rest of Latin America. In 1934, the **Platt Amendment** gave Cuba full independence. When Batista came to power, however, the US backed him completely and refused to acknowledge any other elected leaders.

Cultural Changes in the 1920s and 1930s

Culture and technology changed rapidly in the early 1900s, leading to considerable shifts in popular culture. New technologies, such as the automobile, the radio, the telephone, and electrical appliances became commodities. New modes of entertainment, such as new music, dancing, and the rise of cinema were introduced. Women gained the right to vote in 1920, and the economy had a significant upturn, leading to a culture of consumption in the 1920s. Moral values shifted away from the Victorian standard to allow for more widespread drinking, smoking, dancing, and acceptance of sexuality in media. The 1920s were given the apt name "the Roaring Twenties," which characterized the excitement and optimism of the time. At the end of the decade, however, the stock market crashed, leading into what is known as the Great Depression. As a result of the crash, banks started to fail. Industrial production continued, leading to an abundance of goods with little money to make the purchases. The 1930s were a heavy contrast to the cultural optimism of the 1920s.

World War II

Japan in the Years Before WWII

In 1926, amid growing nationalism, **Hirohito** became the Emperor of Japan. The next year, the Japanese prime minister declared that Japan should dominate Asia, and four years later, Japanese forces invaded **Manchuria**. Some historians consider this to be the beginning of the Second World War. After establishing a puppet regime in Manchuria, the Japanese withdrew from the League of Nations and attacked China. The **Sino-Japanese War** ensued. In 1938, Japan outlined its new vision of **Co-Prosperity Spheres**; Japan would be the industrial center of Asia and would acquire its raw materials from its colonies in the rest of Asia. Japan promoted this idea as an opportunity to break from European imperialism, but it was really just the substitution of one master for another. In 1940, Japan would complete its transformation into a **fascist state** by dissolving all political parties.

Events Leading to World War II in Europe

Still shell-shocked from the First World War, the nations of western Europe were slow to respond to the growing menace of **Nazi Germany**. In general, they pursued a policy of appeasement and isolation. The British prime minister **Neville Chamberlain** was especially committed to using diplomacy over war. Then, in 1936, Hitler sent troops to occupy the **Rhineland**, a strip of territory on the German border. At around the same time, **Mussolini** invaded Ethiopia; the two aggressors, Germany and Italy, entered into an agreement making them the **Axis Powers**. In 1938, Germany annexed Austria and indicated that it was about to attack Czechoslovakia. In response to these actions, Chamberlain brought together Mussolini and Hitler for the **Munich Conference of 1938**. These talks would only briefly suspend German aggression.

Weimar Republic and the Rise of Hitler

After the abdication of the emperor, Germany was ruled by a legislative body known as the **Weimar Republic**. Most Germans felt that this group had been too willing to accept punishment in the treaties that followed the war. Germans also thought that this government was responsible for the **inflation** that crippled the German economy in the post-war period. Germany, then, was vulnerable to the charms of a leader who told them they had nothing about which to be ashamed. This leader was **Adolf Hitler** (1889-1945). A failed artist, Hitler became the head of the **National Socialist**, or **Nazi**, party. His speeches were expressions of ardent nationalism, although often Hitler seemed to be calling for a return to an ideal German state that had never actually existed.

Belief System of the Nazi Party

Led by **Adolf Hitler**, the Nazi party championed the **Aryan race** as superior to all others, especially the "insidious" Jews. Hitler suggested that the noble ambitions of the true German people required ***lebensraum***, or living space. In other words, Germany needed more territory. In its early days, the Nazi party was part of the German republican system; Nazi candidates ran for office and served in the **Reichstag** (German parliament). As Germany suffered through a terrible economic depression in the early 1930s, however, the people became impatient. In 1933, the Reichstag was set on fire, and the Nazis used the opportunity to claim total control of the government. Hitler had already been appointed Chancellor in January 1933. He was able to quickly improve the German economy, mostly through the expansion of the weapon-building industry. At the same time, the new government began to quietly round up Jews, Gypsies, and homosexuals.

Holocaust

As **Germany** sank deeper and deeper into dire economic straits, the tendency was to look for a person or group of people to blame for the problems of the country. With distrust of the **Jewish people** already ingrained, it was easy for German authorities to set up the Jews as scapegoats for Germany's problems.

The Holocaust is the name given to the systematic killing of Jews, Gypsies, homosexuals, and others by the Nazis. **Anti-Semitism** had existed in Europe for millennia, but the Nazis gave it renewed emphasis and, after making numerous false claims about Jews, began persecuting them upon Hitler's rise to power in 1933. Jews were disenfranchised, forced into ghettos, had their property taken, and were finally sent to work and be killed in **concentration camps**. Approximately 6 million Jews were killed during the **Holocaust**. As the situation for the Germans became more dire in the Second World War, Hitler sought to implement what he called the "final solution," in which hundreds of thousands were killed just before the fall of Nazi Germany.

The Allies were aware of rumors of mass slaughter throughout the war, but many discounted the reports. Only when troops went in to liberate the prisoners was the true horror of the concentration camps brought to light.

Review Video: The Holocaust
Visit mometrix.com/academy and enter code: 350695

Consequences of the Holocaust

Many of the Nazi leaders were tried and convicted at the **Nuremberg trials** for their roles in the Holocaust. West Germany would later issue a **Federal Compensation Law**, through which billions of dollars were paid to survivors. During and after the Holocaust, Zionist Jews fled to **Palestine**. Public sympathy with their plight would be one of the main reasons for the creation of **Israel** in 1948. The total destruction of the Jewish community in Europe caused many Jews to question their faith, and those that remained in Europe are markedly more secular than their ancestors. The shock of the Holocaust has also caused many institutions, including the Roman Catholic Church, to consider their own latent anti-Semitism. Unfortunately, the anti-genocide legislation created in response to the Holocaust was not strict enough to rally international support against the **Rwandans** (who slaughtered hundreds of thousands of Tutsis in 1994) or the **Bosnian Serbs and Croats** (who killed thousands of Muslims in the early 1990s).

Pacific Arena in WWII

The **Japanese**, like the Germans, became seduced by the notion of their own racial superiority during the 1930s. As in Germany, this inevitably led to a lust for territorial expansion. By 1941, Japan had conquered Korea, Manchuria, and parts of China. Japan was also threatening to invade American interests in the Philippines. The United States imposed **economic sanctions** on Japan, making it difficult for the Japanese war industry to function. In response, the Japanese launched a surprise attack on the United States by bombing the US naval base of **Pearl Harbor**. After the attack on Pearl Harbor, the United States declared war upon Japan (and Germany, in turn, declared war on the United States). The Japanese made huge territorial gains before the US turned the tide at the **Battles of Midway and Guadalcanal**. The war in the Pacific would take much longer than the war in Europe due to the island-hopping nature of the fight. The unwillingness of the Japanese to surrender made it almost impossible for America to entirely vanquish them without enormous loss of life. So, the United States decided to drop atomic bombs on **Hiroshima** and **Nagasaki** to force Japan to surrender and finally end the war in the Pacific in August 1945.

Beginning and Initial Years of World War II in Europe

After **Chamberlain** had tried to forestall German aggression at the **Munich Conference of 1938**, Germany nevertheless invaded Czechoslovakia in 1939. It was also during this year that Hitler signed a secret agreement with **Stalin** pledging not to attack Russia so long as Russia stayed out of German affairs. Hitler then declared war on and conquered Poland. At this step, Great Britain and France were finally forced to declare war upon Germany. Germany at this point was a dominating military adversary. New advances in motorized military vehicles made it possible for Germany to conquer large areas of land quickly in a new form of warfare called **Blitzkrieg** (lightning war). The **Axis powers** conquered almost the entire European continent, including France, over the course of 1940. Only Great Britain remained in opposition, and the Nazis undertook a ferocious aerial assault on the British, who were by then led by **Winston Churchill**, but failed to do enough damage to make an invasion of the island country practical. Instead, Hitler turned east and decided to violate his truce with Stalin, invading **Russia** in 1941. The Germans overwhelmed much of the Soviet military and advanced deep into Russian territory in a huge surprise offensive.

America's Introduction to WWII

After the First World War, the US became obsessed with isolating itself from foreign conflicts. The **Nye Committee** studied the war and determined that it had been fought for financial reasons and could have been avoided. Isolationist parties achieved some popularity during this period, including the **America First Committee**, led by Charles Lindbergh, and **SOS** (Stop Organized Slaughter). The **Neutrality Laws** of 1935-7 declared that the US could not sell weapons to another country in a time of war and that US citizens could not travel on the ships of a nation at war. In 1937, FDR delivered the **Quarantine Speech**, in which he asserted that the Nazi "disease" must be contained. Finally, after conflict in Europe had escalated considerably, FDR declared that the US needed to help Britain and be an "arsenal of democracy in the world." The **Neutrality Act of 1940** made it legal for the US to sell weapons on a cash and carry basis. In August of 1941, FDR and Churchill drew up the **Atlantic Charter**, which vowed to destroy Nazism, protect the right of self-determination, and create a World Peace Organization.

Buildup to the Attack on Pearl Harbor

A number of events had created a stormy relationship between the US and Japan long before the invasion of Pearl Harbor. The US influence over the **Treaty of Portsmouth**, which ended the Russo-Japanese War, created a great deal of tension between the two countries. The Japanese were also antagonized by Theodore Roosevelt's parade of the **Great White Fleet** and by the **National Origins Act of 1924** and the **Segregation Laws**, which kept Japanese from entering and assimilating into the US. America also had a cordial relationship at this time with Japan's longtime rival, China. As the Japanese became more belligerent, the US froze all Japanese assets in America and denied Japan the purchase of any more oil or scrap metal. The Japanese then launched surprise attacks both on the American naval base at **Pearl Harbor** and on the **Philippines**, where they hoped to secure some oil.

US Involvement in WWII Concerning Europe and Africa

After the Japanese attack on Pearl Harbor in 1941, the US declared **war** on Japan, after which Germany declared war on the US. Before going after Japan, however, the US first attacked Germany; this was done because the US underestimated Japan industrially and militarily, and because the US feared Britain was on the verge of defeat. **Operation Overlord**, the Allied invasion of the European continent at Normandy, was led in part by General **Dwight D. Eisenhower**. The American generals Omar Bradley and George Patton took part in the **Allied Operation Torch**, aimed at taking back North Africa. At the **Battle of the Bulge**, in Belgium, the Germans tried to break the Allied lines, but were unsuccessful, in part because of the heroism of American soldiers.

US Involvement in WWII Concerning Asia and the Pacific

The US strategy for controlling the Pacific was known as "island hopping." In the **Coral Sea Battle of 1942**, Americans stopped the Japanese from taking Australia and New Guinea. In the same year, the **Doolittle raids** of Japanese naval bases boosted American morale. In the **Battle of Midway** (1942), the US sunk four Japanese aircraft carriers. In the **Battle of Leyte Gulf**, General Douglas MacArthur took back the Philippines and also took control of Iwo Jima and Okinawa. During this period, a team of American scientists led by Robert Oppenheimer was developing the **atomic bomb** in Los Alamos, New Mexico. Japan was warned several times by President Truman that the bomb would be used if they did not surrender. Surely enough, Americans dropped atomic bombs on **Hiroshima** on August 6, 1945, and on **Nagasaki** three days later. Japanese leaders surrendered aboard the USS Missouri on August 15, 1945.

Election of 1940 and American Home Front During WWII

In 1940, **FDR** easily defeated the Republican Wendell Willkie. After his election, Roosevelt pledged that every resource would be devoted to winning the war. FDR created a number of war-time bureaucracies, including the **War Production Board** (which was devoted to manufacturing goods for war), the **War Manpower Commission** (which organized the draft and created jobs for women), and the **Office of Price Administration**, which set prices and rations. In total, the US war effort cost between $330 and $360 billion. Most of this cost was covered through taxation and the sale of government bonds. The US frequently denied civil liberties to Japanese Americans during this period, forcing many to live in internment camps. In **Korematsu v. US** (1944), the Supreme Court ruled that the internment camps were legal, but in **ex parte Endo** (1944), the Court adjusted its decision to state that the US could only intern those whose disloyalty could be proven.

Contributions of Media, Minorities, and Women to the War Effort

World War II was a massive undertaking for the United States. Fighting on two war-fronts across two oceans required copious resources and coordination to succeed. This was also the first war in which instantaneous communication was accessible globally. This meant that **control of information** was especially valuable, as information leaks could lead to devastating results. FDR famously pledged that every resource would go to the war efforts. The government, along with the media, promoted patriotic feelings and encouraged enlistment and support from the home front. Many men went to fight directly, and families left at home played a role in funding the efforts through war bonds and victory gardens. In addition, various minority groups played major roles in the war efforts. Notably, the **Tuskegee Airmen** was a capable African American-only aviation group. Native Americans, called **code talkers**, used their native languages to help encode and decode messages on the radio and helped to secure communication. Many Hispanic Americans also served in combat and support roles in the war.

Treatment of Prisoners of War and Civilians and Detainees

Due to the fear of information leaks, the United States detained vast numbers of American citizens, primarily Japanese Americans, but also Italian and German Americans as a means protecting itself from security threats. Similarly, any people exhibiting a seemingly harmful ideology, such as Soviet or communist sympathies, may have been imprisoned or detained. These internment camps led to questioning the validity of the government's ability to detain people based on a presumed threat. The war also saw many imprisonments of enemy soldiers. Allied powers generally treated prisoners of war (POWs) well, though they required the POWs to participate in manual labor. The Axis, however, frequently treated POWs cruelly with torture, starvation, experimentation, and execution. These cruelties were later considered in the war crimes trials as war crimes.

Middle Years and Conclusion of World War II in Europe

The tide turned against Hitler once the United States entered the war. The harsh Russian winter halted the German advance into Russia short of Moscow in 1941. The Germans made further gains in the summer of 1942 but were decisively beaten at the **Battle of Stalingrad** and were slowly pushed back out of Russia from then on. American and British troops landed in North Africa in 1942 and used that as a springboard to invade Italy in 1943. In 1944, the Americans and British opened yet another front with a massive invasion of northern France in the **D-Day landings**. Fighting numerically superior forces on multiple fronts, the Germans steadily lost ground and the Allies pushed into Germany from both East and West in 1945. Surrounded and with the war lost, Hitler committed **suicide** in his bunker in Berlin in April 1945, and the remaining German forces **surrendered** shortly afterward.

Post-War

After the war, Germany and Japan were controlled by a coalition of nations to regulate their reconstruction from the damages of the war and establish peace and accountability moving forward. At the conclusion of the war, various ethical questions had to be considered regarding the responsibility that individuals should take on the war crimes enacted in the holocaust. About six-million Jewish people were killed at the command of Nazi leaders, but often enacted by the hand of lower-ranking soldiers. The **Nuremberg Trials** and the **Tokyo War Crimes Tribunal** sought to prosecute major war criminals and established legal precedent that an individual following orders was still responsible for their own actions. The rebuilding efforts were largely successful in reestablishing Japan and Germany as economically successful countries moving forward.

The United States Since World War II

Foreign Policy during the Cold War Era

Beginnings of The Cold War

After the defeat of the Axis powers in WWII, the United States and Russia entered into a long and often secret conflict, in which each side used diplomatic, economic, and occasionally military forces to try to assert itself as the dominant world power. The first issue on which these nations butted heads was the **rebuilding of Europe**. Germany was divided into an eastern and western section; the western half was democratic and looked to the US for guidance, while Eastern Germany became a communist nation in the USSR's sphere of influence. Russia worked to bring all of its neighbors (including Poland, Czechoslovakia, Hungary, Romania, and Bulgaria) under its control. The western borders of these nations formed what Churchill referred to as the **iron curtain**, dividing communist Eastern Europe from democratic Western Europe.

Yalta Conference

The Yalta Conference was held on an island in the Crimean Sea in February of 1945. It was attended by FDR, Churchill, and Stalin. At the Conference, FDR tried to make sure that Germany would not be split into smaller nations (this would happen later). Stalin "liberated" the countries along the border of Nazi Germany, and in exchange, FDR allowed the Red Army to remain in those countries. This Conference established boundaries and a provisional government for Poland (this provisional government was led by the Soviets and would last until 1989). One of the more important moves of this Conference was that the US and Britain allowed a Communist government under **Mao Zedong** to remain in Mongolia; this group of Communists would eventually take over China in 1949.

Truman and the Fair Deal

When Truman came into office after the death of Franklin Roosevelt in 1945, he was already fighting an uphill battle. Many people felt that the Democrats had controlled the executive branch for too long, and many expected **Truman** to have the personal charisma of FDR. Truman gamely attempted to continue the reforms of the New Deal, which he renamed the **Fair Deal**. Nevertheless, he was frequently thwarted by the Republican Congress. Truman surprisingly won a narrow victory over Dewey in the election of 1948, and continued to pursue reforms in education, health care, and civil rights. He gradually became worn down by his conflicts with Congress, however, and he declined to run in 1952.

Truman Doctrine, Marshall Plan, NATO, and Warsaw Pact

In order to stop the spread of communism in Europe and elsewhere, President Truman asserted his policy of "containment" in the so-called **Truman Doctrine**. This meant that the US would support the anticommunist governments throughout the world. The **Marshall Plan** advanced this policy by supplying aid to war-ravaged countries in Western Europe. When the **Eastern Bloc countries** prevented aid from reaching West Berlin, the US, England, and France organized the **Berlin Airlift** to overcome this obstacle. In 1949, the Western European and North American nations entered into a mutual defense treaty, NATO (North Atlantic Treaty Organization). As a response, the Eastern Bloc nations joined with the Soviet Union in the **Warsaw Pact**.

Korean War

The Korean War took place during the Truman presidency. Korea had been divided after WWII into a **northern half** (under Soviet control) and a **southern half** (under American control). When foreign troops finally withdrew from the peninsula, North Korea attacked South Korea in an attempt to unify. The United Nations Security Council declared that North Korea was an aggressor, and sent troops led by the American General **Douglas MacArthur** to the region. MacArthur had some early victories, but progress slowed when China began to send men and supplies to the North Koreans. Gradually, combat gave way to armistice talks, yet these too seemed to drag on endlessly.

Election of 1952, Eisenhower, and the Suez Canal

General **Dwight Eisenhower**, a Republican, defeated the Democrat Adlai Stevenson in the election of 1952. One of the first crises of the Eisenhower administration concerned the **Suez Canal** in Egypt. The conflict began after Israel attacked Egypt in response to attacks on the new Jewish nation that were launched at Egyptian bases; at the same time, England and France withdrew plans to build a dam on the Suez Canal because of Egypt's recognition of Communist China. Angered by these events, Egyptian President **Nasser** seized the assets of the European company that administered traffic on the canal. The United States was eventually able to defuse the situation; this marked the introduction of the so-called **Eisenhower Doctrine**, in which American troops and money would be used to undermine Communism in various regions around the world.

Anti-Communism in the United States

As the US was becoming more embroiled in the Cold War, Americans became increasingly paranoid about the spread of **Communism**. There were numerous investigations aimed at weeding Communist spies out of the government, and two people, Julius and Ethel Rosenberg, were executed for spying. The leader of much of this was Senator **Joseph McCarthy**, who was famous for promoting and prolonging the "**Red Scare**" as the often-termed witch-hunt for communists in the government was known (Soviet communications released after the fall of the Soviet Union confirmed the vast majority of his accusations). The tide of anti-communism extended into a general disapproval of organized labor. The **Taft-Hartley Act** restricted the ability of labor unions markedly. In order to survive, the nation's two largest labor unions combined, forming the **AFL-CIO**.

Other Domestic Impacts of the Cold War

In addition to the effects of the Red Scare, the Cold War stimulated a vast expansion of the military-industrial complex, developing new technologies and weapons. Relatedly, the United States took massive pride in their budding space program, which led to the creation of NASA and the moon landing in 1969. Other effects included economic growth and educational reform, which could be considered an effect of the massive spending on defense technology.

End of the Cold War

Over time, the leaders of the Soviet Union and United States began to realize the total annihilation that would ensue if nuclear war was declared, and it was agreed that both sides would **disarm**. The two treaties that were signed during the 1970s are known as the **Strategic Arms Limitation Talks (SALT) I and II**. When **Mikhail Gorbachev** came into power in the USSR in 1985, he established a policy of **glasnost**, or "openness." In response to US President Ronald Reagan's military build-up using the might of the US economy, Gorbachev understood that the Soviet Union could not economically compete militarily under a communist system and overcome the military might of the United States. He thus advocated **perestroika**, a gradual metamorphosis of the Soviet economy. In 1991, these reforms culminated in the disintegration of the ruling Communist party, and the **disbanding of the Soviet Union**. This occurred two years after the **Berlin Wall**, which for more than forty years had separated communist and anticommunist Germany, was finally torn down.

Review Video: The End of the Cold War
Visit mometrix.com/academy and enter code: 278032

Middle East from 1947 to 1977

After WWII, the United Nations announced that **Palestine** would be partitioned in order to make room for a new Jewish state. **Israel** was created in 1948. In 1951, the Iranian leader **Mossadegh** nationalized the oil interests, making his government extremely wealthy and powerful. This move would be emulated by future leaders. In 1967, in the **Six-Day War**, Israel routed a coalition of Arab nations, seizing the West Bank, Sinai, and Jerusalem. In 1972, Palestinian terrorists murdered 12 Israeli athletes at the Olympics in Munich. In 1973, the oil-producing Arab nations placed an embargo on shipments to the West, causing major energy crises in the US and Europe. Also, in 1973, Israelis and Arabs battled again in the **Yom Kippur War**. In 1977, Egyptian leader **Anwar Sadat** became the first Arab leader to visit Israel.

Social, Political, and Cultural Movements during the Second Half of the Twentieth Century

Civil Rights Under Eisenhower

For a long time, the problems of black people had been considered a Southern issue; however, massive black migration into the Northern cities made civil rights a national question. In **Brown v. Board of Education** (1954), the Supreme Court ruled that segregation in public schools is unconstitutional. After some southern states defied this decision, Eisenhower was forced to send in federal troops. At the same time, black people were staging nonviolent protests across the south. **Rosa Parks** famously refused to give up her bus seat in Montgomery, Alabama, and four black men staged a sit-in at a whites-only lunch counter in Greensboro, North Carolina. With the **Civil Rights Acts** of 1957 and 1960, black people were given the right to vote, but these acts were not enforced.

US Foreign Policy Under Eisenhower

The Secretary of State under Eisenhower was **John Foster Dulles**, who wanted to pursue an aggressive foreign policy to "roll back Communism." This was also the period in which the national defense budget skyrocketed, as both the US and USSR believed that peace could be maintained by threatening the other side with total annihilation. It was in this climate that the US first became involved in **Vietnam**. The French had been kicked out of this Southeast Asian nation for good in 1954, and the country had been divided into a northern and southern half in the **Geneva Truce** of the same year. The US then tried to bolster the standing of the non-communist leader **Ngo Dinh Diem** in the south, as he batted the communist **Viet Cong**. Increasingly, Eisenhower was funneling money to the anti-communist forces in South Vietnam, believing that if this country became communist, others would follow (the "Domino effect").

Election of 1960, Kennedy and the Space Program, and Assassination of JFK

In the election of 1960, the Democrat **John F. Kennedy** defeated Richard Nixon; this was the first election in which television was a major factor. One of the most important issues of the Kennedy presidency would be the **space race** with the Soviet Union. It was under Kennedy that the **National Aeronautics and Space Administration** was established. Alan Shepard became the first American in space in 1961, and in 1969, Neil Armstrong would become the first human to walk on the moon. Kennedy, unfortunately, would not witness this event: he was shot and killed by **Lee Harvey Oswald** in Dallas in November of 1963. Though some still claim that Oswald was a part of a broader conspiracy, an investigation led by Chief Justice Earl Warren declared that he had acted alone.

Civil Rights During the Kennedy Years

The black struggle for **civil rights** intensified during the Kennedy administration. After integration at Southern universities was mandated, National Guardsmen were deployed to keep the peace. The situation was especially tense in Alabama, where Governor George Wallace declared that segregation would stand in his state forever. In July of 1963, **Martin Luther King, Jr.** led the famous **March on Washington**, during which he made his "I Have a Dream" speech. King would receive the **Nobel Peace Prize** in 1964. The **23rd and 24th amendments** to the Constitution were aimed at redressing the issue of black suffrage; they gave electoral votes to Washington, DC, and eliminated the poll tax.

LBJ and Election of 1964

Lyndon Baines Johnson took over as president after the assassination of Kennedy. He was able to use the "ghost" of the assassinated president to pass the **Civil Rights Act of 1964**. Johnson also declared a "war on poverty," a system of programs aimed at helping the poor. In the election of 1964, the escalating conflict in Vietnam was much in the public's mind, and the Republican candidate, Barry Goldwater, was viewed as a war-monger. The election of Johnson, however, did not keep the US out of Vietnam. After being elected, Johnson promoted legislation under the banner of the "Great Society." He created Medicare and Medicaid with the **Social Security Act of 1965** and established the agency of **Housing and Urban Development**.

Civil Rights Movement During the Johnson Years

The summer of 1964 saw more violence in the South as three civil rights workers were murdered while trying to register voters. After the passage of the **Voting Rights Act of 1965**, Johnson would have to deploy Federal Marshals to escort black people to the polls. Frustrated by the slow advance to equality, many black people became more militant. During the summer of 1967, there were riots in 150 cities, most of which were sparked by economic concerns, as black people felt they were being mistreated in the marketplace. Advocates of **Black Power** joined groups like the Black Panthers and the Mau Mau, and even formerly moderate groups like the SNCC would begin to endorse violence. Many white Americans who sympathized with the black struggle were alienated by this militancy. There were more riots in 1968 after the assassination of Martin Luther King, Jr. in Memphis. The **Civil Rights Act of 1968** gave full rights to black people but contained restrictions aimed at reducing racial violence.

Foreign Policy Under Johnson

After an American ship came under fire from **North Vietnam** in the Gulf of Tonkin, Johnson received a blank check for American involvement in the region. **General Westmoreland** oversaw troops during this period of escalation. Soon, 184,000 American soldiers were in Vietnam, and the government was spending a million dollars every day. Coupled with inflation, this expense bled Johnson's domestic program dry. The **peace movement** in the US took off during this period. Many people protested what they saw as inequities in the draft system (for instance, black people seemed to be unfairly overrepresented). The US problems in Vietnam were exposed to the world during the **Tet Offensive** of January 1968; during this period, the Viet Cong damaged American forces in virtually every city in the region.

Election of 1968 and Domestic Policy of Nixon

In the election of 1968, the Republican **Richard M. Nixon**, who had narrowly lost to Kennedy in 1960, defeated the Democrat Hubert Humphrey. The **Democratic National Convention** had endured violent protests over the Vietnam War. Though much of Nixon's administration would be concerned with the war (and later with the Watergate investigation), he did institute a somewhat successful policy of sharing revenue with states. The economy was languishing in a state of stagflation (high inflation and high unemployment) during this period and thus Nixon tried to jolt it with a ninety-day wage and price freeze. This move, known as the **New Economic Policy** (or Nixonomics) was a total failure.

Nixon and Vietnam

Nixon had won the election on a platform of "Peace with Honor," and upon entering office, he began slowly withdrawing troops from Vietnam. The **Nixon Doctrine** asserted that the US would honor its commitment to South Vietnam with material rather than men. Nixon did, however, order an invasion of purportedly neutral **Cambodia**, where the Viet Cong were stockpiling weapons. It was also during Nixon's presidency that four students at Kent State University were killed by the National Guard during a protest. In the election of 1972, Nixon crushed George McGovern after Foreign Advisor Henry Kissinger claimed that peace was "at hand." After the election, Kissinger and Le Duc Tho would negotiate the **Paris Peace Accords of 1973**.

Watergate Scandal

On June 17, 1972, a break-in was thwarted at the **Democratic National Committee office** at the Watergate Hotel in Washington, DC. It was eventually discovered that the burglars had ties to the Nixon administration. This began the unraveling of an enormous conspiracy of corruption in the Nixon administration. Many of Nixon's advisers would be forced to resign, though Nixon still refused to cooperate with the investigation. Eventually, though, evidence would mount against him, and Nixon would be forced to release tapes of his Oval Office conversations. Nixon **resigned** on August 8, 1974, although he never admitted any guilt. The **Watergate scandal** left a permanent stain on the presidency.

Gerald Ford Interlude

Gerald Ford, a congressman from Michigan, had been appointed vice president under Nixon after the resignation of Spiro Agnew, and became president after Nixon resigned. His was a mostly uneventful term, as the nation recovered from the shocks of Vietnam and Watergate. Ford talked a great deal about battling inflation but never did very much to back up his rhetoric. It was during the Ford administration that **South Vietnam** fell once and for all to the North Vietnamese. Ford's most famous act may have been his full **pardon** of Nixon. Though Ford at the time declared that "our long national nightmare is over," this unpopular move may have cost him the election in 1976.

Election of 1976 and the Carter Administration

The Democratic governor of Georgia, **Jimmy Carter**, defeated the incumbent Gerald Ford in the election of 1976. Carter was popular with black voters and was generally believed to be outside the cesspool of Washington politics. Carter immediately made an $18 billion tax cut, and inflation soared. Carter also made the controversial move of pardoning all those who evaded the draft during the Vietnam War. "As for foreign policy, Carter became known for his humanitarian efforts, working for peace between Israel and Egypt at Camp David and in 2002 earned the Nobel Peace Prize 'for his decades of untiring effort to find peaceful solutions to international conflicts'" (www.nobelprize.org). Carter signed a bill to give the **Panama Canal** back to the Panamanians and endured a severe oil shortage. This, along with the failed rescue of fifty American hostages in Iran, led to Carter's defeat in 1980.

Election of 1980 and Foreign Policy Under Reagan

In the election of 1980, known as the **Conservative Revolution**, **Ronald Reagan** easily defeated Jimmy Carter. Reagan presided over the last few years of the Cold War. In 1983, Reagan authorized the invasion of Grenada, where there was an airstrip that was supposedly being used by the Cubans and the Soviet Union. Later in 1983, a Marine barrack in Lebanon was blown up by terrorists, killing hundreds of American soldiers. Reagan introduced the **"Star Wars" program**, a strategic defense initiative in which incoming missiles would be destroyed from outer space by laser-armed satellites. Reagan promoted the "**Peace through strength**" method of foreign policy, whereby the economic might of the United States would furnish such an intimidating military that the Soviet Union would be unable to compete financially and thus fail. This eventually played a major role in the **fall of the Soviet Union** in 1989. Reagan nevertheless improved relations with the Soviet Union diplomatically, even signing a treaty with Soviet Premier **Mikhail Gorbachev** to ban a certain class of nuclear weapon.

Impact of Policy Changes on Foreign Relationships

Policies in the shadow of the Cold War and the red scare were heavily focused on suppressing the expansion of communism globally. As a result, the United States frequently supported authoritarian leaders and dictatorships in Latin America. This support of non-democratic countries undermined the rise of democracy and human rights, allowing for oppression and political turmoil in many countries. The policies of this time also forged connections between Latin American countries and the economic interests of the United States, leading to unhealthy economic dependency. The ultimate result of these policies included economic damage, social discontent, violations of human rights, and long-lasting global mistrust.

Domestic Affairs Under Reagan

Upon entering office, Reagan implemented **tax cuts** in the hopes of stimulating the economy. While this had a very positive effect on the economy by the end of his first term, the American trade deficit continued to grow wider. Reagan's presidency was tarnished by the **Iran-Contra affair**, in which it was determined that the US had sold weapons to a hostile nation. In 1984, due to an impressive economic recovery and unprecedented growth, Reagan defeated Walter Mondale (whose running mate was Geraldine Ferraro, the first female vice-presidential candidate) in a landslide, winning 49 states electorally. In the case **Wallace v. Jaffree** (1985), the Supreme Court ruled that schools could provide for a moment of silence but could not endorse any particular religion. In **US v. Eichman** (1990), the Court ruled that burning the American flag qualified as expressive conduct and was therefore permitted under the First Amendment.

Election of 1992 and Domestic Policy Under Clinton

The Democratic governor of Arkansas, **Bill Clinton**, defeated the incumbent George H. W. Bush and H. Ross Perot (Independent) in the election of 1992. Clinton tried to reduce the federal deficit. He also pushed for gays to be allowed into the military. Clinton appointed Janet Reno as the first female Attorney General and also reversed most of the restrictions on abortions that had been established by the Reagan and Bush administrations. Clinton's presidency would be plagued by scandals throughout; he and his wife were accused of making illegal land deals in the **Whitewater scandal**, and Clinton would later be **impeached** for lying under oath and obstructing justice in regard to an extramarital affair. A Democrat majority in the Senate elected not to remove him from office.

Election of 1996 and Foreign Policy Under Clinton

In the election of 1996, the incumbent **Bill Clinton** narrowly defeated Kansas Senator Bob Dole. During Clinton's two terms, the United States trade deficit would continue. In the aftermath of the collapse of the Soviet regime, the US gave substantial aid to Russia and many of the new republics. The United States would also supply troops for a **NATO peacekeeping effort** during the Civil War in the former Yugoslavia between the years 1992 and 2000. American troops also participated in peacekeeping missions in Somalia, Bosnia, and Haiti. Finally, Clinton ordered air strikes against Iraq after it was determined that Iraqi leader **Saddam Hussein** had been part of a conspiracy to assassinate President Bush.

Middle East from 1978 to 1985

In 1978, American President **Jimmy Carter** hosted successful peace talks between Egypt and Israel at **Camp David**. The next year, however, a fundamentalist Islamist regime would take power in Iran, and many Americans would be taken hostage, only released upon the election of **Ronald Reagan**. Between 1980 and 1988, Iran and Iraq engaged in a bloody and brutal war, begun when the Iraqi leader **Saddam Hussein** seized territory in eastern Iran. Also, during this period, Afghan rebels were engaged in a prolonged, ultimately successful fight for independence from the Soviets. In 1982, Israel attacked Lebanon, which was harboring the Palestinian leader **Yasser Arafat**. Lebanon would be forced to oust Arafat the next year. Israel would continue attacking Arafat and the **Palestinian Liberation Organization**, and the PLO would continue to sponsor terrorist activities against Israel.

Middle East from 1987 to 2003

In 1987, Syrian troops entered Lebanon and stopped the civil war. Also, during this year, 402 pilgrims died during riots in the Saudi Arabian sacred city of Mecca. In 1988, the Palestinian resistance (known as the Intifada) began in earnest against Israel. Iraq invaded Kuwait in 1990, and after UN sanctions were levied, the US invaded in 1991. The Iraqi soldiers set fire to thousands of Kuwaiti oil wells while retreating. In 1992, Arafat and Israeli PM Yitzhak Rabin shook hands in Washington, and Arafat would soon return to Gaza after years of exile. In 1995, the Israelis and Palestinians signed an agreement giving the Palestinians autonomy in the West Bank and Gaza areas. Despite continuing violence, another agreement was reached in 1998, this one stating that the Palestinians would be granted land in exchange for keeping the peace. Violence continued, however, and in 2003, Israel began construction of a barrier between itself and the Palestinian territories.

New Europe after 1991 through 1998

In 1991, **Gorbachev** resigned as the last president of the USSR, and a number of the Soviet provinces, including Lithuania and Latvia, declared independence. The **Maastricht Treaty**, formally announcing the creation of the European Union, was signed in 1992, and the next year a unified European stock market opened. In the **"Velvet" Revolution of 1993**, Slovakia separated from Czechoslovakia, which became the Czech Republic. Meanwhile, the former USSR was enduring civil strife until **Boris Yeltsin** seized power in 1993. In 1994, Russian troops attacked **Chechnya**, which was trying to achieve independence. In 1998, President Clinton helped broker a peace agreement between the **British** and **North Irish rebels**.

New Europe After 1999

In 1999, the Czech Republic, Poland, and Hungary all joined **NATO**, further eliminating the old divides between western and eastern Europe. The conflict in Chechnya increased during this year, and Yeltsin was succeeded as Russian leader by the former KGB agent Vladimir Putin. An **International Criminal Court** was created in the Hague (Netherlands) in 2002, despite the vehement opposition of the United States. In the late '90s, many of the western European governments had become quasi-socialist, and they spent much of their time debating the immense increase in **immigration**. Meanwhile, the former Soviet states have had a rough transition from command to market economies and are still somewhat economically depressed.

Emergence of the Pacific Rim After 1991

In the 1990s and early years of the 21st century, Japan and China emerged as two major economic powers. Despite suffering a prolonged recession, **Japan** continued to be one of the world's manufacturing leaders. However, several internal scandals have shaken Japanese confidence and have caused many to question the close relations between corporations and government. In **China**, the suffocating communist regime has relaxed its economic strictures somewhat, and the result has been an economic boom. China created several **special economic zones** along its eastern coast to lure foreign business. Now however, Chinese firms control a sizable portion of the market in their own right.

Immigration in the Second Half of the Twentieth Century

In the post-WWII era, many countries needed reconstruction and economic growth, leading to fairly open immigration policies. In the 50s, the 1952 McCarran-Walter Act allowed for a quota system established in the 20s, but restricted immigration from Asia, but made allowances for skilled laborers to be admitted for work. In 1965, the Immigration and Nationality Act removed the quota system that had discriminated against non-European immigrants and shifted its focus to allowing immigration-based labor and employment skills and family unification. The policy shift allowed for a major increase to immigration from other parts of the world. Outside of America, global migration flourished in the second half of the Twentieth Century, sometimes driven by economic motivations and others by continuing war that caused people to seek refuge and asylum in other countries.

Technological and Cultural Changes in the Second Half of the Twentieth Century

The second half of the twentieth century saw huge expansions on the recent inventions of the industrial revolution. Infrastructure was expanded to allow for people to make better use of their cars on better roads and to use electric devices more reliably at home. Space technology, medicine, communication technology, electronics, and household appliances were developed and improved, often alongside the space race and the arms races related to the Cold War. By the 1970s, computers started to assist with tasks in industry and by the 1990s, the world wide web was invented, leading to the information age, where digital information became as important as physical products in the past. These technological expansions also accelerated cultural movements as communications and the powers of mass media continued to expand.

Political and Social Conditions during the Early Twenty-First Century

Election of 2000 and George W. Bush

In the election of 2000, **George W. Bush**, the son of ex-President Bush, defeated Vice President Al Gore, despite losing to Gore in the popular vote. Bush immediately instituted a major tax cut; critics claimed that this tax cut only benefited the very rich. On September 11, 2001, the US suffered the worst **terrorist attack** in its history, as four planes were hijacked and two of them destroyed the **World Trade Center** towers in New York. The attacks were planned and funded by **al-Qaeda**; an Islamic fundamentalist group led by Osama bin Laden. The United States almost immediately launched **Operation Enduring Freedom**, an attack on the Taliban government of Afghanistan that had harbored bin Laden.

Overview of George Bush's Foreign and Domestic Policies

In the election of 1988, the Republican Vice President **George H.W. Bush** defeated Michael Dukakis easily. Under Bush, the **federal deficit** continued to rise, and the US role in the Iran-Contra affair continued to cast a shadow over the executive branch. One of the major crises during the Bush administration was the wreck of the **Exxon Valdez**, which created the largest oil spill ever along the Alaskan coast. Meanwhile, Bush led the US military into the **Persian Gulf War** in 1990-1 after Iraq invaded neighboring Kuwait. American troops routed the Iraqis. It was also during Bush's administration that the **Berlin Wall** fell and the Communist regime in the Soviet Union finally crumbled.

Barack Obama

In 2008, Barack Obama, a senator from Illinois, became the first African American US president. His administration focused on improving the lot of a country suffering from a major recession. His major initiatives included:

- Economic bailout packages
- Improvements in women's rights
- Moves to broaden LGBT rights
- Health care reform legislation
- Reinforcement of the war in Afghanistan

Donald Trump

In 2016, Donald Trump, previously a real estate developer and television personality, was elected 45th president after a tumultuous election in which he won the electoral college but lost the popular vote. Marked by tension between the administration and domestic media, Trump's initiatives included:

- Appointing three Supreme Court Justices: Neil Gorsuch, Brett Kavanaugh, and Amy Coney Barrett
- Passing a major tax reform bill
- Enacting travel and emigration restrictions on eight nations: Iran, Libya, Syria, Yemen, Somalia, Chad, North Korea, and Venezuela
- Recognizing Jerusalem, rather than Tel Aviv, as the capital of Israel
- Responding to the novel coronavirus (SARS-CoV-2) outbreak

Almost completely along party lines, Donald Trump was impeached by the House on charges of abuse of power and obstruction of Congress; he was acquitted by the Senate.

Joe Biden

In 2020, Joe Biden won the election against Donald Trump amidst the backdrop of the COVID-19 pandemic. Biden's vice president was Kamala Harris, the first female and the first Black and South Asian vice president. The period of Biden's presidency was marked by topics including the following:

- Pandemic response and policy
- Racial justice movements
- Economic policy and fallout from the pandemic
- Healthcare policy

Technological Changes of the 21st Century

Continuing the pace of technological advancement from the previous two centuries, the twenty-first century has continued to rapidly expand in technological advancement. Since the invention and proliferation of the internet in the 1990s, the internet has continued to spread to nearly every person in the United States. The improvement of battery functionality and microchip design has created very small devices that can hold up to rigorous computing and internet connectivity anywhere in the country. In addition, social media and communication methodology has dramatically increased. In more recent years, artificial intelligence and machine learning has spread to public use. Robotics, transportation technology, and space technology have all made great strides, introducing all-electric cars and increased access to space-flight technology, entering the privatized and commercialized sector.

Geography Concepts

Overview of Geography Concepts

Geography involves learning about the world's primary **physical and cultural patterns** to help understand how the world functions as an interconnected and dynamic system. Combining information from different sources, geography teaches the basic patterns of climate, geology, vegetation, human settlement, migration, and commerce. Thus, geography is an **interdisciplinary** study of history, anthropology, and sociology. **History** incorporates geography in discussions of battle strategies, slavery (trade routes), ecological disasters (the Dust Bowl of the 1930s), and mass migrations. Geographic principles are useful when reading **literature** to help identify and visualize the setting, and also when studying **earth science**, **mathematics** (latitude, longitude, sun angle, and population statistics), and **fine arts** (song, art, and dance often reflect different cultures). Consequently, a good background in geography can help students succeed in other subjects as well.

Themes of Geography

The five themes of geography are:

- **Location** – This includes relative location (described in terms of surrounding geography such as a river, sea coast, or mountain) and absolute location (the specific point of latitude and longitude).
- **Place** – This includes physical characteristics (deserts, plains, mountains, and waterways) and human characteristics (features created by humans, such as architecture, roads, religion, industries, and food and folk practices).
- **Human-environmental interaction** – This includes human adaptation to the environment (using an umbrella when it rains), human modification of the environment (building terraces to prevent soil erosion), and human dependence on the environment for food, water, and natural resources.
- **Movement** –Interaction through trade, migration, communications, political boundaries, ideas, and fashions.
- **Regions** – This includes formal regions (a city, state, country, or other geographical organization as defined by political boundaries), functional regions (defined by a common function or connection, such as a school district), and vernacular regions (informal divisions determined by perceptions or one's mental image, such as the "Far East").

Review Video: Regional Geography
Visit mometrix.com/academy and enter code: 350378

Areas Covered by Geography

Geography is connected to many issues and provides answers to many everyday questions. Some of the areas covered by geography include:

- Geography investigates global climates, landforms, economies, political systems, human cultures, and migration patterns.
- Geography answers questions not only about where something is located, but also why it is there, how it got there, and how it is related to other things around it.
- Geography explains why people move to certain regions (climate, availability of natural resources, arable land, etc.).
- Geography explains world trade routes and modes of transportation.
- Geography identifies where various animals live and where various crops and forests grow.
- Geography identifies and locates populations that follow certain religions.
- Geography provides statistics on population numbers and growth, which aids in economic and infrastructure planning for cities and countries.

Physical and Cultural Geography and Physical and Political Locations

- **Physical geography** is the study of climate, water, and land and their relationships with each other and humans. Physical geography locates and identifies the earth's surface features and explores how humans thrive in various locations according to crop and goods production.
- **Cultural geography** is the study of the influence of the environment on human behaviors as well as the effect of human activities such as farming, building settlements, and grazing livestock on the environment. Cultural geography also identifies and compares the features of different cultures and how they influence interactions with other cultures and the earth.
- **Physical location** refers to the placement of the hemispheres and the continents.
- **Political location** refers to the divisions within continents that designate various countries. These divisions are made with borders, which are set according to boundary lines arrived at by legal agreements.

Both physical and political locations can be precisely determined by geographical surveys and by latitude and longitude.

Spatial Organization

Spatial organization in geography refers to how things or people are grouped in a given space anywhere on earth. Spatial organization applies to the **placement of settlements**, whether hamlets, towns, or cities. These settlements are located to make the distribution of goods and services convenient. For example, in farm communities, people come to town to get groceries, to attend church and school, and to access medical services. It is more practical to provide these things to groups than to individuals. These settlements, historically, have been built close to water sources and agricultural areas. Lands that are topographically difficult, have few resources, or experience extreme temperatures do not have as many people as temperate zones and flat plains, where it is easier to live. Within settlements, a town or city will be organized into commercial and residential neighborhoods, with hospitals, fire stations, and shopping centers centrally located. All of these organizational considerations are spatial in nature.

IMPORTANT TERMS RELATED TO MAPS

The most important terms used when describing items on a map or globe are:

- **Latitude and longitude** – Latitude and longitude are the imaginary lines (horizontal and vertical, respectively) that divide the globe into a grid. Both are measured using the 360 degrees of a circle.
- **Coordinates** – These are the latitude and longitude measures for a place.
- **Absolute location** – This is the exact spot where coordinates meet. The grid system allows the location of every place on the planet to be identified.
- **Equator** – This is the line at 0° latitude that divides the earth into two equal halves called hemispheres.
- **Parallels** – This is another name for lines of latitude because they circle the earth in parallel lines that never meet.
- **Meridians** – This is another name for lines of longitude. The Prime Meridian is located at 0° longitude, and is the starting point for measuring distance (both east and west) around the globe. Meridians circle the earth and connect at the Poles.

Review Video: Elements of a Map
Visit mometrix.com/academy and enter code: 437727

TYPES OF MAPS

- A **physical map** is one that shows natural features such as mountains, rivers, lakes, deserts, and plains. Color is used to designate the different features.
- A **topographic map** is a type of physical map that shows the relief and configuration of a landscape, such as hills, valleys, fields, forest, roads, and settlements. It includes natural and human-made features.
- A **topological map** is one on which lines are stretched or straightened for the sake of clarity, but retain their essential geometric relationship. This type of map is used, for example, to show the routes of a subway system.
- A **political map** uses lines for state, county, and country boundaries; points or dots for cities and towns; and various other symbols for features such as airports and roads.

MAP STYLES

There are three basic styles of maps:

- **Base maps** – Created from aerial and field surveys, base maps serve as the starting point for topographic and thematic maps.
- **Topographic maps** – These show the natural and human-made surface features of the earth, including mountain elevations, river courses, roads, names of lakes and towns, and county and state lines.
- **Thematic maps** – These use a base or topographic map as the foundation for showing data based on a theme, such as population density, wildlife distribution, hill-slope stability, economic trends, etc.

Scale is the size of a map expressed as a ratio of the actual size of the land (for example, 1 inch on a map represents 1 mile on land). In other words, it is the proportion between a distance on the map and its corresponding distance on earth. The scale determines the level of detail on a map. **Small-scale maps** depict larger areas, but include fewer details. **Large-scale maps** depict smaller areas, but include more details.

Time Zones

Time is linked to **longitude** in that a complete rotation of the Earth, or 360° of longitude, occurs every 24 hours. Each hour of time is therefore equivalent to 15° of longitude, or 4 minutes for each 1° turn. By the agreement of 27 nations at the 1884 International Meridian Conference, the time zone system consists of **24 time zones** corresponding to the 24 hours in a day. Although high noon technically occurs when the sun is directly above a meridian, calculating time that way would result in 360 different times for the 360 meridians. Using the 24-hour system, the time is the same for all locations in a 15° zone. The 1884 conference established the meridian passing through Greenwich, England, as the zero point, or **prime meridian**. The halfway point is found at the 180th meridian, a half day from Greenwich. It is called the **International Date Line**, and serves as the place where each day begins and ends on earth.

Cartography

Cartography is the art and science of **mapmaking**. Maps of local areas were drawn by the Egyptians as early as 1300 BC, and the Greeks began making maps of the known world in the 6th century BC. Cartography eventually grew into the field of geography. The first step in modern mapmaking is a **survey**. This involves designating a few key sites of known elevation as benchmarks to allow for measurement of other sites. **Aerial photography** is then used to chart the area by taking photos in sequence. Overlapping photos show the same area from different positions along the flight line. When paired and examined through a stereoscope, the cartographer gets a three-dimensional view that can be made into a **topographical map**. In addition, a field survey (on the ground) is made to determine municipal borders and place names. The second step is to compile the information and **computer-draft** a map based on the collected data. The map is then reproduced or printed.

Globe and Map Projections

A **globe** is the only accurate representation of the earth's size, shape, distance, and direction since it, like the earth, is **spherical**. The flat surface of a map distorts these elements. To counter this problem, mapmakers use a variety of "**map projections**," a system for representing the earth's curvatures on a flat surface through the use of a grid that corresponds to lines of latitude and longitude. Some distortions are still inevitable, though, so mapmakers make choices based on the map scale, the size of the area to be mapped, and what they want the map to show. Some projections can represent a true shape or area, while others may be based on the equator and therefore become less accurate as they near the poles. In summary, all maps have some distortion in terms of the shape or size of features of the spherical earth.

Types of Map Projections

There are three main types of map projections:

- **Conical** – This type of projection superimposes a cone over the sphere of the earth, with two reference parallels secant to the globe and intersecting it. There is no distortion along the standard parallels, but distortion increases further from the chosen parallels. A Bonne projection is an example of a conical projection, in which the areas are accurately represented but the meridians are not on a true scale.
- **Cylindrical** – This is any projection in which meridians are mapped using equally spaced vertical lines and circles of latitude (parallels) are mapped using horizontal lines. A Mercator's projection is a modified cylindrical projection that is helpful to navigators because it allows them to maintain a constant compass direction between two points. However, it exaggerates areas in high latitudes.

- **Azimuthal** – This is a stereographic projection onto a plane centered so that a straight line from the center to any other point represents the shortest distance. This distance can be measured to scale.

Review Video: Map Projections
Visit mometrix.com/academy and enter code: 327303

Hemispheres and Parallels on the World Map

The definitions for these terms are as follows:

- **Northern Hemisphere** – This is the area above, or north, of the equator.
- **Southern Hemisphere** – This is the area below, or south, of the equator.
- **Western Hemisphere** – This is the area between the North and South Poles. It extends west from the Prime Meridian to the International Date Line.
- **Eastern Hemisphere** – This is the area between the North and South Poles. It extends east from the Prime Meridian to the International Date Line.
- **North and South Poles** – Latitude is measured in terms of the number of degrees north and south from the equator. The North Pole is located at 90°N latitude, while the South Pole is located at 90°S latitude.
- **Tropic of Cancer** – This is the parallel, or latitude, 23½° north of the equator.
- **Tropic of Capricorn** – This is the parallel, or latitude, 23½° south of the equator. The region between these two parallels is the tropics. The subtropics is the area located between 23½° and 40° north and south of the equator.
- **Arctic Circle** – This is the parallel, or latitude, 66½° north of the equator.
- **Antarctic Circle** – This is the parallel, or latitude, 66½° south of the equator.

Review Video: Geographical Features
Visit mometrix.com/academy and enter code: 773539

GPS

Global Positioning System (GPS) is a system of satellites that orbit the Earth and communicate with mobile devices to pinpoint the mobile device's position. This is accomplished by determining the distance between the mobile device and at least three satellites. A mobile device might calculate a distance of 400 miles between it and the first satellite. The possible locations that are 400 miles from the first satellite and the mobile device will fall along a circle. The possible locations on Earth relative to the other two satellites will fall somewhere along different circles. The point on Earth at which these three circles intersect is the location of the mobile device. The process of determining position based on distance measurements from three satellites is called **trilateration**.

Physical and Cultural Features of Geographic Locations and Countries

Physical Features

- **Vegetation zones, or biomes** – Forests, grasslands, deserts, and tundra are the four main types of vegetation zones.
- **Climate zones** – Tropical, dry, temperate, continental, and polar are the five different types of climate zones. Climate is the long-term average weather conditions of a place.

CULTURAL FEATURES

- **Population density** – This is the number of people living in each square mile or kilometer of a place. It is calculated by dividing population by area.
- **Religion** – This is the identification of the dominant religions of a place, whether Christianity, Hinduism, Judaism, Buddhism, Islam, Shinto, Taoism, or Confucianism. All of these originated in Asia.
- **Languages** – This is the identification of the dominant or official language of a place. There are 12 major language families. The Indo-European family (which includes English, Russian, German, French, and Spanish) is spoken over the widest geographic area, but Mandarin Chinese is spoken by the most people.

GEOMORPHOLOGY

The study of landforms is call **geomorphology** or physiography, a science that considers the relationships between *geological structures* and *surface landscape features.* It is also concerned with the processes that change these features, such as erosion, deposition, and plate tectonics. Biological factors can also affect landforms. Examples are when corals build a coral reef or when plants contribute to the development of a salt marsh or a sand dune. Rivers, coastlines, rock types, slope formation, ice, erosion, and weathering are all part of geomorphology. A **landform** is a landscape feature or geomorphological unit. These include hills, plateaus, mountains, deserts, deltas, canyons, mesas, marshes, swamps, and valleys. These units are categorized according to elevation, slope, orientation, stratification, rock exposure, and soil type. Landform elements include pits, peaks, channels, ridges, passes, pools, and plains. The highest order landforms are continents and oceans. Elementary landforms such as segments, facets, and relief units are the smallest homogenous divisions of a land surface at a given scale or resolution.

OCEANS, SEAS, LAKES, RIVERS, AND CANALS

- **Oceans** are the largest bodies of water on earth and cover nearly 71% of the earth's surface. There are five major oceans: Atlantic, Pacific (largest and deepest), Indian, Arctic, and Southern (surrounds Antarctica).
- **Seas** are smaller than oceans and are somewhat surrounded by land like a lake, but lakes are fresh water and seas are salt water. Seas include the Mediterranean, Baltic, Caspian, Caribbean, and Coral.
- **Lakes** are bodies of water in a depression on the earth's surface. Examples of lakes are the Great Lakes and Lake Victoria.
- **Rivers** are a channeled flow of water that start out as a spring or stream formed by runoff from rain or snow. Rivers flow from higher to lower ground, and usually empty into a sea or ocean. Great rivers of the world include the Amazon, Nile, Rhine, Mississippi, Ganges, Mekong, and Yangtze.
- **Canals** are artificial waterways constructed by humans to connect two larger water bodies. Examples of canals are the Panama and the Suez.

Mountains, Hills, Foothills, Valleys, Plateaus, and Mesas

The definitions for these geographical features are as follows:

- **Mountains** are elevated landforms that rise fairly steeply from the earth's surface to a summit of at least 1,000-2,000 feet (definitions vary) above sea level.
- **Hills** are elevated landforms that rise 500-2,000 feet above sea level.
- **Foothills** are a low series of hills found between a plain and a mountain range.
- **Valleys** are a long depression located between hills or mountains. They are usually products of river erosion. Valleys can vary in terms of width and depth, ranging from a few feet to thousands of feet.
- **Plateaus** are elevated landforms that are fairly flat on top. They may be as high as 10,000 feet above sea level and are usually next to mountains.
- **Mesas** are flat areas of upland. Their name is derived from the Spanish word for table. They are smaller than plateaus and often found in arid or semi-arid areas.

Formation of Mountains

Mountains are formed by the movement of geologic plates, which are rigid slabs of rocks beneath the earth's crust that float on a layer of partially molten rock in the earth's upper mantle. As the plates collide, they push up the crust to form mountains. This process is called **orogeny**. There are three basic forms of orogeny:

- If the collision of continental plates causes the crust to buckle and fold, a chain of **folded mountains**, such as the Appalachians, the Alps, or the Himalayas, is formed.
- If the collision of the plates causes a denser oceanic plate to go under a continental plate, a process called **subduction**; strong horizontal forces lift and fold the margin of the continent. A mountain range like the Andes is the result.
- If an oceanic plate is driven under another oceanic plate, **volcanic mountains** such as those in Japan and the Philippines are formed.

Coral Reefs

Coral reefs are formed from millions of tiny, tube-shaped **polyps**, an animal life form encased in tough limestone skeletons. Once anchored to a rocky surface, polyps eat plankton and miniscule shellfish caught with poisonous tentacles near their mouth. Polyps use calcium carbonate absorbed from chemicals given off by algae to harden their body armor and cement themselves together in fantastic shapes of many colors. Polyps reproduce through eggs and larvae, but the reef grows by branching out shoots of polyps. There are three types of coral reefs:

- **Fringing reefs** – These surround, or "fringe," an island.
- **Barrier reefs** – Over the centuries, a fringe reef grows so large that the island sinks down from the weight, and the reef becomes a barrier around the island. Water trapped between the island and the reef is called a lagoon.
- **Atolls** – Eventually, the sinking island goes under, leaving the coral reef around the lagoon.

PLAINS, DESERTS, DELTAS, AND BASINS

- **Plains** are extensive areas of low-lying, flat, or gently undulating land, and are usually lower than the landforms around them. Plains near the seacoast are called lowlands.
- **Deserts** are large, dry areas that receive less than 10 inches of rain per year. They are almost barren, containing only a few patches of vegetation.
- **Deltas** are accumulations of silt deposited at river mouths into the seabed. They are eventually converted into very fertile, stable ground by vegetation, becoming important crop-growing areas. Examples include the deltas of the Nile, Ganges, and Mississippi River.
- **Basins** come in various types. They may be low areas that catch water from rivers; large hollows that dip to a central point and are surrounded by higher ground, as in the Donets and Kuznetsk basins in Russia; or areas of inland drainage in a desert when the water can't reach the sea and flows into lakes or evaporates in salt flats as a result. An example is the Great Salt Lake in Utah.

MARSHES AND SWAMPS AND TUNDRA AND TAIGA

Marshes and swamps are both **wet lowlands**. The water can be fresh, brackish, or saline. Both host important ecological systems with unique wildlife. There are, however, some major differences. **Marshes** have no trees and are always wet because of frequent floods and poor drainage that leaves shallow water. Plants are mostly grasses, rushes, reeds, typhas, sedges, and herbs. **Swamps** have trees and dry periods. The water is very slow-moving, and is usually associated with adjacent rivers or lakes.

Both taiga and tundra regions have many plants and animals, but they have few humans or crops because of their harsh climates. **Taiga** has colder winters and hotter summers than tundra because of its distance from the Arctic Ocean. Taiga is the world's largest forest region, located just south of the tundra line. It contains huge mineral resources and fur-bearing animals. **Tundra** is a Russian word describing marshy plain in an area that has a very cold climate but receives little snow. The ground is usually frozen, but is quite spongy when it is not.

HUMID CONTINENTAL, PRAIRIE, SUBTROPICAL, AND MARINE CLIMATES

- A **humid continental climate** is one that has four seasons, including a cold winter and a hot summer, and sufficient rainfall for raising crops. Such climates can be found in the United States, Canada, and Russia. The best farmlands and mining areas are found in these countries.
- **Prairie climates**, or steppe regions, are found in the interiors of Asia and North America where there are dry flatlands (prairies that receive 10-20 inches of rain per year). These dry flatlands can be grasslands or deserts.
- **Subtropical climates** are very humid areas in the tropical areas of Japan, China, Australia, Africa, South America, and the United States. The moisture, carried by winds traveling over warm ocean currents, produces long summers and mild winters. It is possible to produce a continuous cycle of a variety of crops.
- A **marine climate** is one near or surrounded by water. Warm ocean winds bring moisture, mild temperatures year-round, and plentiful rain. These climates are found in Western Europe and parts of the United States, Canada, Chile, New Zealand, and Australia.

Review Video: Climates
Visit mometrix.com/academy and enter code: 991320

Adaptation to Environmental Conditions

The environment influences the way people live. People **adapt** to **environmental conditions** in ways as simple as putting on warm clothing in a cold environment; finding means to cool their surroundings in an environment with high temperatures; building shelters from wind, rain, and temperature variations; and digging water wells if surface water is unavailable. More complex adaptations result from the physical diversity of the earth in terms of soil, climate, vegetation, and topography. Humans take advantage of opportunities and avoid or minimize limitations. Examples of environmental limitations are that rocky soils offer few opportunities for agriculture and rough terrain limits accessibility. Sometimes, **technology** allows humans to live in areas that were once uninhabitable or undesirable. For example, air conditioning allows people to live comfortably in hot climates; modern heating systems permit habitation in areas with extremely low temperatures, as is the case with research facilities in Antarctica; and airplanes have brought people to previously inaccessible places to establish settlements or industries.

Natural Resources, Renewable Resources, Nonrenewable Resources, and Commodities

Natural resources are things provided by nature that have commercial value to humans, such as minerals, energy, timber, fish, wildlife, and the landscape. **Renewable resources** are those that can be replenished, such as wind, solar radiation, tides, and water (with proper conservation and clean-up). Soil is renewable with proper conservation and management techniques, and timber can be replenished with replanting. Living resources such as fish and wildlife can replenish themselves if they are not over-harvested. **Nonrenewable resources** are those that cannot be replenished. These include fossil fuels such as oil and coal and metal ores. These cannot be replaced or reused once they have been burned, although some of their products can be recycled. **Commodities** are natural resources that have to be extracted and purified rather than created, such as mineral ores.

Review Video: Renewable vs. Nonrenewable Resources
Visit mometrix.com/academy and enter code: 840194

Harmful or Potentially Harmful Interaction with Environment

Wherever humans have gone on the earth, they have made **changes** to their surroundings. Many are harmful or potentially harmful, depending on the extent of the alterations. Some of the changes and activities that can harm the **environment** include:

- Cutting into mountains by machine or blasting to build roads or construction sites
- Cutting down trees and clearing natural growth
- Building houses and cities
- Using grassland to graze herds
- Polluting water sources
- Polluting the ground with chemical and oil waste
- Wearing out fertile land and losing topsoil
- Placing communication lines cross country using poles and wires or underground cable
- Placing railway lines or paved roads cross country
- Building gas and oil pipelines cross country
- Draining wetlands
- Damming up or re-routing waterways
- Spraying fertilizers, pesticides, and defoliants
- Hunting animals to extinction or near extinction

Carrying Capacity and Natural Hazards

Carrying capacity is the maximum, sustained level of use of an environment can incur without sustaining significant environmental deterioration that would eventually lead to environmental destruction. Environments vary in terms of their carrying capacity, a concept humans need to learn to measure and respect before harm is done. Proper **assessment of environmental conditions** enables responsible decision making with respect to how much and in what ways the resources of a particular environment should be consumed. **Energy and water conservation** as well as recycling can extend an area's carrying capacity. In addition to carrying capacity limitations, the physical environment can also have occasional extremes that are costly to humans. **Natural hazards** such as hurricanes, tornadoes, earthquakes, volcanoes, floods, tsunamis, and some forest fires and insect infestations are processes or events that are not caused by humans, but may have serious consequences for humans and the environment. These events are not preventable, and their precise timing, location, and magnitude are not predictable. However, some precautions can be taken to reduce the damage.

Applying Geography to Interpretation of the Past

Space, environment, and chronology are three different points of view that can be used to study history. Events take place within **geographic contexts**. If the world is flat, then transportation choices are vastly different from those that would be made in a round world, for example. Invasions of Russia from the west have normally failed because of the harsh winter conditions, the vast distances that inhibit steady supply lines, and the number of rivers and marshes to be crossed, among other factors. Any invading or defending force anywhere must make choices based on consideration of space and environmental factors. For instance, lands may be too muddy or passages too narrow for certain equipment. Geography played a role in the building of the Panama Canal because the value of a shorter transportation route had to outweigh the costs of labor, disease, political negotiations, and equipment, not to mention a myriad of other effects from cutting a canal through an isthmus and changing a natural land structure as a result.

Applying Geography to Interpretation of the Present and Plans for the Future

The decisions that individual people as well as nations make that may **affect the environment** have to be made with an understanding of spatial patterns and concepts, cultural and transportation connections, physical processes and patterns, ecosystems, and the impact, or "footprint," of people on the physical environment. Sample issues that fit into these considerations are recycling programs, loss of agricultural land to further urban expansion, air and water pollution, deforestation, and ease of transportation and communication. In each of these areas, present and future uses have to be balanced against possible harmful effects. For example, wind is a clean and readily available resource for electric power, but the access roads to and noise of wind turbines can make some areas unsuitable for livestock pasture. Voting citizens need to have an understanding of **geographical and environmental connections** to make responsible decisions.

United States Physical Geography

MAJOR LAND REGIONS OF THE UNITED STATES

The United States can be divided into seven distinct **major land regions**: the Pacific Ranges and Lowlands; the Western Basins and Ranges; the Rocky Mountains; the Ozark-Ouachita Highlands; the Interior Plains; the Coastal Lowlands; and the Appalachian Highlands. Of course, this division does not include Alaska or Hawaii. Some geographers eliminate the Ozark-Ouachita Highlands from the total by classifying the Ozark Plateau as part of the Interior Plains and the Ouachita Mountains as part of the Appalachian Range. Similarly, some geographers combine the Rocky Mountains with the Pacific Ranges and Lowlands into the Pacific Cordillera. In any case, the United States has a total area of about 3.8 million square miles, or about 9.8 million square kilometers.

PACIFIC RANGES AND LOWLANDS REGION OF THE UNITED STATES

The Pacific Ranges and Lowlands region of the United States extends along the western border of the North American continent. On its eastern side, it is bordered by two mountain ranges, the Cascades and the Sierra Nevadas. The Cascade Range includes Lassen Peak (California) and Mount Saint Helens (Washington), both of which are active volcanoes. The Pacific Ranges and Lowlands region runs from northern Washington State to southern California. To the west of the mountain ranges, there are expansive and fertile valleys. These include California's Central Valley, Oregon's Willamette Valley, and Washington's Puget Sound Lowland. To the west of the valleys, there are coastal ranges, some of which are quite dramatic and others of which are relatively low. The Pacific Coast features a number of large bays, including San Diego Bay, San Francisco Bay, Columbia River Bay, and the Puget Sound. In California, the San Andreas Fault extends along the length of the coastal ranges.

ROCKY MOUNTAINS REGION OF THE UNITED STATES

The Rocky Mountains region of the United States primarily consists of North America's largest mountain group. The Rocky Mountains run from northern New Mexico all the way to Alaska. Some of the peaks in the chain are higher than 14,000 feet. Along the lower slopes of the Rockies, there are deep forests, but above the timberline, it is impossible for trees to grow. At the highest elevations, the only plant life that can be sustained is mosses, lichens, and grasses. These jagged mountain ranges include plentiful rivers and streams, and some of North America's most dramatic scenery. Geographers trace an imaginary line, known as the Continental Divide, along the range to separate those areas in which running water flows toward the Pacific Ocean and those in which it flows into the Gulf of Mexico, Atlantic Ocean, or Arctic Ocean. The Rocky Mountains region includes the headwaters of the Rio Grande, Colorado, Missouri, and Colorado Rivers. The first widely used pass through these mountains was at the Wyoming Basin.

OUTLYING AREAS OF THE UNITED STATES

Two states, Hawaii and Alaska, are not part of the conterminous United States. **Alaska** is the largest state in the nation. It has proven to be an excellent source of natural resources, like gold and oil. Because of the frigid climate, though, it has a very small population. **Hawaii** is an archipelago, or collection of islands, in the Pacific Ocean. It is home to several important American military bases. The United States also has possession of several islands in the Pacific Ocean and Caribbean. Of these, Puerto Rico is the most closely aligned with the United States, though it is still largely autonomous. Puerto Rico is designated as a commonwealth. It sends a representative to Washington for committee votes, as do American Samoa, the Virgin Islands, and Guam.

Western Basins and Ranges Region of the United States

The Western Basins and Ranges region of the United States is bordered on the west by the Cascades and Sierra Nevadas and on the east by the Rockies. From north to south, it extends from central Washington to Mexico. This region is characterized by arid terrain, including several large deserts. Death Valley in California contains the lowest point in the United States, at a little less than 300 feet below sea level. To the north, the Great Basin is a large area with several salty and shallow lakes. The largest of these is the Great Salt Lake, which is adjoined by a desert composed in part of a salt bed. On the northern end of the Great Basin, the Columbia Plateau features exceptionally fertile soil, most of which derives from volcanic eruptions in the distant past. However, for the most part, the Western Basins and Ranges region is too dry for large-scale farming, though livestock may be sustained. In the southern part of the Great Basin lies the Colorado Plateau, which includes many deep river gorges, most notably the Grand Canyon.

Ozark-Ouachita Highlands Region of the United States

The Ozark-Ouachita Highlands region of the United States is not always considered an independent geographic region, though it is difficult to group it with any of the larger regions. The Ozark Plateau and Ouachita Mountains lie north of the Coastal Lowlands and south of the Interior Plains. They run through southern Missouri, eastern Oklahoma, and northwest Arkansas. The region is marked by rough, scrubby highlands interlaced with deep gorges. Perhaps the most noteworthy features of the region are the natural caves. There has also been a great deal of profitable mining in this region, primarily for coal and iron ore. Despite a network of springs, streams, and rivers, the land of the Ozark-Ouachita Highlands is not especially good for farming.

Interior Plains Region of the United States

The Interior Plains region of the United States is an enormous expanse of mostly flat land, extending from the Appalachians in the east to the Rockies in the west. This region was mainly formed by the slow passage of massive glaciers during the Ice Age. As these glaciers descended from the north, they removed topsoil in what are now Wisconsin, Minnesota, and Michigan. These glaciers were also responsible for carving out enormous depressions, among them the Great Lakes (Huron, Michigan, Erie, Superior, and Ontario), the largest system of freshwater lakes in the world. Farther south, the glaciers flattened the land and distributed the topsoil from the north, making the land in Indiana, Illinois, Iowa, and Ohio among the best in the world for farming. The region contains a network of rivers and streams, the greatest of which is the Mississippi River. The Mississippi begins in northern Minnesota and flows all the way to New Orleans. The western part of the Interior Plains region is known as the Great Plains; it is grassland used primarily for livestock grazing.

Appalachian Highlands Region of the United States

The Appalachian Highlands region of the United States extends from northern Alabama all the way to northern Maine. It includes mountain ranges like the Blue Ridge, Smokies, Whites, Greens, and Adirondacks. The Blue Ridge Mountains are widely believed to be the oldest range in the world. They extend from northern Georgia to southern Pennsylvania. Several water gaps, or flat passages useful for transportation, are cut through the Blue Ridge by the Delaware, Potomac, and other rivers. To the west of the Blue Ridge, there is a series of high and lowlands known as the Ridge and Valley Region. It includes famous valleys like the Cumberland, Shenandoah, and Rome. The third major feature of this region is the Appalachian Plateau, which runs all the way from Alabama to New York. This area was formed by glaciers and has been mined more extensively than any other area of the United States.

Climate of the United States

The United States is an extremely large nation with a varied topography, so a number of **climate groups** are represented. In the continental United States, there are humid oceanic, humid subtropical, humid continental, desert, semiarid, highland, and subtropical dry summer regions. Climate is significantly impacted by major topographical features, like the Pacific Ocean, Rocky Mountains, and Great Lakes. The highest average temperature is 78.2 degrees Fahrenheit, in Death Valley, California, while the lowest average temperature is 9 degrees Fahrenheit, in Barrow, Alaska. It was near Barrow that the lowest temperature ever in the United States was recorded: -80 degrees Fahrenheit on January 23, 1971. The highest recorded temperature is 134 degrees Fahrenheit in Death Valley on July 10, 1913.

Regions of the United States

Coastal Lowlands Region

The Coastal Lowlands region of the United States runs in a strip along the Atlantic coast, expanding and heading west in the southeast until it terminates in eastern Texas. This region is typically divided into three **sub-regions**: the Gulf Coastal Plain, the Atlantic Coastal Plain, and the Piedmont. The **Gulf Coastal Plain** adjoins the Gulf of Mexico and includes such major rivers as the Mississippi and Rio Grande. The land in this area is exceptionally fertile, and there are also rich deposits of petroleum. The **Atlantic Coastal Plain** runs from Maine to Florida, gradually widening as it heads south. This area is also fertile and is primarily suited for cotton, peanuts, tobacco, and citrus fruits. The Atlantic Coastal Plain includes some large natural harbors, including those at Cape Cod, Boston, and the Chesapeake. The **Piedmont** lies just inland from the Atlantic Coastal Plain. It is characterized by gentle hills and rivers. Along the eastern border of the Piedmont is the Fall Line: rivers that run west across this line feature dramatic rapids and waterfalls, which makes shipping difficult.

Grasslands and Alpine Tundra Region

The United States includes extensive **grasslands**, beginning in the Interior Plains region and stretching out into the basins and plateaus of the Rocky Mountains. These grasslands are covered with plants like side oat, buffalo grass, needle, wheatgrass, and grama. There are also numerous wild herbs growing in these areas. Grasslands used to be grazed by huge populations of buffalo and cattle, but the buffalo were mostly hunted out of existence. The continental United States only has a few instances of **alpine tundra**, mostly in the Rocky Mountains above the tree line. In these regions, vegetation consists mostly of short grasses and flowers that bloom only for a brief period. Very few animals are hardy enough to live exclusively in the tundra.

Humid Oceanic Region

A humid oceanic climate region exists in a narrow band that runs down the northern Pacific Coast of the United States, from Washington State almost to San Francisco. The eastern boundary of this climate region is the Cascade/Sierra Nevada mountain group. A **humid oceanic climate region** is characterized by a moderately warm summer and a moderately cold winter. In other words, temperature variations are slighter in this region than in others. Humid oceanic climates are typical of the western side of continents, where the prevailing winds blow east from the sea onto the land. These regions have a moderate to high level of precipitation throughout the year, mostly in the form of rain. There are very few droughts, heatwaves, or thunderstorms. In general, the relative stability of the ocean's water temperature translates into stable temperatures just inland.

Humid Subtropical Climate Region

A humid subtropical climate region covers much of the Southeastern United States and extends up the Atlantic coast as far as New York City. This climate region exists even over the higher elevations of the southern Appalachian range. It extends into western Texas and Oklahoma. In this climate region, there are very hot summers and relatively mild winters. There is a medium amount of precipitation in all seasons. No season gets significantly more precipitation than the rest. In the winter, there are often large snowstorms related to the rapid passage of westward winds over the open spaces. There are frequent summer thunderstorms, and the southeast coast occasionally encounters tropical storms and hurricanes as well.

Desert and Semiarid Climate Regions

There are desert and semiarid climate regions in the western United States, particularly in the southwest and in the northern regions on either side of the Rocky Mountains. The **deserts** are concentrated in southern New Mexico, Arizona, and California. In both semiarid and desert regions, there is very little precipitation. The variation between day and night temperatures in these regions is often severe, in part because the air is typically very clear and dry. Moisture in the air would tend to mitigate wild swings in temperature, and clouds would retain some of the heat from the day. Deserts receive less precipitation than semiarid climates, though not by much. The **semiarid** regions are generally at a slightly higher elevation.

Subtropical Dry Summer Climate Region

A subtropical dry summer climate region exists in the United States in southern California, from the Pacific Ocean west to the Sierra Nevada Mountains. The subtropical dry summer zone extends up the coast to San Francisco and slightly farther north just inland. Los Angeles is around the southern tip of this climate zone. A **subtropical dry summer climate region** is characterized by hot, dry summers and mild winters. There is a moderate amount of precipitation in the winter and very little in the summer. This is the climate typical of the Mediterranean countries in southern Europe. The subtropical dry summer climate is generally found on the western edge of a continent. In the section of the region closest to the water, the temperatures are more moderate, and there is less variation between summer and winter weather.

Humid Continental Climate Region

A humid continental climate region covers the Northeast and much of the upper Midwest. It encompasses New England and broadens as it extends west, taking in Missouri and eastern Colorado as well as Minnesota. **Humid continental regions** are characterized by mild summers and extremely cold winters. These regions experience an average amount of precipitation in all seasons. Farther inland, the variation between winter cold and summer heat is likely to be greater. Indeed, in places like northern Minnesota, the difference between summer and winter average temperatures can be as much as 65 degrees Fahrenheit. These inland locations also tend to have a bit more precipitation during the summer. The humid continental climate region in the United States is often covered by snow for most of the winter. This snow perpetuates the cold temperatures by reflecting heat back into the atmosphere.

Highland Climate Region

Some isolated highland climate regions exist in the United States along the higher points of the Rocky Mountain and Cascade ranges. To some extent, this climate region even extends south along the Sierra Nevada range. The **highland** designation actually encompasses a number of distinct climate types that are present at different elevations. The progression of climates along the ascending edge of a mountain is not unlike that encountered during travel away from the Equator; as one gains elevation, the climate becomes closer to tundra or even an icecap. Air becomes thinner, vegetation becomes more sparse and low-lying, and precipitation is more likely to be snow or ice. At the highest points of the highland region, the temperature may never rise above freezing.

Subarctic and Tundra Climate Regions

Subarctic and tundra climate regions only exist in the United States in Alaska. The lower two-thirds, approximately, of the state is considered **subarctic**, while the top third is **tundra**. In a subarctic climate region, summers are cool and brief, while winters are long and extremely cold. There is considerably more precipitation during the summer, but any during the winter is likely to be snow and to remain on the ground until spring. Indeed, subarctic regions are typically covered for most of the year. Tundra is drier and colder. The tundra is too cold to support trees, so the only vegetation there is low grasses. A common feature of tundra is permafrost, or permanently frozen ground just under the surface. It is virtually impossible to farm in tundra.

Geography and United States History

Geography of the Continent of North America

North America is the third largest continent in the world. It includes all the mainland of the northern landmass in the western hemisphere, as well as all the related offshore islands that lie north of the Isthmus of Panama. People often will call Canada and the United States "**Anglo-America**," and Mexico, Central America, and the Caribbean "**Middle America**." North America is bounded on the north by the Arctic Ocean, on the west by the Pacific Ocean and the Bering Sea, and on the east by the Atlantic Ocean and the Gulf of Mexico. The Gulf of Mexico is the largest body of water to indent the coast, the second-largest being the Hudson Bay. The Gulf of St. Lawrence and the Gulf of California also indent the coast of North America severely.

Coastal Islands, Highest Point, Longest River, and Other Major Rivers

There are a number of large **islands** off the coast of North America: Greenland, the Arctic Archipelago, the Greater and Lesser Antilles, the Alexander Archipelago, and the Aleutian Islands. The highest point in North America is **Mt. McKinley**, Alaska, and the lowest point is in **Death Valley**. The **Missouri-Mississippi River System** is the longest in North America; it is also the world's largest inland waterway system. Ships are able to enter the heart of North America by means of the Saint Lawrence Seaway. Other major rivers of the North American continent are the Colorado, Mackenzie, Nelson, Rio Grande, St. Lawrence, Susquehanna, Columbia, and Yukon.

Climate of North America

The continent of North America contains every climatic zone, ranging from the tropical rain forests and savannas in the lowlands of Central America to the permanent ice caps in the middle of Greenland. In northern Canada, the climates are mostly subarctic and tundra. These are also found in northern Alaska. The two major mountain ranges of the continent affect the climate greatly. In the interior regions close to the Appalachian and Rocky Mountains, the climate and terrain are mostly semiarid and desert. These areas are largely prevented from receiving westerly winds and storms. Most of North America, however, has a temperate climate and is hospitable to settlement and agriculture.

Physiography of North America

North America can be divided into five regions. The **Canadian Shield** is an area of stable, ancient rock that occupies the northeast corner of the continent, including Greenland. The **Appalachian Mountains** are an old and worn-down mountain system extending from the Gaspe Peninsula to Alabama. The **Atlantic-Gulf Coastal Plain** is a stretch of lowlands running from New England to

Mexico. The **Interior Lowlands** extend from central Canada to the Gulf Coast. The **North American Cordillera** is a mountain system that includes both the Pacific Margin and the Rocky Mountains. Another lesser formation, the **Transverse Volcanic Range**, extends below Mexico City.

NATIVE AMERICANS

NATIVE AMERICANS OF THE NORTHWEST COAST AREA

The main Native American tribes in the Northwest Coast are the **Kwakiutl**, **Haida**, and **Nootka**. These people lived in a densely forested area with a temperate climate and heavy rainfall, and they survived mainly on salmon. The Native Americans in this region built their houses out of wood and made canoes from cedar. These tribes built totem poles in their permanent winter villages, which were elaborately carved with the faces of the tribal animal gods. They had a strict social hierarchy, with chiefs, nobles, commoners, and slaves. The Native Americans of the Pacific Northwest would be largely untouched by Europeans until the 18th century, when **fur trappers** began to encroach upon their territory.

Review Video: Major Native American Regional Groups
Visit mometrix.com/academy and enter code: 550136

NATIVE AMERICANS OF THE PLAINS AREA

The Plains area extends from barely north of the Canadian border to Texas. Before the arrival of Columbus, the tribes in this region were either nomadic or sedentary. The **sedentary** tribes settled in the great river valleys and grew corn, squash, and beans. The **nomads**, meanwhile, moved their goods around on sleds pulled by dogs. They hunted buffalo by driving them into enclosures or by herding them with fires. There was also a fair amount of trade with the sedentary tribes. Many Native American tribes migrated into the Plains region; among them were the **Sioux**, **Comanche**, **Kiowa**, **Navajo**, and **Apache**. The tribes were typically governed by a chief, who would eventually be supplanted in a violent coup.

NATIVE AMERICANS OF THE PLATEAU AREA

The Plateau area runs from just above the Canadian border into the American Southwest. Some of the larger tribes in the region were the **Spokane**, **Nez Perce**, and **Shoshone**. The area where these tribes dwelled was not especially hospitable, so they spent much of their time trying to eke out a living. The tribes in the south gathered fruits and nuts and hunted small animals. The tribes in the north fished for salmon and gathered roots and berries. Later on, these tribes would begin to hunt buffalo. Many of the northern tribes had permanent winter villages, most of which were along waterways. They borrowed the architecture of the tepee from the Plains Native Americans, though some tribes had longhouses covered with bark.

NATIVE AMERICANS OF THE EASTERN WOODLANDS

The Eastern Woodlands extend from the Mississippi River east to the Atlantic Ocean. The tribes of this region included the **Natchez**, **Choctaw**, **Cherokee**, and **Creek**. The people of the northeast region mostly farmed and hunted deer. They used canoes made of birch bark. The people in the Iroquois family of tribes lived either in dome-shaped wigwams or in longhouses, and would typically wear clothing made from the skin of deer, often painting their faces. In the southern part of the Eastern Woodlands, there were seminomadic tribes who survived by hunting, fishing, and gathering. These people hunted with a bow and arrow or with a blowgun. They developed highly detailed pottery and surrounded their villages with elaborate defenses.

NATIVE AMERICANS WHO INHABITED THE REGION NOW KNOWN AS CANADA

The Native Americans that inhabited the region now known as Canada included the **Chippewa**. This region was not especially hospitable to life, and therefore, there was little farming. Instead, the tribes hunted, gathered, fished, and trapped in order to survive. There were many groups of nomadic hunters who moved around from season to season. Caribou was the most popular game, and people would make all kinds of products out of parts of the animal, including caribou shoes, caribou nets, and caribou bags. These people relied on snowshoes to allow them to move quickly and without falling into icy lakes. Many of the tribes in this region had a shaman, a mystic who provided spiritual guidance to the members of the tribe.

NATIVE AMERICANS OF THE SOUTHWEST AREA

The Southwest area extends across Arizona, New Mexico, Colorado, and Utah. A seminomadic people known as the **Basketmakers** hunted with the atlatl, a device that made it possible to throw a spear accurately over a great distance. The tribes in this area lived in pit dwellings, which were partly underground. Later, ancestors of the Pueblo Native Americans would develop community houses set into the side of cliffs and canyons. These **cliff dwellings** often had a ceremonial fire pit, or kiva. These people grew corn, beans, squash, cotton, and tobacco, they killed rabbits with a wooden stick, and they traded their textiles to nomadic tribes for buffalo meat. The tribes of the Southwest also had a complex mythology and religious system.

Economics Concepts

Economics is the study of the ways specific societies **allocate** resources to individuals and groups within that society. Also important are the choices society makes regarding what efforts or initiatives are funded and which are not. Since resources in any society are finite, allocation becomes a vivid reflection of that society's values. In general, the economic system that drives an individual society is based on:

- What goods are produced
- How those goods are produced
- Who acquires the goods or benefits from them

Economics consists of two main categories: **macroeconomics**, which studies larger systems, and **microeconomics**, which studies smaller systems.

Market Economy

A market economy is based on supply and demand. **Demand** has to do with what customers want and need, as well as what quantity those consumers are able to purchase based on other economic factors. **Supply** refers to how much can be produced to meet demand, or how much suppliers are willing and able to sell. Where the needs of consumers meet the needs of suppliers is referred to as a market equilibrium price. This price varies depending on many factors, including the overall health of a society's economy and the overall beliefs and considerations of individuals in society. The following is a list of terms defined in the context of a market economy:

- **Elasticity**—this is based on how the quantity of a particular product responds to the price demanded for that product. If quantity responds quickly to changes in price, the supply/demand for that product is said to be elastic. If it does not respond quickly, then the supply/demand is inelastic.
- **Market efficiency**—this occurs when a market is capable of producing output high enough to meet consumer demand.
- **Comparative advantage**—in the field of international trade, this refers to a country focusing on a specific product that it can produce more efficiently and more cheaply, or at a lower opportunity cost, than another country, thus giving it a comparative advantage in production.

Review Video: Basics of Market Economy
Visit mometrix.com/academy and enter code: 791556

Planned Economy vs. Market Economy

In a **market economy**, supply and demand are determined by consumers. In a **planned economy**, a public entity or planning authority makes the decisions about what resources will be produced, how they will be produced, and who will be able to benefit from them. The means of production, such as factories, are also owned by a public entity rather than by private interests. In **market socialism**, the economic structure falls somewhere between the market economy and the planned economy. Planning authorities determine the allocation of resources at higher economic levels, while consumer goods are driven by a market economy.

Microeconomics

While economics generally studies how resources are allocated, **microeconomics** focuses on economic factors such as the way consumers behave, how income is distributed, and output and input markets. Studies are limited to the industry or firm level rather than an entire country or society. Among the elements studied in microeconomics are factors of production, costs of production, and factor income. These factors determine production decisions of individual firms, based on resources and costs.

Classification of Various Markets by Economists

The conditions prevailing in a given market are used to **classify** markets. Conditions considered include:

- Existence of competition
- Number and size of suppliers
- Influence of suppliers over price
- Variety of available products
- Ease of entering the market

Once these questions are answered, an economist can classify a certain market according to its structure and the nature of competition within the market.

Market Failure

When any of the elements for a successfully competitive market are missing, this can lead to a **market failure**. Certain elements are necessary to create what economists call "**perfect competition**." If one of these factors is weak or lacking, the market is classified as having "**imperfect competition**." Worse than imperfect competition, though, is a market failure. There are five major types of market failure:

- Inadequate competition
- Inadequate information
- Immobile resources
- Negative externalities, or side effects
- Failure to provide public goods

Externalities are side effects of a market that affect third parties. These effects can be either negative or positive.

Factors of Production and Costs of Production

Every good and service requires certain resources, or **inputs**. These inputs are referred to as **factors of production**. Every good and service requires four factors of production:

- Labor
- Capital
- Land
- Entrepreneurship

These factors can be fixed or variable and can produce fixed or variable costs. Examples of **fixed costs** include land and equipment. **Variable costs** include labor. The total of fixed and variable costs makes up the cost of production.

Factor Income

Factors of production each have an associated **factor income**. Factors that earn income include:

- **Labor**—earns wages
- **Capital**—earns interest
- **Land**—earns rent
- **Entrepreneurship**—earns profit

Each factor's income is determined by its **contribution**. In a market economy, this income is not guaranteed to be equal. How scarce the factor is and the weight of its contribution to the overall production process determines the final factor income.

Kinds of Market Structures in an Output Market.

The four kinds of market structures in an output market are:

- **Perfect competition**—all existing firms sell an identical product. The firms are not able to control the final price. In addition, there is nothing that makes it difficult to become involved in or leave the industry. Anything that would prevent entering or leaving an industry is called a barrier to entry. An example of this market structure is agriculture.
- **Monopoly**—a single seller controls the product and its price. Barriers to entry, such as prohibitively high fixed cost structures, prevent other sellers from entering the market.
- **Monopolistic competition**—a number of firms sell similar products, but they are not identical, such as different brands of clothes or food. Barriers to entry are low.
- **Oligopoly**—only a few firms control the production and distribution of products, such as automobiles. Barriers to entry are high, preventing large numbers of firms from entering the market.

Types of Monopolies

Four types of monopolies are:

- **Natural monopoly**—a single supplier has a distinct advantage over the others.
- **Geographic monopoly**—only one business offers the product in a certain area.
- **Technological monopoly**—a single company controls the technology necessary to supply the product.
- **Government monopoly**—a government agency is the only provider of a specific good or service.

Actions Taken by the US Government to Control Monopolies

The US government has passed several acts to regulate businesses, including:

- **Sherman Antitrust Act (1890)**—this prohibited trusts, monopolies, and any other situations that eliminated competition.
- **Clayton Antitrust Act (1914)**—this prohibited price discrimination.
- **Robinson-Patman Act (1936)**—this strengthened provisions of the Clayton Antitrust Act, requiring businesses to offer the same pricing on products to any customer.

The government has also taken other actions to ensure competition, including requirements for public disclosure. The **Securities and Exchange Commission (SEC)** requires companies that provide public stock to provide financial reports on a regular basis. Because of the nature of their business, banks are further regulated and required to provide various information to the government.

Marketing and Utility

Marketing consists of all of the activity necessary to convince consumers to acquire goods. One major way to move products into the hands of consumers is to convince them that any single product will satisfy a need. The ability of a product or service to satisfy the need of a consumer is called **utility**. There are four types of utility:

- **Form utility**—a product's desirability lies in its physical characteristics.
- **Place utility**—a product's desirability is connected to its location and convenience.
- **Time utility**—a product's desirability is determined by its availability at a certain time.
- **Ownership utility**—a product's desirability is increased because ownership of the product passes to the consumer.

Marketing behavior will stress any or all of these types of utility when marketing to the consumer.

Producers Determining What Customers Desire for Their Products

Successful marketing depends not only on convincing customers they need the product but also on focusing the marketing towards those who already have a need or desire for the product. Before releasing a product into the general marketplace, many producers will **test** markets to determine which will be the most receptive to the product. There are three steps usually taken to evaluate a product's market:

- **Market research**—this involves researching a market to determine if it will be receptive to the product.
- **Market surveys**—a part of market research, market surveys ask consumers specific questions to help determine the marketability of a product to a specific group.
- **Test marketing**—this includes releasing the product into a small geographical area to see how it sells. Often test marketing is followed by wider marketing if the product does well.

Major Elements of a Marketing Plan

The four major elements of a marketing plan are:

- **Product**—this includes any elements pertaining directly to the product, such as packaging, presentation, or services to include along with it.
- **Price**—this calculates the cost of production, distribution, advertising, etc., as well as the desired profit to determine the final price.
- **Place**—this determines which outlets will be used to sell the product, whether traditional outlets such as brick and mortar stores or through direct mail or internet marketing.
- **Promotion**—this involves ways to let consumers know the product is available, through advertising and other means.

Once these elements have all been determined, the producer can proceed with production and distribution of his product.

Distribution Channels

Distribution channels determine the route a product takes on its journey from producer to consumer, and can also influence the final price and availability of the product. There are two major forms of distributions: wholesale and retail. A **wholesale distributor** buys in large quantities and then resells smaller amounts to other businesses. **Retailers** sell directly to the consumers rather than to businesses. In the modern marketplace, additional distribution channels have grown up with the rise of markets such as club warehouse stores as well as purchasing through catalogs or over the internet. Most of these newer distribution channels bring products more directly to the consumer, eliminating the need for middlemen.

Distribution of Income in a Society

Distribution of income in any society ranges from poorest to richest. In most societies, income is not distributed evenly. To determine **income distribution**, family incomes are ranked from lowest to highest. These rankings are divided into five sections called **quintiles**, which are compared to each other. The uneven distribution of income is often linked to higher levels of education and ability in the upper classes but can also be due to other factors such as discrimination and existing monopolies. The **income gap** in America continues to grow, largely due to growth in the service industry, changes in the American family unit, and reduced influence of labor unions. **Poverty** is defined by comparing incomes to poverty guidelines. Poverty guidelines determine the level of income necessary for a family to function. Those below the poverty line are often eligible for assistance from government agencies.

Macroeconomics

Macroeconomics examines economies on a much larger level than microeconomics. While **microeconomics** studies economics on a firm or industry level, **macroeconomics** looks at economic trends and structures on a national level. Variables studied in macroeconomics include:

- Output
- Consumption
- Investment
- Government spending
- Net exports

The overall economic condition of a nation is defined as the **Gross Domestic Product**, or GDP. GDP measures a nation's economic output over a limited time period, such as a year.

Review Video: Microeconomics and Macroeconomics
Visit mometrix.com/academy and enter code: 538837

Review Video: Gross Domestic Product
Visit mometrix.com/academy and enter code: 409020

Types of Consumer Behavior

The two major types of consumer behavior as defined in macroeconomics are:

- **Marginal propensity to consume (MPC)** defines the tendency of consumers to increase spending in conjunction with increases in income. In general, individuals with greater income will buy more. As individuals increase their income through job changes or growth of experience, they will also increase spending.
- **Utility** is a term that describes the satisfaction experienced by a consumer in relation to acquiring and using a good or service. Providers of goods and services will stress utility to convince consumers they want the products being presented.

Ways to Measure the Gross Domestic Product of a Country

The two major ways to measure the Gross Domestic Product of a country are:

- The **expenditures approach** calculates the GDP based on how much money is spent in each individual sector.
- The **income approach** calculates the GDP based on how much money is earned in each sector.

Both methods yield the same results, and both of these calculation methods are based on four **economic sectors** that make up a country's macro-economy:

- Consumers
- Business
- Government
- Foreign sector

Types of Earnings Generated by an Economy Considered to Calculate GDP

Several factors must be considered in order to accurately calculate the GDP using the incomes approach. **Income factors** are:

- Wages paid to laborers, or compensation of employees (CE)
- Rental income derived from land
- Interest income derived from invested capital
- Entrepreneurial income

Entrepreneurial income consists of two forms. **Proprietor's income** is income that comes back to the entrepreneur himself. **Corporate profit** is income that goes back into the corporation as a whole. Corporate profit is divided by the corporation into corporate profits taxes, dividends, and retained earnings. Two other figures must be subtracted in the incomes approach. These are **indirect business taxes**, including property and sales taxes, and **depreciation**.

Effects of Population of a Country on the Gross Domestic Product

Changes in population can affect the calculation of a nation's **GDP**, particularly since GDP and GNP (Gross National Product) are generally measured per capita. If a country's economic production is low but the population is high, the income per individual will be lower than if the income is high and the population is lower. Also, if the population grows quickly and the income grows slowly, individual income will remain low or even drop drastically.

Population growth can also affect overall **economic growth**. Economic growth requires both that consumers purchase goods and workers produce them. A population that does not grow quickly enough will not supply enough workers to support rapid economic growth.

Ideal Balance to be Obtained in an Economy

Ideally, an economy functions efficiently, with the **aggregate supply**, or the amount of national output, equal to the **aggregate demand**, or the amount of the output that is purchased. In these cases, the economy is stable and prosperous. However, economies more typically go through **phases**. These phases are:

- **Boom**—GDP is high and the economy prospers
- **Recession**—GDP falls and unemployment rises
- **Trough**—the recession reaches its lowest point
- **Recovery**—unemployment lessens, prices rise, and the economy begins to stabilize again

These phases tend to repeat in cycles that are not necessarily predictable or regular.

Unemployment and Inflation

When demand outstrips supply, prices are driven artificially high, or are **inflated**. This occurs when too much spending causes an imbalance in the economy. In general, inflation occurs because an economy is growing too quickly. When there is too little spending, and supply has moved far beyond demand, a **surplus** of product results. Companies cut back on production and reduce the number of employees, and **unemployment** rises as people lose their jobs. This imbalance occurs when an economy becomes sluggish. In general, both these economic instability situations are caused by an imbalance between supply and demand. Government intervention may be necessary to stabilize an economy when either inflation or unemployment becomes too serious.

Different Forms of Unemployment

- **Frictional**—when workers change jobs and are unemployed while waiting for new jobs
- **Structural**—when economic shifts reduce the need for workers
- **Cyclical**—when natural business cycles bring about loss of jobs
- **Seasonal**—when seasonal cycles reduce the need for certain jobs
- **Technological**—when advances in technology result in the elimination of certain jobs

Any of these factors can increase unemployment in certain sectors.

Inflation is classified by the overall rate at which it occurs:

- **Creeping inflation**—this is an inflation rate of about 1%-3% annually.
- **Walking inflation**—this is an inflation rate of 3%-10% annually.
- **Galloping inflation**— a severe inflation rate above 10 percent (to upwards of 100 percent and beyond) annually. Highly detrimental to the economy, this deeply impacts the lower and middle class populus.
- **Hyperinflation**— an inflation rate over 50% monthly or 500+ percent annually. Hyperinflation usually leads to complete monetary collapse in a society. Individuals are unable to have enough income to purchase their needed goods.

Government Intervention Policies that Can Help Mitigate Inflation and Unemployment

When an economy becomes too imbalanced, either due to excessive spending or not enough spending, **government intervention** often becomes necessary to put the economy back on track. Government fiscal policy can take several forms, including:

- Contractionary policy
- Expansionary policy
- Monetary policy

Contractionary policies help counteract inflation. These include increasing taxes and decreasing government spending to slow spending in the overall economy. **Expansionary policies** increase government spending and lower taxes in order to reduce unemployment and increase the level of spending in the economy overall. **Monetary policy** can take several forms and affects the amount of funds available to banks for making loans.

Study and Quantification of Populations and Population Growth

Populations are studied by **size**, rates of **growth** due to immigration, the overall **fertility rate**, and **life expectancy**. For example, though the population of the United States is considerably larger than it was two hundred years ago, the rate of population growth has decreased greatly, from about three percent per year to less than one percent per year.

In the US, the fertility rate is fairly low, with most choosing not to have large families, and life expectancy is high, creating a projected imbalance between older and younger people in the near future. In addition, immigration and the mixing of racially diverse cultures are projected to increase the percentages of Asians, Hispanics, and African Americans.

Functions and Types of Money

Money is used in three major ways:

- As an accounting unit
- As a store of value
- As an exchange medium

In general, money must be acceptable throughout a society in exchange for debts or to purchase goods and services. Money should be relatively scarce, its value should remain stable, and it should be easily carried, durable, and easy to divide up. There are three basic types of money: commodity, representative, and fiat. **Commodity money** includes gems or precious metals. **Representative money** can be exchanged for items such as gold or silver that have inherent value. **Fiat money**, or legal tender, has no inherent value but has been declared to function as money by the government. It is often backed by gold or silver but not necessarily on a one-to-one ratio.

Types of Money Available in the US and Economists' Measure of It

Money in the US is not just currency. When economists calculate the amount of money available, they must take into account other factors, such as deposits that have been placed in checking accounts, debit cards, and "near moneys," such as savings accounts, that can be quickly converted into cash. Currency, checkable deposits and traveler's checks, referred to as **M1**, are added up, and then **M2** is calculated by adding savings deposits, CDs, and various other monetary deposits. The final result is the total quantity of available money.

Aspects of Monetary Policy and the Role of the Federal Reserve System

The Federal Reserve System, also known as the **Fed**, implements all monetary policy in the US. Monetary policy regulates the amount of money available in the American banking system. The Fed can decrease or increase the amount of available money for loans, thus helping regulate the national economy. Monetary policies implemented by the Fed are part of expansionary or contractionary monetary policies that help counteract inflation or unemployment. The **discount rate** is an interest rate charged by the Fed when banks borrow money from them. A lower discount rate leads banks to borrow more money, leading to increased spending. A higher discount rate has the opposite effect.

How Banks Function

Banks earn their income by **loaning** out money and charging **interest** on those loans. If less money is available, fewer loans can be made, which affects the amount of spending in the overall economy. While banks function by making loans, they are not allowed to loan out all the money they hold in deposit. The amount of money they must maintain in reserve is known as the **reserve ratio**. If the reserve ratio is raised, less money is available for loans and spending decreases. A lower reserve ratio increases available funds and increases spending. This ratio is determined by the Federal Reserve System.

Open Market Operations

The Federal Reserve System can also expand or contract the overall money supply through **open market operations**. In this case, the Fed can buy or sell **bonds** it has purchased from banks or individuals. When the Fed buys bonds, more money is put into circulation, creating an expansionary situation to stimulate the economy. When the Fed sells bonds, money is withdrawn from the system, creating a **contractionary** situation to slow an economy suffering from inflation. Because of international financial markets, however, American banks often borrow and lend money in markets outside the US. By shifting their attention to international markets, domestic banks and other businesses can circumvent whatever contractionary policies the Fed may have put into place.

Major Characteristics of International Trade

International trade can take advantage of broader markets, bringing a wider variety of products within easy reach. By contrast, it can also allow individual countries to specialize in particular products that they can produce easily, such as those for which they have easy access to raw materials. Other products, more difficult to make domestically, can be acquired through trade with other nations. **International trade** requires efficient use of **native resources** as well as sufficient **disposable income** to purchase native and imported products. Many countries in the world engage extensively in international trade, but others still face major economic challenges.

Major Characteristics of a Developing Nation

The five major characteristics of a developing nation are:

- Low GDP
- Rapid growth of population
- Economy that depends on subsistence agriculture
- Poor conditions, including high infant mortality rates, high disease rates, poor sanitation, and insufficient housing
- Low literacy rate

Developing nations often function under oppressive governments that do not provide private property rights and withhold education and other rights from women. They also often feature an extreme disparity between upper and lower classes, with little opportunity for the lower classes to improve their position.

Stages of Economic Development

Economic development occurs in three stages that are defined by the activities that drive the economy:

- Agricultural stage
- Manufacturing stage
- Service sector stage

In developing countries, it is often difficult to acquire the necessary funding to provide equipment and training to move into the advanced stages of economic development. Some can receive help from developed countries via foreign aid and investment or international organizations such as the **International Monetary Fund** or the **World Bank**. Having developed countries provide monetary, technical, or military assistance can help developing countries move forward to the next stage in their development.

Obstacles Developing Nations Face Regarding Economic Growth

Developing nations typically struggle to overcome obstacles that prevent or slow economic development. Major **obstacles** can include:

- Rapid, uncontrolled population growth
- Trade restrictions
- Misused resources, often perpetrated by the government
- Traditional beliefs that can slow or reject change

Corrupt, oppressive governments often hamper the economic growth of developing nations, creating huge **economic disparities** and making it impossible for individuals to advance, in turn preventing overall growth. Governments sometimes export currency, called **capital flight**, which is detrimental to a country's economic development. In general, countries are more likely to experience economic growth if their governments encourage entrepreneurship and provide private property rights.

Problems When Industrialization Occurs Too Quickly

Rapid growth throughout the world leaves some nations behind and sometimes spurs their governments to move forward too quickly into **industrialization** and **artificially rapid economic growth**. While slow or nonexistent economic growth causes problems in a country, overly rapid industrialization carries its own issues. Four major problems encountered due to rapid industrialization are:

- Use of technology not suited to the products or services being supplied
- Poor investment of capital
- Lack of time for the population to adapt to new paradigms
- Lack of time to experience all stages of development and adjust to each stage

Economic failures in Indonesia were largely due to rapid growth that was poorly handled.

Importance of E-Commerce in Today's Marketplace

The growth of the internet has brought many changes to our society, not the least of which is the modern way of business. Where supply channels used to move in certain necessary ways, many of these channels are now bypassed as **e-commerce** makes it possible for nearly any individual to set up a direct market to consumers, as well as direct interaction with suppliers. Competition is fierce. In many instances, e-commerce can provide nearly instantaneous gratification, with a wide variety of products. Whoever provides the best product most quickly often rises to the top of a marketplace. How this added element to the marketplace will affect the economy in the future remains to be seen. Many industries are still struggling with the best ways to adapt to the rapid, continuous changes.

Knowledge Economy and Possible Effect on Future Economic Growth

The knowledge economy is a growing sector in the economy of developed countries, and includes the trade and development of:

- Data
- Intellectual property
- Technology, especially in the area of communications

Knowledge as a resource is steadily becoming more and more important. What is now being called the **Information Age** may prove to bring about changes in life and culture as significant as those brought on by the Agricultural and Industrial Revolutions.

Cybernomics

Related to the knowledge economy is what has been dubbed "**cybernomics**," or economics driven by e-commerce and other computer-based markets and products. Marketing has changed drastically with the growth of cyber communication, allowing suppliers to connect one-on-one with their customers. Other issues coming to the fore regarding cybernomics include:

- Secure online trade
- Intellectual property rights
- Rights to privacy
- Bringing developing nations into the fold

As these issues are debated and new laws and policies developed, the face of many industries continues to undergo drastic change. Many of the old ways of doing business no longer work, leaving industries scrambling to function profitably within the new system.

Civics Concepts

US Government and Citizenship

Principles of the Constitution

The six basic principles of the Constitution are:

1. **Popular Sovereignty** – The people establish government and give power to it; the government can function only with the consent of the people.
2. **Limited Government** – The Constitution specifies limits on government authority, and no official or entity is above the law.
3. **Separation of Powers** – Power is divided among three government branches: the legislative (Congress), the executive (President), and the judicial (federal courts).
4. **Checks and Balances** – This is a system that enforces the separation of powers and ensures that each branch has the authority and ability to restrain the powers of the other two branches, thus preventing tyranny.
5. **Judicial Review** – Judges in the federal courts ensure that no act of government is in violation of the Constitution. If an act is unconstitutional, the judicial branch has the power to nullify it.
6. **Federalism** – This is the division of power between the central government and local governments, which limits the power of the federal government and allows states to deal with local problems.

Classic Forms of Government

Forms of government that have appeared throughout history include:

- **Feudalism** – This is based on the rule of local lords who are loyal to the king and control the lives and production of those who work on their land.
- **Classical republic** – This form is a representative democracy. Small groups of elected leaders represent the interests of the electorate.
- **Absolute monarchy** – A king or queen has complete control of the military and government.
- **Authoritarianism** – An individual or group has unlimited authority. There is no system in place to restrain the power of the government.
- **Dictatorship** – Those in power are not held responsible to the people.
- **Autocracy** – This is rule by one person (despot), not necessarily a monarch, who uses power tyrannically.
- **Oligarchy** – A small, usually self-appointed elite rules a region.
- **Liberal democracy** – This is a government based on the consent of the people that protects individual rights and freedoms from any intolerance by the majority.
- **Totalitarianism** – All facets of the citizens' lives are controlled by the government.

Influences of Philosophers on Political Study

Ancient Greek philosophers **Aristotle** and **Plato** believed political science would lead to order in political matters, and that this scientifically organized order would create stable, just societies.

Thomas Aquinas adapted the ideas of Aristotle to a Christian perspective. His ideas stated that individuals have certain rights, but also certain duties, and that these rights and duties should determine the type and extent of government rule. In stating that laws should limit the role of government, he laid the groundwork for ideas that would eventually become modern constitutionalism.

Niccolò Machiavelli, author of *The Prince*, was a proponent of politics based solely on power.

Parliamentary and Democratic Systems of Government

In a **parliamentary system**, government involves a legislature and a variety of political parties. The head of government, usually a Prime Minister, is typically the head of the dominant party. A head of state can be elected, or this position can be taken by a monarch, such as in Great Britain's constitutional monarchy system.

In a **democratic system** of government, the people elect their government representatives. The term democracy is a Greek term that means "for the rule of the people." There are two forms of democracy—direct and indirect. In a direct democracy, each issue or election is decided by a vote where each individual is counted separately. An indirect democracy employs a legislature that votes on issues that affect large number of people whom the legislative members represent. Democracy can exist as a Parliamentary system or a Presidential system. The US is a presidential, indirect democracy.

Bill of Rights

The **United States Bill of Rights** was based on principles established by the **Magna Carta** in 1215, the 1688 **English Bill of Rights**, and the 1776 **Virginia Bill of Rights**. In 1791, the federal government added 10 amendments to the United States Constitution that provided the following **protections**:

- Freedom of speech, religion, peaceful assembly, petition of the government, and petition of the press
- The right to keep and bear arms
- No quartering of soldiers on private property without the consent of the owner
- Regulations on government search and seizure
- Provisions concerning prosecution
- The right to a speedy, public trial and the calling of witnesses
- The right to trial by jury
- Freedom from excessive bail or cruel punishment
- These rights are not necessarily the only rights
- Powers not prohibited by the Constitution are reserved to the states

Review Video: Bill of Rights
Visit mometrix.com/academy and enter code: 585149

Making a Formal Amendment to the Constitution

So far, there have been only **27 amendments** to the federal Constitution. There are four different ways to change the constitution: two methods for proposal and two methods for ratification:

1. An amendment is proposed by a two-thirds vote in each house of Congress and ratified by three-fourths of the state legislatures.
2. An amendment is proposed by a two-thirds vote in each house of Congress and ratified by three-fourths of the states in special conventions called for that purpose.

3. An amendment is proposed by a national convention that is called by Congress at the request of two-thirds of the state legislatures and ratified by three-fourths of the state legislatures.
4. An amendment is proposed by a national convention that is called by Congress at the request of two-thirds of the state legislatures and ratified by three-fourths of the states in special conventions called for that purpose.

Division of Powers

The **division of powers** in the federal government system is as follows:

- **National** – This level can coin money, regulate interstate and foreign trade, raise and maintain armed forces, declare war, govern United States territories and admit new states, and conduct foreign relations.
- **Concurrent** – This level can levy and collect taxes, borrow money, establish courts, define crimes and set punishments, and claim private property for public use.
- **State** – This level can regulate trade and business within the state, establish public schools, pass license requirements for professionals, regulate alcoholic beverages, conduct elections, and establish local governments.

There are three types of **delegated powers** granted by the Constitution:

1. **Expressed or enumerated powers** – These are specifically spelled out in the Constitution.
2. **Implied** – These are not expressly stated, but are reasonably suggested by the expressed powers.
3. **Inherent** – These are powers not expressed by the Constitution but ones that national governments have historically possessed, such as granting diplomatic recognition.

Powers can also be classified as reserved or exclusive. **Reserved powers** are not granted to the national government, but not denied to the states. **Exclusive powers** are those reserved to the national government, including concurrent powers.

Stages of Extending Suffrage in the US

Originally, the Constitution of 1789 provided the right to vote only to white male property owners. Through the years, suffrage was extended through the following five stages.

1. In the early 1800s, states began to eliminate **property ownership** and **tax payment qualifications**.
2. By 1810, there were no more **religious tests** for voting. In the late 1800s, the 15th Amendment protected citizens from being denied the right to vote because of **race or color**.
3. In 1920, the 19th Amendment prohibited the denial of the right to vote because of **gender**, and women were given the right to vote.
4. Passed in 1961 and ratified in 1964, the 23rd Amendment added the voters of the **District of Columbia** to the presidential electorate and eliminated the poll tax as a condition for voting in federal elections. The **Voting Rights Act of 1965** prohibited disenfranchisement through literacy tests and various other means of discrimination.
5. In 1971, the 26th Amendment set the minimum voting age at **18 years of age**.

Major Supreme Court Cases

Out of the many Supreme Court rulings, several have had critical historical importance. These include:

- **Marbury v. Madison** (1803) – This ruling established judicial review as a power of the Supreme Court.
- **Dred Scott v. Sandford** (1857) – This decision upheld property rights over human rights in the case of a slave who had been transported to a free state by his master, but was still considered a slave.
- **Brown v. Board of Education** (1954) – The Court ruled that segregation was a violation of the Equal Protection Clause and that the "separate but equal" practice in education was unconstitutional. This decision overturned the 1896 Plessy v. Ferguson ruling that permitted segregation if facilities were equal.
- **Miranda v. Arizona** (1966) – This ruling compelled the reading of Miranda rights to those arrested for crimes the law. It ensured that confessions could not be illegally obtained and that citizen rights to fair trials and protection under the law would be upheld.

> **Review Video: Marbury vs. Madison**
> Visit mometrix.com/academy and enter code: 573964
>
> **Review Video: The Dred Scott Act**
> Visit mometrix.com/academy and enter code: 364838

Famous Speeches in US History that Defined Government Policy, Foreign Relations, and American Spirit

Among the best-known speeches and famous lines known to modern Americans are the following:

- The **Gettysburg Address** – Made by Abraham Lincoln on November 19, 1863, it dedicated the Gettysburg battleground's cemetery.
- The **Fourteen Points** – Made by Woodrow Wilson on January 18, 1918, this outlined Wilson's plans for peace and the League of Nations.
- **Address to Congress** – Made by Franklin Roosevelt on December 8, 1941, it declared war on Japan and described the attack on Pearl Harbor as "a day which will live in infamy."
- **Inaugural Address** – Made by John F. Kennedy on January 20, 1961, it contained the famous line: "Ask not what your country can do for you, ask what you can do for your country."
- **Berlin Address** – Made by John F. Kennedy on June 26, 1963, it contained the famous line "Ich bin ein Berliner," which expressed empathy for West Berliners in their conflict with the Soviet Union.
- "**I Have a Dream**" and "**I See the Promised Land**" – Made by Martin Luther King, Jr. on August 28, 1963 and April 3, 1968, respectively, these speeches were hallmarks of the Civil Rights Movement.
- **Brandenburg Gate speech** – Made by Ronald Reagan on June 12, 1987, this speech was about the Berlin Wall and the end of the Cold War. It contained the famous line "Tear down this wall."

Closed and Open Primaries in a Direct Primary System

The **direct primary system** is a means for members of a political party to participate in the selection of a candidate from their party to compete against the other party's candidate in a general election. A **closed primary** is a party nominating election in which only declared party members can vote. Party membership is usually established by registration. Currently, 26 states and the District of Columbia use this system. An **open primary** is a party nominating election in which any qualified voter can take part. The voter makes a public choice at the polling place about which primary to participate in, and the choice does not depend on any registration or previous choices. A **blanket primary**, which allowed voters to vote in the primaries of both parties, was used at various times by three states. The Supreme Court ruled against this practice in 2000.

Important Documents in United States History and Government

The following are among the greatest **American documents** because of their impact on foreign and domestic policy:

- Declaration of Independence (1776)
- The Articles of Confederation (1777)
- The Constitution (1787) and the Bill of Rights (1791)
- The Northwest Ordinance (1787)
- The Federalist Papers (1787-88)
- George Washington's Inaugural Address (1789) and Farewell Address (1796)
- The Alien and Sedition Act (1798)
- The Louisiana Purchase Treaty (1803)
- The Monroe Doctrine (1823); The Missouri Compromise (1830)
- The Compromise of 1850
- The Kansas-Nebraska Act (1854)
- The Homestead Act (1862)
- The Emancipation Proclamation (1863)
- The agreement to purchase Alaska (1866)
- The Sherman Anti-Trust Act (1890)
- Theodore Roosevelt's Corollary to the Monroe Doctrine (1905)
- The Social Security Act (1935) and other acts of the New Deal in the 1930s; The Truman Doctrine (1947); The Marshall Plan (1948)
- The Civil Rights Act (1964)

Federal Taxes

The four types of **federal taxes** are:

- **Income taxes on individuals** – This is a complex system because of demands for various exemptions and rates. Further, the schedule of rates can be lowered or raised according to economic conditions in order to stimulate or restrain economic activity. For example, a tax cut can provide an economic stimulus, while a tax increase can slow down the rate of inflation. Personal income tax generates about five times as much as corporate taxes. Rates are based on an individual's income, and range from 10 to 35 percent.
- **Income taxes on corporations** – The same complexity of exemptions and rates exists for corporations as individuals. Taxes can be raised or lowered according to the need to stimulate or restrain the economy.
- **Excise taxes** – These are taxes on specific goods such as tobacco, liquor, automobiles, gasoline, air travel, and luxury items, or on activities such as highway usage by trucks.
- **Customs duties** – These are taxes imposed on imported goods. They serve to regulate trade between the United States and other countries.

United States Currency System

The Constitution of 1787 gave the United States Congress the central authority to **print or coin money** and to **regulate its value**. Before this time, states were permitted to maintain separate currencies. The currency system is based on a **modified gold standard**. There is an enormous store of gold to back up United States currency housed at Fort Knox, Kentucky. Paper money is actually **Federal Reserve notes** and coins. It is the job of the Bureau of Engraving and Printing in the Treasury Department to design plates, special types of paper, and other security measures for bills and bonds. This money is put into general circulation by the Treasury and Federal Reserve Banks, and is taken out of circulation when worn out. Coins are made at the Bureau of the Mint in Philadelphia, Denver, and San Francisco.

Employment Act of 1946

The **Employment Act of 1946** established the following entities to combat unemployment:

- The **Council of Economic Advisers** (CEA) – Composed of a chair and two other members appointed by the President and approved by the Senate, this council assists the President with the development and implementation of US economic policy. The Council members and their staff, located in the Executive Office, are professionals in economics and statistics who forecast economic trends and provide analysis based on evidence-based research.
- The **Economic Report of the President** – This is presented every January by the President to Congress. Based on the work of the Council, the report recommends a program for maximizing employment, and may also recommend legislation.
- **Joint Economic Committee** (JEC) – This is a committee composed of 10 members of the House and 10 members of the Senate that makes a report early each year on its continuous study of the economy. Study is conducted through hearings and research, and the report is made in response to the president's recommendations.

Qualifications of a US Citizen

Anyone born in the US, born abroad to a US citizen, or who has gone through a process of **naturalization** to become a citizen, is considered a **citizen** of the United States. It is possible to lose US citizenship as a result of conviction of certain crimes such as treason. Citizenship may also be lost if a citizen pledges an oath to another country or serves in the military of a country engaged in hostilities with the US. A US citizen can also choose to hold dual citizenship, work as an expatriate in another country without losing US citizenship, or even renounce citizenship if he or she so chooses.

Rights, Duties, and Responsibilities Granted to or Expected from US Citizens

Citizens are granted certain rights under the US government. The most important of these are defined in the **Bill of Rights**, and include freedom of speech, religion, assembly, and a variety of other rights the government is not allowed to remove.

Duties of a US citizen include:

- Paying taxes
- Loyalty to the government, though the US does not prosecute those who criticize or seek to change the government
- Support and defend the Constitution
- Serve in the Armed Forces as required by law
- Obeying laws as set forth by the various levels of government.

Responsibilities of a US citizen include:

- Voting in elections
- Respecting one another's rights and not infringing upon them
- Staying informed about various political and national issues
- Respecting one another's beliefs

United States Political Systems

Representative Democracy

In a system of government characterized as a representative democracy, voters elect **representatives** to act in their interests. Typically, a representative is elected by and responsible to a specific subset of the total population of eligible voters; this subset of the electorate is referred to as a representative's constituency. A **representative democracy** may foster a more powerful legislature than other forms of government systems; to compensate for a strong legislature, most constitutions stipulate that measures must be taken to balance the powers within government, such as the creation of a separate judicial branch. Representative democracy became popular in post-industrial nations where increasing numbers of people expressed an interest in politics, but where technology and census counts remained incompatible with systems of direct democracy. Today, the majority of the world's population resides in representative democracies, including constitutional monarchies that possess a strong representative branch.

Democracy

Democracy, or rule by the people, is a form of government in which power is vested in the people and in which policy decisions are made by the majority in a decision-making process such as an election that is open to all or most citizens. Definitions of democracy have become more generalized and include aspects of society and political culture in democratic societies that do not necessarily represent a form of government. What defines a democracy varies, but some of the characteristics of a democracy could include the presence of a middle class, the presence of a civil society, a free market, political pluralism, universal suffrage, and specific rights and freedoms. In practice however, democracies do have limits on specific freedoms, which are justified as being necessary to maintain democracy and ensure democratic freedoms. For example, freedom of association is limited in democracies for individuals and groups that pose a threat to government or to society.

Presidential/Congressional System

In a **presidential system**, also referred to as a **congressional system**, the legislative branch and the executive branches are elected separately from one another. The features of a presidential system include a *president* who serves as both the head of state and the head of the government, who has no formal relationship with the legislative branch, who is not a voting member, who cannot introduce bills, and who has a fixed term of office. *Elections* are held at scheduled times. The president's *cabinet* carries out the policies of the executive branch and the legislative branch.

Political Parties

A **political party** is an organization that advocates a particular ideology and seeks to gain power within government. The tendency of members of political parties to support their party's policies and interests relative to those of other parties is referred to as partisanship. Often, a political party is comprised of members whose positions, interests and perspectives on policies vary, despite having shared interests in the general ideology of the party. As such, many political parties will have divisions within them that have differing opinions on policy. Political parties are often placed on a political spectrum, with one end of the spectrum representing conservative, traditional values and policies and the other end of the spectrum representing radical, progressive value and policies.

Types of Party Systems

There is a variety of **party systems**, including single-party systems, dominant-party systems, and dual-party systems. In a **single-party system**, only one political party may hold power. In this type of system, minor parties may be permitted, but they must accept the leadership of the dominant party. **Dominant-party systems** allow for multiple parties in opposition of one another, however the dominant party is the only party considered to have power. A **two-party system**, such as in the United States, is one in which there are two dominant political parties. In such a system, it is very difficult for any other parties to win an election. In most two-party systems, there is typically one right wing party and one left wing party.

Democratic Party

The **Democratic Party** was founded in 1792. In the United States, it is one of the two dominant political parties, along with the Republican Party. The Democratic Party is to the left of the Republican Party. The Democratic Party began as a conservative party in the mid-1800s, shifting to the left during the 1900s. There are many factions within the Democratic Party in the United States. The **Democratic National Committee (DNC)** is the official organization of the Democratic Party, and it develops and promotes the party's platform and coordinates fundraising and election strategies. There are Democratic committees in every US state and most US counties. The official symbol of the Democratic Party is the donkey.

Republican Party

The **Republican Party** is often referred to as the **GOP**, which stands for *Grand Old Party*. The Republican Party is considered socially conservative and economically neoliberal relative to the Democratic Party. Like the Democratic Party, there are factions within the Republic Party that agree with the party's overall ideology, but disagree with the party's positions on specific issues. The official symbol of the Republican Party is the elephant. The **Republican National Committee (RNC)** is the official organization of the Republican Party, and it develops and promotes the party's platform and coordinates fundraising and election strategies. There are Republican committees in every US state and most US counties.

Political Campaigns

A **political campaign** is an organized attempt to influence the decisions of a particular group of people. Examples of campaigns could include elections or efforts to influence policy changes. One of the first steps in a campaign is to develop a **campaign message**. The message must then be delivered to the individuals and groups that the campaign is trying to reach and influence through a campaign plan. There are various ways for a campaign to communicate its message to the intended audience, including public media; paid media such as television, radio and newspaper ads, billboards and the internet; public events such as protests and rallies; meetings with speakers; mailings; canvassing; fliers; and websites. Through these efforts, the campaign attempts to attract additional support and, ultimately, to reach the goal of the campaign.

Voting

Voting is a method of decision making that allows people to express their opinion or preference for a candidate or for a proposed resolution of an issue. In a democratic system, voting typically takes place as part of an **election**. An individual participates in the voting process by casting a vote, or a **ballot**; ballots are produced by states A *secret ballot* can be used at polls to protect voters' privacy. Individuals can also vote via *absentee ballot*. In some states voters can write-in a name to cast a vote for a candidate that is not on the ballot. Some states also use *straight ticket voting*, allowing the voter to vote for one party for all the elected positions on the ballot.

US Elections

In the United States, **officials** are elected at the federal, state and local levels. The first two articles of the Constitution, as well as various amendments, establish how **federal elections** are to be held. The **President** is elected indirectly, by electors of an electoral college. Members of the electoral college nearly always vote along the lines of the popular vote of their respective states. Members of **Congress** are directly elected. At the state level, state law establishes most aspects of how elections are held. There are many elected offices at the state level, including a governor and state legislature. There are also elected offices at the local level.

Voter Eligibility

The United States Constitution establishes that individual people are permitted to **vote** in elections if they are citizens of the United States and are at least eighteen years old. The **fifteenth** and **nineteenth amendments** of the United States Constitution stipulate that the right to vote cannot be denied to any United States citizen based on race or sex, respectively. States regulate voter eligibility beyond the minimum qualifications stipulated by the United States Constitution. Depending on the regulations of individual states, individuals may be denied the right to vote if they are convicted criminals.

Advantages and Disadvantages to Two-Party System

Advocates of the **two-party system** argue that its advantages are that they are stable because they enable policies and government to change slowly rather than rapidly due to the relative lack of influence from small parties representing unconventional ideologies. In addition, they seem to drive voters toward a middle ground and are less susceptible to revolutions, coups, or civil wars. Among the critiques of the two-party system is the claim that stability in and of itself is not necessarily desirable, as it often comes at the expense of democracy. Critics also argue that the two-party system promotes negative political campaigns, in which candidates and their respective parties only take positions on issues that will differentiate themselves from their opponents, rather than focusing on policy issues that are of significance to citizens. Another concern is that if one of the two major parties becomes weak, a dominant-party system may develop.

Campaign Message

Political campaigns consist of three main elements, which are the campaign message, the money that is necessary to run the campaign, and the "machine," or the capital that is necessary to run the campaign. A campaign message is a succinct statement expressing why voters should support the campaign and the individual or policy associated with that campaign. The message is one of the most significant aspects of a political campaign, and a considerable amount of time, money and effort is invested in devising a successful campaign message, as it will be repeated throughout the campaign and will be one of the most identifying factors of the campaign.

Modern Election Campaigns in the US

Political campaigns in the US have changed and continue to change as advances in technology permit varied campaign methods. Campaigns represent a civic practice, and today they are a high profit industry. The US has an abundance of professional political consultants that employ highly sophisticated campaign management strategies and tools. The election process varies widely between the federal, state and local levels. Campaigns are typically controlled by individual candidates, rather than by the parties that they are associated with. Larger campaigns utilize a vast array of media to reach their targeted audiences, while smaller campaigns are typically limited to direct contact with voters, direct mailings and other forms of low-cost advertising to reach their audiences. In addition to fundraising and spending done by individual candidates, party committees and political action committees also raise money and spend it in ways that will advance the cause of the particular campaign they are associated with.

Voter Registration

Individuals have the responsibility of **registering to vote**. Every state except North Dakota requires citizens to register to vote. In an effort to increase voter turnout, Congress passed the **National Voter Registration Act** in 1993. This Act is also known as "Motor Voter," because it required states to make the voter registration process easier by providing registration services through drivers' license registration centers, as well as through disability centers, schools, libraries, and mail-in registration. Some states are exempt because they permit same-day voter registration, which enables voters to register to vote on the day of the election.

Presidential Elections

The President of the United States is elected **indirectly**, by members of an **electoral college**. Members of the electoral college nearly always vote along the lines of the popular vote of their respective states. The winner of a presidential election is the candidate with at least 270 electoral college votes. It is possible for a candidate to win the electoral vote, and lose the popular vote. Incumbent Presidents and challengers typically prefer a balanced ticket, where the President and Vice President are elected together and generally balance one another with regard to geography, ideology, or experience working in government. The nominated Vice Presidential candidate is referred to as the President's *running mate*.

Electoral College

Electoral college votes are cast by state by a group of electors; each elector casts one electoral college vote. State law regulates how states cast their electoral college votes. In all states except Maine and Nebraska, the candidate winning the most votes receives all the state's electoral college votes. In Maine and Nebraska two electoral votes are awarded based on the winner of the statewide election, and the rest go to the highest vote-winner in each of the state's congressional districts. Critics of the electoral college argue that it is undemocratic because the President is elected indirectly as opposed to directly, and that it creates inequality between voters in different states because candidates focus attention on voters in swing states who could influence election results. Critics argue that the electoral college provides more representation for voters in small states than large states, where more voters are represented by a single electoral than in small states and discriminates against candidates that do not have support concentrated in a given state.

Congressional Elections

Congressional elections are every two years. Members of the **House of Representatives** are elected for a two year term and elections occur every two years on the first Tuesday after November 1st in even years. A Representative is elected from each of the 435 House districts in the US House elections usually occur in the same year as Presidential elections. Members of the **Senate** are elected to six year terms; one-third of the Senate is elected every two years. Per the Seventeenth Amendment to the Constitution, which was passed in 1913, Senators are elected by the electorate of states. The country is divided into **Congressional districts**. Critics argue that this division eliminates voter choice, sometimes creating areas in which Congressional races are uncontested. Every ten years **redistricting** of Congressional districts occurs. However, redistricting is often partisan and therefore reduces the number of competitive districts. The division of voting districts resulting in an unfair advantage to one party in elections is known as gerrymandering. Gerrymandering has been criticized as being undemocratic.

State and Local Elections

State elections are regulated by state laws and constitutions. In keeping with the ideal of separation of powers, the legislature and the executive are elected separately at the state level, as they are at the federal level. In each state, a **Governor** and a **Lieutenant Governor** are elected. In some states, the Governor and Lieutenant Governor are elected on a joint ticket, while in other states they are elected separately from one another. In some states, executive positions such as Attorney General and Secretary of State are also elected offices. All members of state legislatures are elected, including state senators and state representatives. Depending on the state, members of the state supreme court and other members of the state judiciary may be chosen in elections. Local government can include the governments of counties and cities. At this level, nearly all government offices are filled through an election process. Elected local offices may include sheriffs, county school boards, and city mayors.

Campaign Finance and Independent Expenditures

An individual or group is legally permitted to make unlimited **independent expenditures** in association with federal elections. An independent expenditure is an expenditure that is made to pay for a form of communication that supports the election or defeat of a candidate; the expenditure must be made independently from the candidate's own campaign. To be considered independent, the communication may not be made with the cooperation or consultation with, or at the request or suggestion of, any candidate, any committees or political party associated with the candidate, or any agent that acts on behalf of the candidate. There are no restrictions on the amount that anyone may spend on an independent expenditure, however, any individual making an independent expenditure must report it and disclose the source of the funds they used.

Campaign Finance and Activities of Political Parties

Political parties participate in federal elections at the local, state and national levels. Most **party committees** must register with the **Federal Election Committee** and file reports disclosing federal campaign activities. While party committees may contribute funds directly to federal candidates, the amounts that they contribute are restricted by the campaign finance contribution limits. National and state party committees are permitted to make additional **coordinated expenditures**, within limits, to assist their nominees in general elections. However, national party committees are not permitted to make unlimited **independent expenditures**, also known as soft money, to support or oppose federal candidates. State and local party committees are also not permitted to use soft money for the purpose of supporting or opposing federal candidates, but they are allowed to spend soft money, up to a limit of $10,000 per source, on voter registration and on efforts aimed at increasing voter participation. All party committees are required to register themselves and file disclosure reports with the Federal Election Committee once their federal election activities exceed specified monetary limits.

Public Opinion

Public opinion represents the collective attitudes of individual members of the adult population in the United States of America. There are many varied forces that may influence public opinion. These forces include *public relations efforts* on the part of political campaigns and political parties. Another force affecting political opinion is the *political media* and the *mass media*. Public opinion is very important during elections, particularly Presidential elections, as it is an indicator of how candidates are perceived by the public and of how well candidates are doing during their election campaigns. Public opinion is often measured and evaluated using survey sampling.

MASS MEDIA AND PUBLIC OPINION

The **mass media** is critical in developing public opinion. In the short term people generally evaluate information they receive relative to their own beliefs; in the long term the media may have a considerable impact on people's beliefs. Due to the impact of the media on an individual's beliefs, some experts consider the effects of the media on an individual's independence and autonomy to be negative. Others view the impact of the media on individuals as a positive one, because the media provides information that expands worldviews and enriches lives, and fosters the development of opinions that are informed by many sources of information. A critical aspect of the relationship between the media and public opinion is who is in control of the knowledge and information that is disseminated through the media. Whoever controls the media can propagate their own agenda. The extent to which an individual interprets and evaluates information received through the media can influence behaviors such as voting patterns, consumer behavior, and social attitudes.

Practice Test #1

1. The idea that the purpose of the American colonies was to provide Great Britain with raw materials and a market for its goods is an expression of:

a. Free trade
b. Most favored nation status
c. Mercantilism
d. Laissez-faire capitalism

2. Although Roosevelt's New Deal solved many problems, it also did which of the following?

a. Failed to provide direct relief to the poor
b. Had little effect on the problem of unemployment
c. Raised the national debt
d. Weakened labor unions

3. The legislative structure set forth in the US Constitution was determined by:

a. The Virginia Plan
b. The New Jersey Plan
c. The Connecticut Compromise
d. The Plan of Charles Pinckney

4. Which of the following is NOT true regarding the early colonization of New York?

a. Dutch fur traders first created the New Amsterdam settlement on Manhattan Island in 1624.
b. King Charles II of England entitled his brother James to conquer New Amsterdam in 1664.
c. James, Duke of York, prohibited assemblies in New York as he was against representation.
d. Colonel Richard Nicols granted very few civil or political rights to the New York colonials.

5. What did the Mason-Dixon Line divide?

a. The East from the West before the western states were incorporated
b. The East from the West along the Mississippi River
c. The North from the South before the Civil War
d. The Senate from the House of Representatives

6. Which of the following is NOT a true statement regarding the Louisiana Purchase?

a. Jefferson sent a delegation to Paris to endeavor to purchase only the city of New Orleans from Napoleon.
b. Napoleon, anticipating US intrusions into Louisiana, offered to sell the US the entire Louisiana territory.
c. The American delegation accepted Napoleon's offer, though they were only authorized to buy New Orleans.
d. The Louisiana Purchase, once it was completed, increased the territory of the US by 50% overnight.

7. Which of the following was an effect of industrialization in the United States?

a. Large growth in city populations
b. A general shift from self-employment to being employed by others
c. Increased economic/employment opportunities for women
d. All of the above

8. Before the Civil War, to which of the following did Southern states object?

a. An increase in Southern tobacco production
b. An increase in tariffs on Northern manufactured goods
c. An increase in western mining for gold
d. An increase in the voting rights of slaves

9. What would be the BEST title for this list that summarizes what all of the items on the list have in common?

- Communist North Korea invaded South Korea in 1950.
- President Truman worried that the Soviet Union and China planned to expand communism throughout Asia.
- The United Nations passed a resolution in 1950 urging United Nations member countries to give assistance to South Korea in their battle against North Korea.

a. Reasons Why the Policy of Containment was Ineffective
b. Reasons for United States Involvement in the Korean War
c. Reasons for the Popularity of McCarthyism in the United States
d. Reasons Why the House Un-American Activities Committee Formed

10. During World War I, which group joined with the Central Powers after it formed?

a. Austria-Hungary
b. Germany
c. Ottoman Empire
d. Italy

11. In 2002, President George W. Bush cited certain countries as being part of an "axis of evil." Which country was NOT part of that description?

a. Iran
b. Iraq
c. North Korea
d. Afghanistan

12. What significance did *Brown* v. *Board of Education of Topeka* have on the system if education in the United States?

a. Students were educated separately but equally.
b. Students were taught creationism.
c. Students were taught evolution.
d. The "separate but equal" ruling was reversed.

13. In 1973, the US Congress passed the War Powers Act. How did the Act reassert congressional authority relative to that of the President?

a. It mandated congressional approval for funding war-related expenses.
b. It required the President to submit regular reports to Congress regarding conflicts lasting more than 60 days.
c. It restricted the power of the President to suspend key elements of the Constitution.
d. It limited the length of time the President can dispatch combat troops without congressional approval.

14. Which of the following most accurately describes the group that invaded the Bay of Pigs in 1961?

a. Members of the US CIA
b. A group of Cuban exiles
c. The people of Cuba
d. CIA-sponsored Cuban exiles

15. Which of the following BEST describes the significance of the US Supreme Court's decision in the Dred Scott case?

a. The ruling effectively declared slavery to be a violation of the Constitution.
b. The ruling guaranteed full citizenship rights to freed slaves.
c. The ruling turned many Southerners against the Supreme Court.
d. The ruling furthered the gap between North and South and hastened the Civil War.

16. Which of the following was used as a justification for increased US military presence in Vietnam?

a. France's defeat at the Battle of Điện Biên Phủ
b. The Gulf of Tonkin incident
c. The Fall of Saigon
d. The Geneva Accords of 1954

17. Which of the following grievances is NOT listed in the Declaration of Independence?

a. He has plundered our seas, ravaged our coasts, burnt our towns, and destroyed the lives of our people.
b. He has cleaved us in twain, set betwixt the desire for Peace and the demand of Justice for those aggrieved.
c. He has erected a multitude of New Offices, and sent hither swarms of Officers to harass our people and eat out their substance.
d. He has affected to render the Military independent of and superior to the Civil Power.

Refer to the following for question 18:

- A Wilderness Protection Act saved forestland from being developed
- The Elementary and Secondary Education Act provided money for public schools
- Medicare was started to help elderly with the costs of health care
- A Housing Act provided money to build low-income housing
- Pollution controls became stronger due to the Air and Water Quality Acts
- Standards were raised for safety in consumer products
- A Food Stamp program was enacted
- Head Start's preschool programs for poor children were created
- The Corporation for Public Broadcasting was created, providing many public television and radio stations

18. All of the programs on the above list fall under what category of programs?

a. President Franklin D. Roosevelt's New Deal programs
b. President John F. Kennedy's Civil Rights programs
c. President Lyndon B. Johnson's Great Society programs
d. President Richard M. Nixon's American Welfare programs

19. Carrie Chapman Catt founded the League of Women Voters in 1920 in response to which of the following historical events?

a. The election of President Woodrow Wilson.
b. The passage of the Nineteenth Amendment to the Constitution.
c. The breakup of the National Women's Party.
d. The end of World War I.

20. Which of the following statements is NOT true about the Gilded Age in America?

a. The Gilded Age was the era of the "robber barons" in the business world.
b. The Gilded Age got its name from the excesses of the wealthy upper class.
c. The Gilded Age had philanthropy Carnegie called the "Gospel of Wealth".
d. The Gilded Age is a term whose origins have not been identified clearly.

21. Martin Luther King, Jr. and Malcolm X were both important figures in the American civil rights movement. Which of the following statements best describes a difference between their respective approaches to civil rights?

a. Martin Luther King, Jr. advocated nonviolence; Malcolm X advocated self-defense against white aggression.
b. Martin Luther King, Jr. mobilized ordinary citizens; Malcolm X focused on working with local white political leaders.
c. Martin Luther King, Jr. related Christianity to civil rights; Malcolm X did not link religion to civil rights.
d. Martin Luther King, Jr. promoted Black Nationalism; Malcolm X did not.

22. What was generally the sentiment towards Chinese laborers in the United States in the 1880s?

a. Chinese laborers were viewed as cheap laborers and were generally discriminated against.
b. Chinese laborers were highly valued members of US society.
c. Chinese laborers were forced out of the country.
d. Chinese laborers were welcomed through several immigration laws.

23. Which of the following statements is false regarding the Puritans?

a. In terms of their theology, the Puritans were considered Calvinists.
b. Many Puritans agreed with radical views that criticized the Swiss Calvinists.
c. Many of those identified as Calvinists opposed the Puritans.
d. The Restoration and the Uniformity Act reunified the Puritan movement and the Church of England.

24. Who may write a bill?

a. Anyone
b. A member of the House
c. A Senator
d. Any member of Congress

25. How did the Truman Doctrine shape US foreign policy after World War II?

a. It influenced President Truman's decision to create commissions on civil rights.
b. It shaped the US role in rebuilding the economies of postwar Europe.
c. It led the US government to refrain from interfering with the US economy.
d. It led to US military involvement in countries such as Korea.

26. Which of the following exemplifies the multiplier effect of large cities?

a. The presence of specialized equipment for an industry attracts even more business.
b. The large population lowers the price of goods.
c. Public transportation means more people can commute to work.
d. A local newspaper can afford to give away the Sunday edition.

27. The two new states admitted under the Missouri Compromise of 1820 were Missouri and what other state?

a. Ohio
b. Alabama
c. Kansas
d. Maine

28. Which of the following territories was acquired last by the United States?

a. The Texas Annexation
b. Oregon Country
c. The Gadsden Purchase
d. The Mexican Cession

29. What major US event took place around the same time that the Judiciary Act set up the federal judiciary system?

a. The Neutrality Act was passed.
b. The United States entered WWII.
c. The Korean War ended.
d. George Washington was inaugurated president.

30. Thomas Paine's *Common Sense* influenced which American document that ultimately helped shape the Constitution?

a. The Articles of Confederation
b. The Declaration of Independence
c. The Bill of Rights
d. The Treaty of Greenville

31. The writers of *The Federalist Papers* published under the pen name "Publius." Who were the authors?

a. James Madison, John Jay, and Alexander Hamilton
b. George Washington, Thomas Jefferson, and James Madison
c. Alexander Hamilton, Benjamin Franklin, and Thomas Jefferson
d. Benjamin Franklin, John Jay, and Thomas Jefferson

32. Which of the following is considered more a cause than an effect of the Industrial Revolution?

a. Emergence of socialism
b. Emergence of capitalism
c. The Romantic movement
d. The Protestant work ethic

Refer to the following for question 33:

United States Foreign Trade 1960–1970

(by Category Percentages)

Category	**1960**		**1970**	
	Exports	Imports	Exports	Imports
Chemicals	8.7	5.3	9.0	3.6
Crude materials (except fuel)	13.7	18.3	10.8	8.3
Food and beverages, including tobacco	15.6	22.5	11.8	15.6
Machinery and transport	34.3	9.7	42.0	28.0

33. From 1960 to 1970, which of the following categories had the greatest difference between percentage of exports and imports?

a. chemicals
b. crude materials
c. food and beverages
d. machinery and transport

34. Of the following demonstrations of Soviet disagreements with the US after World War II, which was the first to transpire?

a. The Soviet Union backed Communist control of Hungary and Romania.
b. The Soviet Union endorsed Communist control of Czechoslovakia.
c. The Soviets did not allow conservatives to serve in the Communist government imposed on Poland.
d. Soviets refused to take part in the international Baruch Plan because they mistrusted American motives.

35. Of the following international diplomatic conferences, which one made US-Soviet differences apparent?

a. The Potsdam conference
b. The conference at Yalta
c. Dumbarton Oaks conference
d. The Tehran conference

36. Which of the following was NOT an immediate effect of rapid urban growth in the 1800s?

a. Poor sanitation conditions in the cities
b. Epidemics of diseases in the cities
c. Inadequate police and fire protection
d. Widespread urban political corruption

37. Of the following, which statement about the US economy in the 1990s is correct?

a. By the year 2000, the US economy was increasing at a rate of 5% a year.
b. The rate of unemployment in America at this time dropped to 6%.
c. The rates of productivity and of inflation in the US were about the same.
d. The US stock market's total value had doubled in only six years.

38. Which of the following best defines American GDP?

a. The value, in American dollars, of all goods and services produced within American borders during one calendar year
b. The value, in American dollars, of all goods and services produced by American companies during one calendar year
c. The total value, in American dollars, of all American household incomes during one calendar year
d. The value, in American dollars, of a "market basket" of goods and services in one year divided by the value of the same market basket in a previous year multiplied by 100

39. The Seven Years' War, called the French and Indian War by the Colonists:

a. Was the precursor to the American Revolution
b. Was a conflict related to European colonization
c. Primarily took place in Canada
d. Ended European conquests

Refer to the following for question 40:

ERA in US History	Approximate Dates	Defining Characteristics of this Era
Gilded Age or Progressive Era	1890-1914	The era was called "gilded" because of expanded wealth and prosperity. "Progressive" describes the politics of the time that called for social reforms and eliminating corruption in government.
World War I Era	1914-1918	The US was involved in fighting a war in Europe.
Roaring Twenties	1918-1928	
Great Depression	1929-1940	
World War II Era	1941-1945	
Cold War Era	1945-1964	

40. Which defining characteristic listed below should go in the row for describing the Roaring Twenties Era?

a. After a World War, America wanted to help rebuild Europe and prevent the Soviet Union's possible expansion of communism.
b. After the stock market crash, many businesses failed and unemployment became high.
c. The US was involved in fighting a war with Allies against Germany, Japan, and Italy.
d. The economy was strong with a great demand for new products, while culture in this era, also known as the "Jazz Age," became more experimental.

41. The Trail of Tears was:

a. The forced removal of British soldiers after the American Revolution
b. The forced evacuation of Cherokee peoples into Oklahoma
c. The forced evacuation of freed slaves from the South after the Civil War
d. The tears of Betsy Ross while she sewed the first American flag

42. The results of increased production of crops and a managed approach to agriculture is called:

a. The industrial revolution
b. The information revolution
c. The agricultural revolution
d. The scientific revolution

43. Which of the following is NOT true regarding the Whiskey Rebellion?

a. Washington's dispatching federal troops did not resolve the revolt, a setback for the government.
b. An excise tax levied on whiskey was central to Treasury Secretary Hamilton's revenue program.
c. Farmers in Pennsylvania objected to the excise tax on whiskey, and were refusing to pay the tax.
d. Farmers in Pennsylvania committed acts of terrorism against tax collectors over the whiskey tax.

44. Inflation has what effects?

a. Harms all members of an economy
b. Helps all members of an economy
c. Harms no members of an economy
d. Harms some members of an economy, helps others

45. Which of the following statements is true regarding movements toward reform in America during the 1840s?

a. American society was undergoing changes, which made conditions unstable and uncertain.
b. During this period of time, the traditional values of American society were being challenged.
c. The Romantic Movement, a reaction to the Enlightenment, was supportive of reforms.
d. All of the above statements are true.

46. Civic responsibility differs from personal responsibility in that the subject matter of civic responsibility is mainly which of the following?

a. Fair reporting of government actions
b. Fair dealings between governments
c. A person's responsibilities as a citizen
d. A person's responsibilities as a government worker

47. How did isolationism most influence American society in the decade following World War I?

a. It shaped a temporarily strong economy as the US avoided the troubled economies of postwar Europe.
b. It led to a system of admitting immigrants according to quotas based on their national origins.
c. It guided the US government's decision to strengthen its navy as a safeguard against foreign attacks.
d. It influenced the collapse of trade deals, allowing US companies access to oil in Colombia and in Middle Eastern countries.

48. The annexation of Texas by the United States in 1845 is best described as of which of the following?

a. An effort to help stem the spread of slavery west of the Mississippi
b. Part of an effort to fulfill Manifest Destiny
c. An expression of principles set forth in the Monroe Doctrine
d. An effort to improve relations between the United States and Mexico

Refer to the following for question 49:

United States Foreign Trade 1960–1970

(by Category Percentages)

Category	**1960**		**1970**	
	Exports	Imports	Exports	Imports
Chemicals	8.7	5.3	9.0	3.6
Crude materials (except fuel)	13.7	18.3	10.8	8.3
Food and beverages, including tobacco	15.6	22.5	11.8	15.6
Machinery and transport	34.3	9.7	42.0	28.0

49. Which category saw the greatest percentage decrease in imports between 1960 and 1970?

a. chemicals
b. crude materials
c. food and beverages
d. machinery and transport

50. With the end of Reconstruction in 1877, which of the following was true regarding African Americans in the South?

a. They soon took control of state legislatures
b. They formed a new political party to protect their own interests
c. They were able to rise quickly into the economic middle class
d. They were kept from voting by poll taxes and literacy tests

51. Which of the following is considered to be the largest cause of death among Native Americans following the arrival of European colonists in North America?

a. Wounds from wars with the European settlers
b. Wounds from wars with the other Native American tribes
c. European diseases
d. Exposure during the wintry, forced marches on which the European settlers forced them

Refer to the following for question 52:

The Black Experience in America, author Norman Coombs describes a 1960s sit-in:

> "In a matter of weeks, student sit-ins were occurring at segregated lunch counters all across the South. College and high school students by the thousands joined the Civil Rights Movement. These students felt the need to form their own organization to mobilize and facilitate the spontaneous demonstrations which were springing up everywhere."

52. Student "sit-ins" in the 1960s BEST exemplified which democratic process?

a. Inciting fear to motivate change
b. Litigating
c. Lobbying
d. Non-violent protesting

53. Which of these was NOT an immediate consequence of the Age of Exploration?

a. The development of more accurate navigation instruments
b. The introduction of new foods and other goods to Europe
c. The decline of England as a world power
d. The discovery of new lands where people might seek a better life

54. Which statement about factors related to the growth of the US economy between 1945 and 1970 is NOT correct?

a. The Baby Boom's greatly increased birth rates contributed to economic growth during this time.
b. The reduction in military spending after World War II contributed to the stronger US economy.
c. Government programs and growing affluence nearly quadrupled college enrollments in 20 years.
d. Increased mobility and bigger families caused fast suburban expansion, especially in the Sunbelt.

55. Who headed the National Association for the Advancement of Colored People (NAACP) in 1910, founded and edited the NAACP's journal *The Crisis*, and wrote many "muckraking" articles for *The Crisis* about civil rights for African Americans?

a. W.E.B. DuBois
b. Matthew Gaines
c. Marcus Garvey
d. Booker T. Washington

56. When President Warren Harding called for a "Return to Normalcy" in 1920, the BEST summary of what he meant would be...

a. A return to the high employment rate that had dominated the US during World War I
b. A return to peaceful times and a focus on domestic issues, as opposed to a focus on international war
c. A return to a period of high immigration rates that were contributing to a diverse culture and growing economy in the US
d. A return to finding more territories, such as Puerto Rico and Guam acquired during the Spanish-American War, for expanding US markets

57. Which of the following statements regarding events in the Middle East that took place during the Reagan administration is NOT correct?

a. Israel invaded Lebanon to get rid of the Palestine Liberation Organization's camps there.
b. When a terrorist bombing killed 240 US Marines, Reagan escalated military action.
c. Lebanon was already in the midst of a civil war when Israeli troops invaded the country.
d. President Reagan deployed US Marines to Lebanon in 1982 on a peacekeeping mission.

58. Which of the following statements is NOT true regarding the events of September 11, 2001, in the US?

a. Shortly after that date the US defeated the Taliban and captured Al-Qaeda leader Osama bin Laden.
b. On September 11, 2001, Muslim terrorists flew two hijacked airplanes into the World Trade Center in New York.
c. On September 11, 2001, Muslim terrorists flew a hijacked passenger airliner into the Pentagon in Arlington, Virginia.
d. An airplane hijacked by Muslim terrorists crashed in Pennsylvania after passengers resisted the terrorists.

59. Which of the following were causes of The Dust Bowl?

I. Wind erosion
II. Too many cultivated fields being left fallow at once
III. Severe droughts

a. I, II, & III
b. I & II
c. I & III
d. II & III

60. The end of Reconstruction was marked by which event?

a. The assassination of Abraham Lincoln
b. Ratification of the 14th Amendment
c. The impeachment of Andrew Johnson
d. The withdrawal of federal troops from the South

Answer Key and Explanations for Test #1

1. C: Mercantilism is the economic theory that nations advance the goal of accumulating capital by maintaining a balance of trade such that the value of exports exceeds that of imports. Great Britain maintained colonies to provide an inexpensive source of raw materials while creating markets for the goods manufactured in England. Under free trade, governments refrain from hindering the international exchange of goods and services. Nations that are granted most favored nation status are assured of enjoying equal advantages in international trade. A laissez-faire capitalist economy would theoretically be completely free of government regulation.

2. C: To achieve Roosevelt's goals, a great deal of money had to be spent, and the national debt skyrocketed. Millions of poor families received welfare, many jobs were created, and labor unions were strengthened with passage of the National Labor Relations Act.

3. C: The Connecticut Compromise was the plan that finally determined how the states would be represented in the government. During the Constitutional Convention or Philadelphia Convention, delegates drafting the Constitution disagreed on this point. The Virginia Plan (A), proposed by the Virginia delegation based on James Madison's ideas, held that states should be represented in proportion to their population sizes. Accordingly, the Virginia Plan was called the "large states plan." William Paterson proposed the New Jersey Plan (B). The New Jersey delegation objected to the Virginia Plan, as proportional representation could give unfair advantages to bigger states like Virginia and crowd out smaller states like New Jersey. The New Jersey Plan was called the "small states plan." It was rejected by the convention but helped small states have their point heard. The Plan of Charles Pinckney (D) of South Carolina has fewer recorded details as Pinckney did not present a written copy, and only James Madison's notes about it remain. The Convention did not debate Pinckney's plan. The Connecticut Compromise (C), proposed by Robert Sherman, reached a balance between large and small states by stipulating the House of Representatives numbers would be in proportion to the states' populations while each state would have equal representation in the Senate, with two Senators. This combined elements of both the Virginia/large states and New Jersey/small states plans. It took delegates 42 days to agree to this conclusion, but the Connecticut Compromise finally resolved the issue of state representation.

4. D: It is not true that Colonel Nicols granted very few civil or political rights to New York colonials. In fact, he gave them as many civil and political rights as possible to make up for the fact that James, Duke of York, who conquered New Amsterdam with his brother King Charles II's authorization (B), was strongly against representation for colonists, and prohibited any representative assemblies in his renamed New York (C). James gave in to their demands in the 1680s, but upon his accession to the throne of England in 1685, he went back on his word. It is true that before the English conquered the New York territories, New Amsterdam on Manhattan Island was a trading settlement of the New Netherlands made by Dutch explorers to facilitate the Dutch West India Company's fur trade with the indigenous peoples (A).

5. C: The Mason-Dixon Line was the manifestation of a border dispute between the British colonies of Pennsylvania, Maryland, and Delaware. It effectively separated, or illustrated, a cultural divide between North and South before the Civil War.

6. D: The Louisiana Purchase actually increased the US's territory by 100% overnight, not 50%. The Louisiana territory doubled the size of the nation. It is true that Jefferson initially sent a delegation to Paris to see if Napoleon would agree to sell only New Orleans to the United States. It is also true that Napoleon, who expected America to encroach on Louisiana, decided to avoid this by offering to sell the entire territory to the US It is likewise true that America only had authority to buy New Orleans. Nevertheless, the delegation accepted Napoleon's offer of all of Louisiana. Due to his belief in strict interpretation of the Constitution, Jefferson did require approval from Congress to make the purchase. When his advisors characterized the purchase as being within his purview based on the presidential power to make treaties, Congress agreed.

7. D: The industrialization of the United States led to an overall decrease in the number of farmers as people moved from the country to the city in search of the new jobs created by industrialization. This move also resulted in fewer Americans being self-employed, as they instead became wage earners working for other people. Industrialization also led to an overall increase in economic and employment opportunities for women. Many of these opportunities took the form of what we now sometimes think of as "pink collar" jobs such as typing and stenography.

8. B: Southern states provided raw materials that were manufactured into commodities in Northern states. Southerners resented paying taxes to Northern states for these products (textiles, furniture, etc.).

9. B: While all the titles have a connection of some kind to at least one or two items on the given list, choice B provides the BEST title for the list to show what all the items have in common: reasons for US involvement in the Korean War. The policy of containment may have been partially effective, because Korea was only one country falling to communism. The United Nations item would probably not fall under a title about containment, McCarthyism, or the HUAC committee, because those were all more internal to the US only. The UN was encouraging nations to get involved in the Korean War, so it fits under that title.

10. C: The Ottoman Empire joined with the Central Powers in 1914 during World War I. The original Triple Alliance was formed by Austria-Hungary, Germany, and Italy in 1882 and renewed in 1902. The Ottoman Empire signed the Turco-German Alliance in August 1914, joining with the Central Powers. In October 1914, with the bombing of Russian ports on the Black Sea, Turkey formally entered World War I. The Allied Powers of the Triple Entente (Great Britain, France, and Russia) declared war on the Ottoman Empire in November 1914.

11. D: In 2002, the United States was involved with nation building in Afghanistan.

12. D: In 1954 the Warren Court unanimously reversed the separate but equal ruling of *Plessy* v. *Ferguson* in 1896.

13. D: Under the War Powers Act of 1973, the President can send combat troops to battle (or to an area where hostilities are imminent) for only 60 days, with the possibility of extending this period of time to 90 days. In order to keep deployed troops in place (or to send additional troops) after this period of time has elapsed, the President must seek Congressional approval, either in the form of a mandate or in the form of a declaration of war. Option A can be eliminated because Congress was responsible for approving war-related funding prior to the War Powers Act, which did not affect this responsibility. Neither option B nor option C accurately describes the importance of the War Powers Act.

14. D: The 1961 Bay of Pigs invaders would best be described as Cuban exiles sponsored by the CIA. It was not members of the CIA themselves (A). It was a group of Cuban exiles (B), but this answer is not as correct as choice D, which further specifies that these Cuban exiles were sponsored by the CIA. They were also trained by the CIA and supported by US armed forces. The people of

Cuba (C) did not invade nor did they support the invasion. In fact, the invasion was quashed by Cuban armed forces within three days.

15. D: In the Dred Scott decision of 1857, the Court ruled that no slave or descendant of slaves could ever be a United States citizen. It also declared the Missouri Compromise of 1820 to be unconstitutional, clearing the way for the expansion of slavery in new American territories. This ruling pleased Southerners and outraged the North, further dividing the nation and setting the stage for war.

16. B: The emergence and increasing acceptance of the Domino Theory became a driving force in how the United States made foreign policy decisions after the Cold War. America's involvement in Vietnam was largely structured around containing the spread of Communism. However, it was not until the Gulf of Tonkin incident in 1964 that provided justification for increased US military presence in Vietnam.

17. B: The Declaration of Independence recognized the British Empire's government as being headed by the King of England, under whom the various local parliaments and legislative bodies served to enact laws for the peoples whom they represented. The Founding Fathers decided that because the colonies did not have the right to elect members of Parliament, Parliament should not pass laws for them. The Declaration of Independence lists 27 total grievances and has served as an inspiration for other revolutionary movements since its inception.

18. C: All the programs listed were part of President Lyndon B. Johnson's Great Society programs. The students' general knowledge of social studies should place most of those programs within the 1960s time period, making Presidents Kennedy or Johnson the best guesses. But because many of the programs do not have to do with civil rights, Johnson becomes the best guess for a student to make over the other choices provided.

19. B: Carrie Chapman Catt (1859-1947) was serving her second term as president of the National American Woman Suffrage Association when the Nineteenth Amendment granted the vote to American women. Elected to the presidency in 1913, Wilson announced his support of women's suffrage in 1918. The National Woman's Party, which continues to function as an educational organization, was founded in 1917 to fight for the passage of a Constitutional amendment to guarantee women's suffrage. World War I ended in 1919.

20. D: It is not true that the Gilded Age is a term whose origins have not been identified clearly. In 1873, Mark Twain and Charles Dudley Warner co-authored a book entitled *The Gilded Age: A Tale of Today*. Twain and Warner first coined this term to describe the extravagance and excesses of America's wealthy upper class, who became richer than ever due to industrialization. Furthermore, the Gilded Age was the era of the "robber barons" such as John D. Rockefeller, Cornelius Vanderbilt, J.P. Morgan, and others. Because they accumulated enormous wealth through extremely aggressive and occasionally unethical monetary manipulations, critics dubbed them "robber barons" because they seemed to be elite lords of robbery. While these business tycoons grasped huge fortunes, some of them—such as Andrew Carnegie and Andrew Mellon—were also philanthropists, using their wealth to support and further worthy causes such as literacy, education, health care, charities, and the arts. They donated millions of dollars to fund social improvements. Carnegie himself dubbed this large philanthropic movement the "Gospel of Wealth." Another characteristic of the Gilded Age was the Beaux Arts architectural style, a neo-Renaissance style modeled after the great architectural designs of the European Renaissance. The Panic of 1893 ended the Gilded Age and began a severe four-year economic depression. The Progressive Era followed these events.

21. A: While Martin Luther King is famous for his advocacy of nonviolence, Malcolm X defended self-defense against aggression by white people. In the course of his work, King did indeed mobilize ordinary citizens; however, Malcolm X did not focus on working with local white political leaders, but instead focused on black communities. This eliminates option B. Malcolm X also sometimes spoke against black citizens practicing Christianity, linking the practice of that religion in part to oppression; this eliminates option C. Finally, option D can be rejected because King did not promote Black Nationalism, while Malcolm X did.

22. A: In 1880, ill sentiment was high against Chinese laborers. This sentiment lead to the reversal of the Burlingame Treaty of 1868, and thus legal immigration was stopped for a period of 10 years.

23. D: Because the Puritans took on a Reformed theology, they were in this sense Calvinists. However, many Puritans endorsed radical views that criticized such Calvinists as John (Jean) Calvin and Huldrych (Ulrich) Zwingli in Switzerland. Not only were Puritans critical of Calvinists despite their mutual Reformed approaches, reciprocally many Calvinists were opposed to the Puritans as well. The Puritan movement changed less in American colonies than in England during the 1660s. Following the Restoration (1660) and the Uniformity Act (1662) in England, nearly all of the Puritan clergy objected and left the Church of England, thereby creating a dramatic change in the movement in that country. Nevertheless, in America, the Puritans who had emigrated from England continued their original Puritan traditions for a longer time, as they had neither the same Anglican Church as in England nor the legislation restoring earlier church status against which the English Puritans had reacted.

24. A: Anyone may write a bill, but only a member of Congress can introduce a bill. The President often suggests bills. Bills can change drastically throughout the review process.

25. D: The Truman Doctrine was intended to prevent Greece and Turkey from becoming communist countries. However, its broad language had implications beyond those two nations, suggesting that US policy generally should be to aid people who resisted outside forces attempting to impose communist rule. This doctrine led to US involvement in Korea and Vietnam, where US forces fought against communist forces in those nations. The United States did have a plan for assisting the European economies, but it was the Marshall Plan, not the Truman Doctrine. This eliminates choice B. While President Truman did establish a President's Committee on Civil Rights, it was not as a result of the Truman Doctrine. This eliminates answer A. Finally, when inflation plagued the postwar US economy, the federal government took measures to address inflation and other economic issues, rather than steering clear of them. This eliminates choice C.

26. A: One example of the multiplier effect of large cities would be if the presence of specialized equipment for an industry attracted even more business. Large cities tend to grow even larger for a number of reasons: they have more skilled workers, they have greater concentrations of specialized equipment, and they have already-functioning markets. These factors all make it easier for a business to begin operations in a large city than elsewhere. Thus, the populations and economic productivity of large cities tend to grow quickly. Some governments have sought to mitigate this trend by clustering groups of similar industries in smaller cities.

27. D: Under the Missouri Compromise, Maine would be admitted as a free state while Missouri would enter as a slave state. Slavery would be prohibited in the former Louisiana Territory north of the 36°30' parallel except in the new state of Missouri. Ohio had entered the Union in 1803 under the Northwest Ordinance. Alabama had been admitted as a slave state shortly before the Missouri Compromise. After years of bloody conflict, Kansas entered the Union as a free state in 1861.

28. C: The Gadsden Purchase of 1853 added a small strip of Mexican land in southern Arizona and New Mexico that provided a valuable railroad route to California. Texas was annexed in 1845. The Oregon border dispute between the United States and Great Britain was settled in 1846. The Mexican Cession was part of the Treaty of Guadalupe Hidalgo in 1848.

29. D: The Judiciary Act established the Supreme Court, district courts, circuit courts, and the office of attorney general in 1789. George Washington was inaugurated president in 1789.

30. B: Published in early 1776, *Common Sense* condemned hereditary kingship. The pamphlet was popular in Colonial America, and even George Washington noticed its effect on the general population. Later that same year, Jefferson drafted the Declaration of Independence.

31. A: James Madison, John Jay, and Alexander Hamilton published *The Federalist* in the *Independent Journal* and other publications in New York. It was a response to the Anti-Federalists in New York, who were slow to ratify the Constitution because they feared it gave the central government too much authority.

32. D: The Protestant work ethic is considered by many historians to have contributed to the Industrial Revolution. In Britain, where industrialization started, financial stability encouraged investment in industry, and the eventual dominance of Protestantism is believed to have contributed to a class of entrepreneurs who believed in education, technological progress, and hard work. The other choices are considered effects of industrialization. Mass production enabled the privately owned, for-profit enterprises that characterize capitalist economic systems. Socialism developed as a criticism of capitalism; Karl Marx argued that capitalism polarized societies into owners versus workers. Marx also viewed capitalism as a necessary precursor to socialism within the logical progression of economies. Romanticism also developed in reaction against mechanization and involved using art and literature to contrast nature with the dark side of scientific progress.

33. D: Machinery and transport jumped from 34.3 to 42.0 percent in exports. Also, they went from 9.7 to 28.0 percent in imports. Chemicals increased exports from 8.7 to 9.0. Imports declined from 5.3 to 3.6. So, choice A is incorrect. Crude material exports declined from 13.7 to 10.8. For imports, they declined from 18.3 to 8.3. So, this makes choice B incorrect. The decline in exports of food and beverages was just under 4 percent, and imports declined 7 percent. So, choice C is not correct.

34. C: The earliest instance of Soviet-US differences was in 1945 when the USSR establishment of a communist government in Poland, which prohibited conservative participation (C). In 1947, the Soviets backed the Communist control of Hungary and Romania (A). In 1948, the Soviets also supported communist rule in Czechoslovakia (B). Later the USSR refused to participate in the Baruch Plan (D), which aimed to set up an international agency to manage the use of atomic energy. This action demonstrated an unwillingness to cooperate with other nations in the interest of peace. These events signified the beginning of the Cold War.

35. A: The postwar conference that brought US-Soviet differences to light was the Potsdam conference in July of 1945. The conference at Yalta, in February of 1945, resulted in the division of Germany into Allied-controlled zones. The Dumbarton Oaks conference (1944) established a Security Council, on which with the US, England, Soviet Union, France, and China served as the five permanent members. Each of the permanent members had veto power, and a General Assembly, with limited power, was also established. The Tehran conference included FDR's proposal for a new international organization to take the place of the League of Nations. This idea would later be realized in the form of the United Nations.

36. D: Political corruption was not an immediate effect of the rapid urban growth during this time. The accelerated growth of cities in America did soon result in services being unable to keep up with that growth. The results of this included deficiencies in clean water delivery and garbage collection, causing poor sanitation. That poor sanitation led to outbreaks of cholera and typhus, as well as typhoid fever epidemics. Police and fire fighting services could not keep up with the population increases, and were often inadequate. With people moving to the cities at such a fast rate, there were also deficits in housing and public transportation.

37. C: The rates of both productivity and inflation in the US were approximately 2% by 2000. By this time, the US economy was not increasing at a rate of 5% a year (A) but of 4% a year. Almost half of industrial growth contributing to economic prosperity was due to the "information revolution" made possible by the invention of the PC. The rate of unemployment in America at this time had not gone down to 6% (B) but to 4.7%. The stock market in the US had not just doubled in six years (D); it had actually quadrupled from 1992-1998 due to the increase in American households that owned stocks or bonds. Most of this ownership resulted from tax law changes regulating retirement accounts.

38. A: GDP (Gross Domestic Product) is restricted to value produced within borders, whereas GNP (Gross National Product) is focused on value produced by companies regardless of borders.

39. B: The Seven Years' War was a global military conflict. In the Americas, the conflict was largely between Western European countries, particularly Great Britain and France.

40. D: It gives the correct defining characteristic of the **Roaring Twenties** Era. The economy was strong with a great demand for new products, while culture in this era, also known as the "Jazz Age," became more experimental. A student might pick choice A, which defines the Cold War Era, if he or she focuses on the fact that it is also an era immediately following a World War. A student can rule out the other choices if they know how to correctly define the World War II and Great Depression Eras.

41. B: The Trail of Tears was the forcible removal of Native American tribes from their homes in the Southeastern US to Oklahoma. The name came due to the high number of Native Americans who died on the journey.

42. C: The agricultural revolution. A dependable food supply is essential to all populations. The agricultural revolution, an organized, almost scientific approach to agriculture, increased the food supply necessary for a growing world population.

43. A: When the President sent federal troops, this caused the Whiskey Rebellion to end, which resolved the situation and added to the new government's credibility. It did not result in a setback for the government. It is true that the whiskey tax was central to Hamilton's revenue program (B). It is true that farmers in western states, including Pennsylvania, did not want to pay this tax (C). It is also true that in addition to objecting to the tax and refusing to pay it, a group of farmers in Pennsylvania terrorized tax collectors to make their point (D). It is true that Washington responded to the farmers' terrorism by sending around 15,000 soldiers to quell the Whiskey Rebellion in 1794.

44. D: While rising prices may hurt many members of an economy, those same rising prices may benefit other members of the same economy. For example, rising prices may help those who sell goods and services and are able to keep their costs of production low, increasing their profit margin. Meanwhile, rising prices can hurt consumers because their income is now able to purchase fewer goods and services than before.

45. D: All of the statements regarding movements for reform in 1840s America are true. This was a period of change in society, meaning that conditions were unstable and people felt uncertainty (A). Additionally, many Americans during this time were challenging the old traditions and values (B). Romanticism began in Europe and spread to the New World as a reaction against the rationalism of the Enlightenment in both places. Romantics, preferring emotions over reason, had an optimistic belief in the basic goodness of humanity and in its ability to become better, which lent itself well to ideas of reform (C). The movements for reform during this time were centered in the Northeastern states, particularly in the New England states.

46. C: The main subject matter of civic responsibility is a person's responsibilities as a citizen. By contrast, the main subject matter of personal responsibility is one's responsibilities as a person. For example, keeping a promise to a friend is often a matter of personal responsibility because such a duty arises from the friendship. Serving on a jury when called to do so is an example of civic responsibility because such a duty arises from the person's citizenship. None of the other options given accurately describe the main subject matter of civic responsibility. For example, while a journalist might see accurate reporting of government actions as his or her civic responsibility, such reporting is not the main subject matter of civic responsibility and is also a responsibility that arises from that journalist's employment. Similar reasoning applies to a person's responsibilities as a government worker. This eliminates options A and D. Civic responsibility does not primarily concern inter-government relations; this eliminates option B.

47. B: After World War I, the United States passed the Immigration Act of 1924, which regulated the number of immigrants in part according to their national origin. The United States sought to avoid the problems of Europe and other nations by limiting the number of foreigners who entered the United States. Option A can be rejected because quite soon after World War I, both inflation and unemployment were significant problems in the United States. Option C can be rejected because in the years immediately following World War I, the United States did not build its navy even to the extent allowed by treaty. Finally, option D can be rejected because after World War I, the United States made arrangements for the US to have access to oil in Colombia and in Middle Eastern countries.

48. B: The term "Manifest Destiny" originated with the annexation of Texas as Americans began to envision a nation that spread from coast to coast. Texas entered the union as a slave state. The Monroe Doctrine addressed European intervention in the Western Hemisphere, which was not an issue in the annexation of Texas. Mexican resentment of the annexation was a factor in the Mexican War, which began the following year.

49. B: Crude material imports declined by 10 percentage points. All other categories saw imports that declined less than 10 points over the decade. Chemicals decreased in that time by only 1.7 percent. So, this makes choice A incorrect. Choice C is also incorrect. Food and beverages decreased during those ten years by just over 7 percent. Imports of machinery and transport nearly tripled, rather than decreased. This means that choice D is incorrect.

50. D: Although the Thirteenth, Fourteenth, and Fifteenth Amendments guaranteed certain legal protection to African Americans, Southern whites were able to retain power by enacting various restrictions on voting. Lacking formal education and deprived of their right to vote, freed slaves were unable to attain political or economic power in the South.

51. C: While wounds from war most certainly killed more than a few, European disease laid waste to vast swaths of Native American people who had no immunity to the foreign diseases which the

Europeans carried. The forced marches took place in the mid-19th century under Andrew Jackson's presidency and are thus removed from the time frame in question.

52. D: Student sit-ins were an example in the 1960s of non-violent protesting that took place mostly under the guidance and philosophy of Martin Luther King, Jr. These were not displays of Black Power to incite fear, although those also occurred separately in the 1960s under leaders such as Malcolm X. Sit-ins were not a form of lobbying or litigation, although those are also non-violent in their nature.

53. C: Exploration between the 15th and 17th centuries resulted in contact between European cultures and many previously unknown or little-known cultures. Navigation techniques improved, food and other goods were imported, and the New World began to be settled. Rather than declining in influence, England became a more prominent imperial power during this era.

54. B: There was not a reduction in military spending after the war. Although the manufacturing demand for war supplies and the size of the military decreased, the government had increased military spending from $10 billion in 1947 to more than $50 billion by 1953—a more than fivefold increase. This increase strengthened the American economy. Other factors contributing to the strengthened economy included the significantly higher birth rates during the Baby Boom from 1946 to 1957, which stimulated the growth of the building and automotive industries by increased demand. Government programs, such as the GI Bill (the Servicemen's Readjustment Act of 1944), other veterans' benefits, and the National Defense Education Act all encouraged college enrollments, which increased by nearly four times. Additionally, larger families, increased mobility and low-interest loans offered to veterans led to suburban development and growth as well as increased home construction. Improvements in public health were also results of the new affluence; the rate of infant deaths decreased significantly, and as a result, from 1946–1957, the American life span rose from 67 to 71 years. Moreover, Dr. Jonas Salk developed the polio vaccine in 1955, which virtually wiped out poliomyelitis, preventing many deaths and disabilities in children.

55. A: W.E.B. DuBois was a famous African American muckraking journalist for the NAACP's magazine in the early 1900s. Booker T. Washington was a contemporary of DuBois, but not a muckraking journalist. Gaines was a former slave who became a Texas State Senator, but Gaines died in 1900 and therefore could not be the correct answer. Marcus Garvey had a writing career advocating civil rights, but in a newspaper he started called *The Negro World*.

56. B: It is the BEST summary for what President Warren Harding meant by a "Return to Normalcy." He was calling for a return to peaceful times and a focus on domestic issues, as opposed to a focus on international war. Choice A is a good guess because the president would want a good economy, and industry had been busy during WWI before falling off slightly after the war. But choice B is the best answer. He was not calling for going out in search of more territories or for higher immigration rates.

57. B: Reagan did not escalate military action in response to a terrorist bombing that killed 240 US Marines. Reagan sent the Marines to Lebanon in 1982 as part of a peacekeeping effort after Israel invaded Lebanon on a mission to eradicate its PLO camps. At the time, Lebanon was already engaged in a civil war. When the terrorist attack killed 240 Marines, Reagan withdrew the rest of the troops rather than escalate the action.

58. A: It is not true that the US captured Osama bin Laden shortly after the attacks. On October 7, the US attacked the Taliban regime in Afghanistan and defeated it in November, so these events did occur shortly after September 11, 2001, but bin Laden was not captured and killed until nearly ten years later, on May 2, 2011. It is true that Muslim terrorists flew two of the four American airplanes they had hijacked into the twin towers of the World Trade Center in New York City (B). They flew the third of the four planes into the US Department of Defense's headquarters, the Pentagon building in Arlington, Virginia, (C) near Washington, D.C. The fourth plane crashed in a field near Shanksville, Pennsylvania, after some of the passengers on board tried to overtake the terrorists (D). President George W. Bush announced a "war on terrorism" after these attacks killed a total of 2,995 people.

59. A: The Dust Bowl was a period of time, largely coinciding with the Great Depression, in which severe droughts, poor farming techniques, wind erosion and several other factors led to the collapse of farming in the southern Plains states. High grain prices had encouraged farmers to over-cultivate their fields and to bring previously uncultivated land under cultivation, leading to soil depletion and an overall loss in soil moisture as farmers would frequently burn their wheat stubble. This was a problem because the long grasses in the Plains states had previously been instrumental in keeping the soil in place. This loss meant that windstorms now began picking up soil, eroding fields and destroying crops. The Dust Bowl resulted in thousands of farmers losing their farms. Many of them traveled to California where they worked as migrant farm workers. John Steinbeck's *The Grapes of Wrath* tells the story of one family who lost their farm in Oklahoma due to the Dust Bowl.

60. D: The last federal troops were removed from the South in 1877 following the inauguration of Republican President Rutherford b. Hayes. The goals of reunifying the country and establishing functional state governments in the South were not marked by Lincoln's assassination in 1865, ratification of the 14th Amendment in 1868, or the 1868 impeachment of Andrew Johnson.

Practice Test #2

1. The strategy of containment was a major element of American foreign policy during:

a. The Spanish-American War
b. World War I
c. World War II
d. The Cold War

2. On a geographical map, which of the following requires using a ratio to interpret?

a. The key or legend
b. The compass rose
c. The scale of miles
d. The lines in a grid

3. The "laissez-faire" economists of the late 1800s, before Progressives had more influence, believed that businesses were best regulated by which entity?

a. Federal government
b. State or local governments
c. Trust-busting laws
d. Marketplace forces

4. Which of the following is NOT a correct statement regarding the Pilgrims?

a. The Pilgrims left England in 1620 on the ship known as the *Mayflower* and landed at Cape Cod.
b. The Pilgrims were led by William Bradford with a charter from the London Company.
c. The Pilgrims were a group of Puritans who left England to escape religious persecution.
d. The Pilgrims were a group of separatists who migrated to leave the Church of England.

5. Why was US industrialization confined to the Northeast until after the Civil War?

a. Because the Civil War delayed the development of water-powered manufacturing
b. Because the Northeast had faster-running rivers than the rivers found in the South
c. Because Slater's first cotton mill with horse-drawn production lost so much money
d. Because the technical innovations for milling textiles had not as yet been invented

6. In LBJ's Great Society program, which of the following was NOT included?

a. Medicare
b. Voting rights
c. Federal aid to education
d. Ending the Vietnam War

7. How were the Mexican-American War and the US annexation of Texas connected?

a. Mexico had informed Texas that an agreement to join the United States was the same as a declaration of war.
b. The Mexican War began as Texas's war of independence.
c. Mexico wanted Texas to remain independent as a buffer between itself and the US and declared war in hopes of halting the annexation.
d. There was no relation. Mexico did not care what Texas did.

8. The Lincoln-Douglas debates resulted in

a. the declaration of Illinois as a slave state.
b. the split of the Democratic Party.
c. the election of Douglas as president in 1860.
d. the election of Lincoln to the senate in 1858.

9. Marxism had a profound influence on the development of

a. the Bolshevik political movement.
b. Autumn Harvest Uprising.
c. the National Socialist German Workers' Party
d. the Greek Civil war

10. In economic terms, which of the following is considered investment?

a. Buying a new home computer
b. Construction of a new manufacturing plant
c. Purchase of a college education
d. Selling finished goods to a customer

11. Which of the following is NOT true about the Second Great Awakening?

a. This movement was a reaction against the Enlightenment emphasis on rationalism.
b. This movement emphasized individualized, personalized, emotional religious faith.
c. This movement was characterized by the participation of large numbers of women.
d. This movement's individualistic nature contradicted nationalism and expansionism.

12. Of the following, who was NOT a dispatch rider notifying Americans of British troop movements reported by American surveillance in 1775?

a. Paul Revere
b. William Dawes
c. John Parker
d. Samuel Prescott

13. The 1783 Treaty of Paris included which of the following agreements?

a. Boundaries were established for the United States, including the southern tip of Florida as the southernmost boundary.
b. Britain was allowed to keep both Canada and Florida as imperial British territories under the terms of the Treaty of Paris.
c. The treaty stipulated that all private creditors in Britain were prohibited from making future debt collections from Americans.
d. Britain and the other most powerful countries of Europe recognized the United States' independence as a nation.

14. During the Civil Rights era of the 1950s, which of the following events furthered the civil rights cause?

a. The Supreme Court's decision in *Brown v. Board of Education of Topeka*
b. Governor Orval Faubus' actions relative to Little Rock High School
c. Eisenhower's use of the 101st Airborne Division to protect students
d. Both A and C

15. What is the main reason that the Federal Reserve Board lowers interest rates?

a. To lower prices
b. To stimulate consumer spending
c. To encourage international trade
d. To keep inflation low

16. As used in geographical maps, which of the following is a synonym for the term *latitude?*

a. Longitude
b. Parallel
c. Meridian
d. Coordinate

17. The link between female activists and the temperance movement in the 19th century is best explained by concerns regarding the relationship between alcohol and:

a. Racial violence
b. Lost productivity
c. Domestic violence
d. Infertility

18. In a market economy, what is the theoretical basis for the price of an individual good?

a. Central Control
b. Supply and Demand
c. Cost Gouging
d. Income and Industry

Refer to the following for question 19:

> In this excerpt from *The Black Experience in America*, author Norman Coombs describes 1941 negotiations between civil rights activist A. Philip Randolph, who was planning a March on Washington by African Americans, and President Franklin D. Roosevelt:
>
> "Finally, Roosevelt contacted Randolph and offered to issue an executive order barring discrimination in defense industries and promised to put "teeth" in the order, provided Randolph call off the march. When Randolph became convinced that Roosevelt's intentions were sincere, he complied.
>
> Roosevelt fulfilled his promise by issuing Executive Order 8802, which condemned discrimination on the grounds of race, color, or creed. Then, he established the Fair Employment Practices Commission and assigned to it the responsibility for enforcing the order."

19. What conclusion can BEST be made based on this excerpt?

a. Jobs for African Americans increased during World War II because of manpower needs and because of an anti-discrimination order from the president
b. Jobs for African Americans increased during World War II because of manpower needs alone, and the anti-discrimination order was probably not really needed
c. A. Philip Randolph was just bluffing about planning a March on Washington
d. President Franklin D. Roosevelt was not really worried about African Americans marching on Washington, but he gave in to Randolph's request for an Executive Order anyway

20. Which of the following methods was NOT used by suffragettes in their attempt to get the 19th Amendment (allowing women the right to vote) passed?

a. Marches
b. Nonviolent protests
c. Speeches and written articles
d. Payments to key senators to help the cause

21. When was the first American transcontinental railroad finished?

a. 1862
b. 1890
c. 1869
d. 1865

22. What would be the BEST title to summarize this list?

- Poor agricultural practices
- Years of drought
- Lack of ground cover to hold soil in place
- High winds on the plains

a. Causes of the 1935 Dust Bowl
b. Effects of the 1935 Dust Bowl
c. Issues for the 1970s Era Rust Belt
d. Issues for the 1970s Era Sun Belt

23. The Underground Railroad was primarily:

a. A route for abolitionists to smuggle weapons
b. A route for slave owners to traffic slaves
c. A means for slaves to travel to free states
d. A strategy for state control of railway construction

24. The price of oil drops dramatically, saving soda pop manufacturers great amounts of money spent on making soda pop and delivering their product to market. Prices for soda pop, however, stay the same. This is an example of what?

a. Sticky prices
b. Indiscriminate costs
c. Stable demand
d. Aggregate expenditure

25. Which of the following is NOT true regarding the Virginia Companies?

a. One of these companies, the Virginia Company of Plymouth, made its base in North America.
b. One of these companies, the Virginia Company of London, made its base in Massachusetts.
c. One company had a charter to colonize America between the Hudson and Cape Fear rivers.
d. One company had a charter to colonize America from the Potomac River to north Maine.

26. Which of these is true concerning the French Revolution, America, and Europe?

a. When France's revolution spread and they went to war with other European countries, George Washington allied with the French.
b. During the time period around 1792, American merchants were trading with countries on both sides of the war.
c. American traders conducted business with various countries, profiting the most from the British West Indies.
d. The Spanish navy retaliated against America for trading with the French by capturing American trading ships.

27. Which of these presidents most greatly expanded the power of the presidency?

a. Thomas Jefferson
b. Herbert Hoover
c. Lyndon Johnson
d. Ronald Reagan

28. During World War II, Japanese Americans in internment camps were denied the right to be brought before a court to challenge the legality of their imprisonment. This was a violation of which constitutional right?

a. Right against involuntary servitude
b. Right to habeas corpus
c. Right to assemble
d. Right to vote

29. The concept of due process in the Fifth Amendment to the U.S. Constitution protects individuals in which of the following ways?

a. Guaranteeing a citizen's right to a trial by jury within a reasonable timeframe
b. Restricting the government's ability to remove basic rights without following the law
c. Guaranteeing a citizen's right to equal protection under the law
d. Restricting the government's ability to remove basic rights without dire cause

30. The First Amendment to the Constitution deals mainly with which of the following?

a. The right of free expression
b. The right to a speedy and public trial
c. Protection from cruel and unusual punishment
d. Freedom from unreasonable search and seizure

31. Which of the following statements regarding immigration to America during the 1980s is NOT true?

a. Twice as many immigrants came to America during the 1980s than during the 1970s.
b. Latin Americans comprised the largest proportion of immigrants to America in the 1980s.
c. Most immigrants to the US in the 1980s were Latin American, Asian, and Caribbean.
d. The 1986 Immigration Reform and Control Act impeded illegal Mexican immigration.

32. Which of the following written works did Thomas Paine publish after the American Revolution?

a. *Common Sense*
b. *Rights of Man*
c. *The Age of Reason*
d. *Rights of Man* and *The Age of Reason*

33. Which of the following did NOT contribute to ending America's neutrality in World War I?

a. Germany's telegram to Mexico that proposed they form an alliance if the US entered the war
b. Germany's declaration of a war on Russia after Archduke Ferdinand's assassination
c. Germany's sinking the British ship Lusitania, which killed 128 American passengers
d. Germany's declaration of unrestricted submarine warfare on all ships in the war zone

34. After the Civil War, urban populations increased. This growth was likely due to:

a. An increased reliance on agriculture
b. The Industrial Revolution
c. Prohibition
d. Slavery persisting in some areas

35. In the early 1950s, the birthrate in the US kept climbing steadily each year, from around 3.6 million births in 1950 to 4.3 million births in 1957. Which phrase BEST describes this post war phenomenon, and tells an effect of the phenomenon?

a. "Baby Boom," benefitted the US economy and led to a greater demand for consumer products
b. "Women Quitting Work Effect," caused an increase in employment opportunities for men
c. "Soldiers Returning Effect," caused more out-of-wedlock births
d. "Baby Bust," led to decreased prosperity in the 1950s

36. Which reason or reasons BEST explain why the US Office of War Information included famous stars such as Ethel Merman in their radio broadcasts in the 1940s?

a. To build morale, raise spirits, and help convince women they needed to stay home while men went to war
b. To build morale, raise spirits, and help convince women to apply for wartime work
c. To convince women to buy tickets to Broadway shows to support the US economy during wartime
d. To convince women to buy movie tickets to support the US economy during wartime

37. Which of the following was NOT a tax levied on the American colonies by the British government in the 1760s and '70s?

a. The Sugar Act of 1764
b. The Stamp Act of 1765
c. The Lead Act of 1772
d. The Tea Act of 1773

38. Which of the following did NOT contribute to differences in the lives of New England colonists vs. the lives of Chesapeake colonists during the 17th century?

a. In Virginia and Maryland, female settlers greatly outnumbered male settlers.
b. New England colonists had significantly longer life expectancies than did Chesapeake colonists.
c. New England colonists had a better organized, more stable society than did Chesapeake colonists.
d. New England colonists had educational advantages over Chesapeake colonists.

Refer to the following for question 39:

Westward Migration

Year	Estimated Number of People Headed West
1844	2,000
1849	30,000
1854	10,000
1859	30,000
1864	20,000

39. Given the increase of population, which of the following statements is most likely to be true?

a. More children were being born in 1849 and 1859.
b. Most of the new migrants were women who wanted to open businesses.
c. The Civil War increased the westward migration.
d. Cities and towns in the West grew and supported many businesses.

40. Which of the following represents a discretionary expense?

a. Textbook
b. Rent
c. DVD
d. Groceries

41. Which country put the first satellite in space in 1957?

a. Russia
b. United States
c. Germany
d. Korea

42. A group that grew in numbers as a result of the Industrial Revolution was:

a. Small farmers.
b. Unskilled workers.
c. Skilled craftsmen.
d. The rural population.

43. What was the purpose of Lyndon Johnson's Great Society?

a. To eliminate poverty and racial injustice in America
b. To erase the last vestiges of the Great Depression from the American economic landscape
c. To encourage economic prosperity through trickledown economics
d. To increase educational standards in the United States

44. Following World War I, African Americans migrated in great numbers to the north for what reason?

a. New federal laws banned employment discrimination in the northern states.
b. Returning African-Americans veterans were not used to the rural economy of the South.
c. Greater job opportunities were available in northern cities.
d. Northern states had passed laws to assure equal voting rights for all Americans.

45. Which of the following was a method that the government in Nazi Germany used gain control of German children?

a. Mandating membership in government sponsored youth organizations
b. Including propaganda in textbooks
c. Mandating activities scheduled to conflict with church services and interfere with family life
d. All of the above

46. Power divided between local and central branches of government is a definition of what term?

a. Bicameralism
b. Checks and balances
c. Legislative oversight
d. Federalism

47. Which of the following helped prepare the US for entry into World War I?

a. The National Defense Act
b. The Navy Act
c. The Revenue Act
d. All of the above

48. Which of the following was an example of violence in cities that occurred as a result of rapid urbanization in America in the 1830s?

a. Democrats opposed Whigs in New York City so strenuously that the state militia was called in.
b. Both New York City and Philadelphia experienced a series of racial riots during the mid-1830s.
c. A Catholic convent was attacked and plundered by a violent mob in New York City in 1834.
d. All of the above occurred in American cities during the 1830s.

49. The "sit-ins" of the civil rights movement during the 1960s were most important to which subsequent reform?

a. Integration of the United States armed forces
b. Banning of literacy tests as a requirement for voter registration
c. Integration of lunch counters, theaters, and other businesses
d. The Supreme Court decision outlawing "separate but equal" schools

50. Which of the following examples is protected as an expression of free speech?

a. Draftees of the Vietnam War who burned their draft cards.
b. A radio personality who states on air that the President should be shot over his most recent budget proposal.
c. Pro-life protesters who carry "wanted" signs displaying the photos and home/work addresses of abortion providers during a legally sanctioned protest.
d. A high school teacher who allows her students to use profanity when creating poetry.

51. What invention increased the value and demand for slaves in the South?

a. the combine
b. the steam engine
c. the cotton gin
d. the automobile

52. Which of the following is NOT a way that the Internet has affected worldwide economies?

a. It made near instantaneous communication possible.
b. It caused an overall increase in the cost of transactions.
c. It increased consumer access to goods.
d. It decreased the barriers to entry in retail situations.

53. Which statement about relations between the Middle East and the US and Europe in the 1950s is NOT correct?

a. President Nasser of Egypt refused to align with the US in the Cold War.
b. President Eisenhower removed US funding from the Aswan Dam in 1956.
c. President Nasser nationalized the Suez Canal, which was owned by England.
d. In 1956, Egypt attacked Israel, and England and France joined in the war.

54. Which statement regarding US international trade policy in the 1990s is NOT correct?

a. In 1994, the General Agreement on Tariffs and Trade (GATT) was approved by Congress.
b. The 57 countries that signed the GATT agreed to remove or reduce many of their tariffs.
c. The GATT created the World Trade Organization (WTO) to settle international trade differences.
d. The NAFTA (North American Free Trade Agreement), ratified in 1994, had originally been set up by George H.W. Bush's administration.

55. Unlike slaves, who were considered to be the property of their masters, which of the following was true regarding most indentured servants in colonial times?

a. They received wages for their labor
b. They were generally treated kindly by their employers
c. They were highly educated
d. They voluntarily entered into servitude

56. How did the ruling in *Marbury v. Madison* alter the Supreme Court's power in the federal government?

a. It lessened it. The Supreme Court was concerned about the possibility of judges overturning laws enacted by voters through referendums and took away that power.
b. It increased it. The decision in *Marbury v. Madison* gave the Supreme Court its now traditional right to overturn legislation.
c. It increased it. The decision in *Marbury v. Madison* strengthened the Supreme Court's Constitutional right to overturn legislation.
d. There was no change. *Marbury v. Madison* was a case involving a president who was unwilling to obey laws enacted by his predecessor; there was nothing about the case or decision that would have more than a cursory connection to federal powers of government

57. In 1890, the US government passed the Sherman Antitrust Act. The Act has been most influential in restricting anticompetitive practices by:

a. Outlawing acts that restrained interstate trade
b. Its use in dissolving the Standard Oil trust
c. Outlawing acts that restrained intrastate trade
d. By its use in dissolving the AT&T monopoly

58. Which of the following is NOT a true statement about the Second World War?

a. It was a war wherein nations mobilized civilian as well as military resources.
b. It was a war wherein nations destroyed civilian as well as military personnel.
c. It eventually became known as "The War to End All Wars."
d. It was the first war in history to detonate nuclear devices.

59. What was the immediate result of the Lincoln-Douglas debates?

a. Lincoln's election to the United States Senate
b. Douglas's election to the United States Senate
c. Lincoln's election to the Illinois State Senate
d. Lincoln's election as President of the United States

Refer to the following for question 60:

United States Foreign Trade 1960–1970

(by Category Percentages)

Category	**1960**		**1970**	
	Exports	Imports	Exports	Imports
Chemicals	8.7	5.3	9.0	3.6
Crude materials (except fuel)	13.7	18.3	10.8	8.3
Food and beverages, including tobacco	15.6	22.5	11.8	15.6
Machinery and transport	34.3	9.7	42.0	28.0

60. In 1960, which of the following categories had the greatest disparity between percentage of both exports and imports?

a. Chemicals
b. Crude materials
c. Food and beverages
d. Machinery and transport

Answer Key and Explanations for Test #2

1. D: Formulated during the Truman administration and enduring throughout the Cold War, the policy of containment was intended to prevent the spread of Communism after World War II. It served as a rationale for many military decisions during the Korean and Vietnamese conflicts.

2. C: In cartography, the scale of miles on a map enables us to estimate actual distances between places. For example, a map's scale of miles may state that one inch equals 500 miles. Thus, a ratio is required to interpret this information: by measuring with a ruler, if we see that the distance on the map between two cities, states, or countries equals six inches, then we can estimate the actual distance between these locations to be 3,000 miles. The key or legend (A) on a map identifies what the different symbols and colors used in the map indicate. The compass rose (B) on a map shows north, south, east, and west directions so we can see the orientations of different places. The lines in a grid (D) on a map indicate latitudes, or parallels, which run east-west, and longitudes, or meridians, which run north-south. By finding the intersection of latitude and longitude coordinates for a given place, we can determine its absolute location.

3. D: It is the best description of what laissez-faire economists believed, which is that marketplace forces were enough to regulate businesses. In contrast, most Progressives wanted more trust-busting laws and federal, state, and local government intervention to help regulate businesses that were perhaps producing unsafe products, forming monopolies to drive up prices, or taking advantage of working people.

4. C: The Pilgrims were not Puritans seeking to escape religious persecution in England. They were actually English Separatists (D) who believed there was no fixing the Church of England, and thus chose to separate from it. They did embark on the *Mayflower* in 1620, and storms drove the ship to land at Cape Cod, Massachusetts (A). Their leader was William Bradford, and they had been given a charter by the London Company to settle America (B) south of the Hudson River.

5. B: US industrialization was confined to the Northeast until after the Civil War because the Northeast had faster-running rivers than the South. The earliest American factories used horse-drawn machines. When waterpower was developed and proved superior, the Northeast's faster rivers were more suited to water-powered mills than the South's slower rivers. The war did not delay the development of waterpower. Waterpower was developed before the Civil War in the late 1790s. Steam power, a more efficient alternative to waterpower, was developed after the Civil War and eventually replaced waterpower. With steam-powered engines, industry could spread to the South, since steam engines did not depend on rapidly running water like water-powered engines. While British emigré Samuel Slater's first cotton mill using horse-drawn production did lose a lot of money, this was not a reason for industrial delay. In fact, Slater's Beverly Cotton Manufactory in Massachusetts, the first American cotton mill, in spite of its financial problems, was successful in both its volume of cotton production and in developing the water-powered technology that ultimately would succeed the horse-drawn method. Slater's second cotton mill in Pawtucket, Rhode Island, was water-powered. Industrial delay was not because milling technology had not yet been invented. Slater learned of new textile manufacturing techniques as a youth in England, and he brought this knowledge to America in 1789.

6. D: The war ended during Nixon's administration, not during LBJ's term. The Great Society program included legislation to create Medicare (A), eliminate obstacles hindering the right to vote (B), provide federal funding for education (C), and establish the Department of Housing and Urban

Development (HUD). The Great Society also included a number of programs aimed at alleviating poverty. Johnson's social reform accomplishments were overshadowed by the Vietnam War during his last two years in office.

7. A: The Texas Rebellion began in 1835 when a group of Texan leaders declared independence from Mexico. Texas won independence in 1836, but the US initially held back on plans for annexation due to concerns that such an act would lead to war with Mexico. In 1845, however, the US Senate ratified the treaty and Texas became the country's 28th state on December 29 of that year. The war with Mexico, which had broken off diplomatic relations with the US in 1844 when the treaty was agreed upon, began in 1846 following news of skirmishes between American and Mexican forces along the Rio Grande.

8. B: The debates between Lincoln, a Republican, and Douglas, a Democrat, resulted in Douglas making statements about slavery that the South would not accept. This resulted in the split of the Democratic Party and the defeat of Douglas in the presidential election in 1860.

9. A: Marxism is a term applied to the political, economic, and social theories advanced by Marx and Engels. Marx's theories had a profound influence on the development of Socialist movements and were the basis for the Bolshevik political movement lead by Lenin.

10. B: Any expenditure that will increase a firm's future productivity is considered investment. Of the items listed, only the construction of a new plant matches the definition.

11. D: It is not true that the Second Great Awakening's individualistic nature contradicted nationalism and expansionism. While it did have an individualistic nature, this evangelical movement, which started in 1801 at the first camp meeting in Cane Ridge, Kentucky, also created significant nationalistic feelings. These later resurfaced in the expansionist beliefs of Manifest Destiny. Therefore, the Second Great Awakening actually influenced nationalism and expansionism rather than contradicting them. In fact, the social implications of the Second Great Awakening later helped to ignite the major reform movements of the 1830s and 1840s. This movement was definitely a reaction to Enlightenment's focus on rationalism (A), and it did emphasize a type of religious faith that was individual, personal, and emotional (B). Women (C) participated in this movement in large numbers.

12. C: Paul Revere and William Dawes were both dispatch riders who set out on horseback from Massachusetts to spread news of British troop movements across the American countryside around the beginning of the War of Independence. John Parker was the captain of the Minutemen militia, who were waiting for the British at Lexington, Massachusetts. Samuel Prescott, a young physician, joined Paul Revere and William Dawes along their route.

13. D: The Treaty of Paris of 1783 did state that Britain and the other leading European countries now recognized the United States of America as an independent country. This treaty also set boundaries, but the southern tip of Florida was not the southern boundary (A). It was the northern boundary of Florida, which became a Spanish territory. Therefore, it is not true that Britain kept both Canada and Florida under this treaty (B). Canada did remain a British territory under its terms, but Britain had to cede Florida to Spain. The Treaty of Paris also gave private British creditors freedom to collect debts from Americans, not the reverse (C). The treaty also stipulated that property confiscated from loyalists during the war should be given back, not kept. Other terms of the Treaty of Paris included that the western boundary of the United States would be the Mississippi River.

14. D: Both answer A and answer C furthered the civil rights cause, but answer B impeded this cause. In the case of *Brown v. Board of Education of Topeka*, the Supreme Court's 1954 ruling stated that schools segregated by race are by nature not equal. This ruling was monumental in the NAACP's fight against school segregation. Orval Faubus, Governor of Arkansas, tried to prevent Little Rock High School's integration in 1957 (B). The situation escalated to the point that President Eisenhower nationalized the Arkansas National Guard and sent the 101st Airborne Division to protect the high school students from harm (C). These actions furthered civil rights by showing the government's defense of school integration.

15. B: Lower interest rates allow banks to lend out more money, which serves to stimulate consumer spending. Increased spending tends to raise, not lower, prices, which also increases inflation. The Federal Reserve Board is not actively involved in international trade.

16. B: Latitudes are lines that run east and west on geographical maps, and are also called parallels. Longitudes (A) are lines that run north and south, so longitude is not a synonym for latitude. Longitudes are also called meridians (C), so meridian is a synonym for longitude, not latitude. Coordinates (D) are the numbers of degrees assigned to various longitudes and latitudes.

17. C: Women, including notable women's rights activists such as Susan B. Anthony, figured importantly in the temperance movement of the 19th century in the United States. Many women were motivated not only by the association of saloons with gambling and prostitution, but by the association of alcohol and domestic violence. Lost productivity was a concern held by figures such as Henry Ford, but figured less prominently with respect to women's role in the temperance movement. This eliminates option B. Option D, infertility, was not a motivating factor. Regarding option A, some women's rights activists were also concerned about race relations and racial injustice, but a specific concern about racial violence was not a primary motivating factor behind the drive for temperance.

18. B: In a pure market economy, price is typically seen as a reflection of supply and demand. A larger supply will result in a lower price and a greater demand will result in a lower price.

19. A: It is the best conclusion to be made based on the facts in the excerpt: Jobs for African Americans increased during World War II because of manpower needs and because of an anti-discrimination order from the president. The jobs would not have come without the executive order because there was still a lot of discrimination against African Americans in the 1940s (as is described in Coombs' book, paragraphs just before and after this excerpt). Roosevelt was concerned about Randolph planning a march because of how it might appear to US enemies during the war, and Randolph was not bluffing. Randolph said discrimination by whites, not his march, was the reason that the US would appear in a poor light to enemies or other countries.

20. D: Payments to senators were not a method used by suffragettes trying to get the 19th Amendment allowing women the right to vote passed. They did use all of the other methods, however, such as speeches, writing articles, nonviolent protesting, and marching.

21. C: The first transcontinental railroad was finished in 1869 (C) on May 10. Construction on the railroad was begun in 1862 (A) but not completed until seven years later. After completion, economic depression prevented more railroad building until the 1890s (B). In 1865 (D), there were 35 000 miles of railroad track in the country; by 1890 (B), there were 200 000 miles. The first transcontinental railroad connected the Central Pacific Railroad, which began in Sacramento, California, to the Union Pacific Railroad, which began in Omaha, Nebraska, in Utah.

22. A: It is the BEST title for the list, The Causes of the 1935 Dust Bowl. The lack of ground cover was a cause of the Dust Bowl, but could also be considered a possible effect of dust storms also. But that is the only item on the list that would also be an effect of the Dust Bowl. The Sun Belt also had some years of drought, but the other items would not fit for Sun Belt as much, or for the Rust Belt except for possibly poor agricultural practices.

23. C: The Underground Railroad was not necessary literally a railroad but a series of clandestine paths to move runaway and freed slaves out of Southern States prior to 1865.

24. A: The phenomenon of "sticky prices" refers to prices that stay the same even though it seems they should change (either increasing or decreasing).

25. B: The Virginia Company of London was based in London, not Massachusetts. It had a charter to colonize American land between the Hudson and Cape Fear rivers. The other Virginia Company was the Virginia Company of Plymouth, which was based in the American colony of Plymouth, Massachusetts. It had a charter to colonize North America between the Potomac River and the northern boundary of Maine. Both Virginia Companies were joint-stock companies, which had often been used by England for trading with other countries.

26. B: In 1792, when the French Revolution turned into European war, American traders conducted business with both sides. It is not true that Washington allied with the French at this time. Washington issued a Proclamation of Neutrality in 1792 when the French went to war with European countries. While they did trade with both sides, American merchants profited the most from the French West Indies, not the British West Indies. The Spanish navy did not retaliate against America for trading with the French. Though Spain was an ally of Britain, it was the British who most often seized American ships and forced their crews to serve the British navy. Edmond-Charles Genêt, or Citizen Genêt, a French ambassador to the United States during the French Revolution, defied Washington's policy of neutrality by encouraging the American people to support the French. Washington was embarrassed by this violation. He did not agree with it.

27. C: Johnson exerted his presidential power to advance the Great Society agenda and to enact major civil rights legislation. He also conducted a war in Vietnam without Congressional declaration. Jefferson, Hoover, and Reagan were all outspoken advocates of limiting the role of government, including the executive branch.

28. B: Students who know the meaning of "right to habeas corpus" will know that it means the right to be brought before a court, which was unconstitutionally denied to Japanese Americans in internment camps during World War II. The other options are all rights which were also violated against Japanese Americans in camps, but not in this particular example of not getting a court date. A student who does not know the meaning of *habeas corpus* may be able to use process of elimination about the other rights (although they may confuse "assembling" with going to a court, or confuse "involuntary servitude" with camp "imprisonment") in order to get the correct answer.

29. B: Under the Fifth Amendment to the U.S. Constitution, the government may not strip certain basic rights from citizens without following the law. In the language of the Fifth Amendment itself, a person shall not "be deprived of life, liberty, or property without due process of law." Of all the options, option B is the only one that accurately describes the concept of due process as understood in the Fifth Amendment. Because due process does not explicitly guarantee a trial by jury within a reasonable timeframe, nor equal protection under the law (concepts covered elsewhere in the Constitution), options A and C can be rejected. Option D can be rejected because the Constitution restricts the government's ability to take away certain rights without following the law, not without a "dire cause" (such as the threat of imminent attack).

30. A: The First Amendment addresses freedom of speech, assembly, religion, and the press. A speedy trial is covered in the Sixth Amendment, cruel and unusual punishment in the Eighth Amendment, and search and seizure in the Fourth Amendment.

31. D: The statement that the 1986 Immigration Reform and Control Act impeded illegal Mexican immigration is not true. This legislation punished employers with sanctions for hiring undocumented employees, but despite this the illegal immigration of Mexicans to America was largely unaffected by the law. It is true that twice as many people immigrated to America in the 1980s than in the 1970s: the number reached over nine million in the 1980s. It is true that the majority of immigrants were Latin American. In addition to Latin Americans, other large groups of immigrants in the 1980s were Asians and Caribbean inhabitants.

32. D: The written works Thomas Paine published *after* the American Revolution (1765-1783) were both *Rights of Man* and *The Age of Reason*. His *Rights of Man* (B) was published in 1791 in response to Edmund Burke's pamphlet *Reflections on the Revolution in France*, which criticized the French Revolution. Paine's *Rights of Man* defended the French Revolution. *The Age of Reason* (C) was a book Paine published in 1793-1794, which advocated deism and rationalism while criticizing traditional Christian beliefs and institutionalized religions. *Common Sense (A)* was a pamphlet Paine published in 1776, which was widely read and very influential to the American Revolution. Paine also published a series of pro-revolutionary pamphlets from 1776-1783 entitled *The American Crisis.*

33. B: Germany's declaration of war on Russia in 1914, following the assassination of Archduke Ferdinand, did not contribute to ending American neutrality in World War I. Once Germany declared war, England, France, Italy, Russia, and Japan joined as the Allied Powers against the Central Powers of Germany and Austria-Hungary, and US President Woodrow Wilson declared America's neutrality. When Germany designated the area surrounding the British Isles as a war zone in February 1913, and warned all ships from neutral countries to stay out of the zone, an end to American neutrality was prompted. President Wilson responded to Germany's declaration by proclaiming that America would hold Germany responsible for any American losses of life or property. When Germany sank the British passenger vessel Lusitania, 128 American passengers were killed. This further eroded Wilson's resolve to remain neutral. In February 1917, Germany declared unrestricted submarine warfare on any ship in the war zone; this signified that ships from any country would face German attack. President Wilson's reaction to this declaration was to cease diplomatic relations with Germany. Meanwhile, England intercepted a telegram from Germany to Mexico asking Mexico to join forces with Germany if the US joined the Allies. This infuriated the American public. President Wilson then asked for a declaration of war on Germany on April 2, 1917, which Congress approved.

34. B: Growth of industry was concentrated in urban areas, which cyclically drew laborers into cities, growing the population of cities and increasing efficiency and quality in industry.

35. A: While an argument could be made that choice B is also correct, there was not a phenomenon actually named the "Women Quitting Work Effect," so choice A is the BEST choice for describing the phenomenon illustrated by the given statistic. The statistic shows the post war Baby Boom, and its effect was to increase the economy and consumer demand for products. Choice D describes the opposite of a Baby Boom, so it is not correct, and choice C was not a historical phenomenon.

36. B: Students who know about the US Office of War Information should know that the purpose was to get out messages that would build morale and raise spirits. They also tried to recruit women for wartime work during WWII. They sometimes used famous stars such as Ethel Merman to further appeal to women. Their purpose was not to sell Broadway or movie tickets, nor was it to encourage women to stay at home.

37. C: The Sugar Act of 1764 raised import duties on goods which were not of British origin, including sugar, while reducing the import tax on molasses. The Stamp Act of 1765 was a tax of paper and printed products, intended to help the British government recoup some of the costs of the French and Indian War. It was extremely unpopular with the colonists and was repealed in 1766. Lead was one of the goods taxed under the Townshend Acts, enacted in 1767, but it did not receive its own specific tax act. The Tea Act of 1773 was another unpopular tax and led to tea boycotts and was the catalyst for the Boston Tea Party.

38. A: Women settlers outnumbering male settlers was not something that contributed to the differences between life in the New England colonies and life in the Chesapeake colonies. It was the other way around - in Virginia and Maryland, men greatly outnumbered women due to these colonies' large tobacco farms, which required men as workers. New England colonists did have life expectancies that were between 15 and 20 years longer than did Chesapeake colonists (B). Because Puritans lived longer, came to America with their families (most Chesapeake colonists came as individual indentured servants), and were a more homogeneous population, society in colonial New England was better organized and more stable than in the Chesapeake colonies (C). Puritans were also great believers in literacy because they felt it was so important to be able to read the Bible, so they had educational advantages over the colonies to the south (D). Because of the disproportionate sex ratio and the shorter life spans of Chesapeake settlers, their family and social lives were not as continuous or as stable as in New England. A combination of smaller farms, cottage industries, trading, fishing and ship building industries, and the resulting emergence of Boston as a chief international seaport all contributed to local prosperity in New England.

39. D: With an increasing population, cities and towns sprang up and became sites of hotels, brothels, laundries, and saloons. Answer A is not likely; most of the migration consisted of men coming to seek their fortunes and planning to return east. The key term in answer B is *most.* Although the women who went west often did establish businesses, most of the new migrants were men. The Civil War did not begin until 1860, more than a decade after the Gold Rush. The harsh climate conditions were not the only reason for the deaths that occurred during western migration. In any case, death would not be a contributor to increased population.

40. C: Purchasing a DVD is a discretionary expense because it is based on personal desire rather than need. In other words, it is an expense made at the discretion of the consumer. Discretionary expenses are those over which a consumer has the most control. A comprehensive budget must include discretionary expenses as well as fixed and variable expenses. Fixed expenses, such as rent, are the same every month. Variable expenses, including groceries, school supplies, and heating oil, are always present but vary in amount over the course of a year.

41. A: Germany developed rocket technology and the United States put a man on the moon in 1969.

42. B: As production shifted to factories, a large number of unskilled workers were needed to operate the machinery that was beginning to put many skilled craftsmen out of work. As farms grew larger and increasingly mechanized, the number of people who owned their own farm began to decrease. The rural population declined as people flocked to the cities in search of employment.

43. A: Lyndon Johnson became president following the assassination of John F. Kennedy on November 22, 1963. The Great Society was a series of social programs implemented under the direction of Lyndon Johnson. The Great Society's goal was to eliminate poverty and racial injustice in America. The Great Society began with economic reforms including a tax cut and the creation of the Office of Economic Opportunity. From there, it grew to include the enacting of laws creating the Medicare and Medicaid systems to assist the elderly and poor with their health care costs, respectively. Educational and Housing reforms followed.

44. C: World War I sparked a frenzy of production in the factories of Chicago, New York, and other northern cities, and a decrease in European immigration created a serious labor shortage. Workers from the South were actively recruited by factory owners. The federal government did not interfere with discriminatory hiring practices until long after World War I, and the Voting Rights Act was not passed until 1965. African-American veterans from the South returned to the same rural economy in which they had grown up.

45. D: All of the answers are ways in which the Nazi government attempted to gain control of German children.

46. D: Federalism is the division of power between the national government and state governments. The framers of the Constitution wanted a stronger national government than the one created by the Articles of Confederation, but many Anti-Federalists worried that a strong central government would become too powerful. To address this concern, the Constitution created a federal system that shares power between national and state governments. It also included checks and balances to keep any one branch of the national government from gaining too much power. The phrase "checks and balances" most commonly refers to the division of the Federal government into the executive, legislative, and judicial branches.

47. D: All of these laws prepared the US for entry into World War I. The National Defense Act of 1916 (A) expanded America's armed forces, and the Navy Act (B), also in 1916, expanded the US Navy. In that same year, the Revenue Act (C) created new taxes to finance the growth of America's military.

48. D: All of these are examples of urban violence in 1830s America. Political differences between Democrats and Whigs in New York City escalated into such violent fighting that the state militia was called in to subdue the disagreeing parties (A). Race riots broke out in New York City and Philadelphia during this decade (B). An angry mob in New York even went so far as to raid a Catholic convent in 1834 (C). All of these events were attributable to the very rapid influx of people to the cities, causing mob violence and street crime to grow out of control.

49. C: Sit-ins were peaceful protests during which both African-American and Caucasian participants protested segregated, or "whites-only," businesses by sitting at such establishments and asking to be served. These protests led to the integration of lunch counters and other businesses. In 1954, the Supreme Court ruled in *Brown v. Board of Education* that public schools could not be separate and equal; this ruling occurred independently of sit-ins. This eliminates choice D. The sit-ins did not focus on either integration of the armed forces, or on literacy tests as requirements for voter registration. Though reforms regarding these issues were passed, they were not directly a result of sit-ins. This eliminates choices A and B respectively.

50. B: Despite the constitutional guarantee of free speech, it is not absolute. There are certain restrictions in which laws regulate defamation, slander, libel, conspiracy and occasions when speech has the potential of causing "imminent harm." During the Vietnam War era, draftees would publicize their displeasure by burning their draft cards—this action actually constituted a federal crime. School employees are required to be socially responsible, and are libel to discipline if their actions encourage delinquency or profanity. The laws prohibit threats against the President only when it represents a real threat, not "political hyperbole."

51. C: Eli Whitney invented the cotton gin in 1794. The gin enabled one worker to produce 50 pounds of cleaned cotton in one day. This made cotton a profitable crop and increased the demand for and value of slaves in the South.

52. B: The Internet has increased the number of methods in which near-instantaneous communication is possible, indirectly improving the economy by opening new channels for communication at great distances. The internet has also generally caused a decrease in transaction costs and barriers to entry in retail situations (e.g., it is much less expensive to start a website to sell your goods than it is to open a physical store). The Internet has also increased consumer access to goods by making it easier for consumers to locate what they want.

53. D: In 1956, Egypt did not attack Israel. On October 29, 1956, Israel attacked Egypt. England and France did join this war within two days. It is true that Egyptian President Gamal Abdul Nasser refused to take America's side in the Cold War. In reaction to his refusal, President Eisenhower's administration pulled its funding from the Aswan Dam project in Egypt. Nasser then nationalized the British-owned Suez Canal. Eisenhower further declared in 1957 that America would provide aid to any country in the Middle East facing Communist control. Pursuant to Eisenhower's declaration, the US invaded Lebanon in 1958 to resolve a conflict in government.

54. B: The GATT countries did agree to abolish or decrease many of their tariffs, but this agreement did not include only 57 countries. The number of signatories was much larger, totaling 117 countries. The GATT was approved by Congress in 1994. In addition to having 117 countries agree to increase free trade, the GATT also set up the World Trade Organization (WTO) for the purpose of settling any differences among nations related to trade. Another instance of free trade policy established in the 1990s was the Senate's ratification of NAFTA. The negotiation of this agreement was originally made by the first Bush administration, with President Bush and the leaders of Canada and Mexico signing it in 1992, but it still needed to be ratified. When he was elected President following the senior Bush's term, Bill Clinton also supported NAFTA, and the Senate ratified it in 1994.

55. D: Indentured servants agreed to work for a set period of time in exchange for transportation to the New World and such basic necessities as food and shelter. They did not receive wages and were generally not highly-educated people. Employers often viewed indentured servants with scorn and treated them as harshly as they treated slaves.

56. B: *Marbury v. Madison* started with the election of Thomas Jefferson as third President of the United States. The lame-duck Congress responded by issuing a large number of judicial patents, which the incoming president and Secretary of State refused to deliver to their holders. Marbury, who was to receive a patent as Justice of the Peace, sued to demand delivery. What makes this case important is the decision which declared the judiciary's ability to overturn legislation that conflicted with the Constitution. The case states:

"It is emphatically the province and duty of the judicial department to say what the law is. Those who apply the rule to particular cases must, of necessity, expound and interpret that rule. If two laws conflict with each other, the courts must decide on the operation of each.

"So if a law be in opposition to the Constitution; if both the law and the constitution apply to a particular case, so that the court must either decide that case conformably to the law, disregarding the Constitution; or conformably to the Constitution, disregarding the law; the court must determine which of these conflicting rules governs the case. This is of the very essence of judicial duty.

"If, then, the courts are to regard the Constitution, and the Constitution is superior to any ordinary act of the legislature, the Constitution, and not such ordinary act, must govern the case to which they both apply."

Later, the ruling states: "The judicial power of the United States is extended to all cases arising under the Constitution." It was in this way that the Supreme Court achieved its now traditional ability to strike down laws and to act as the final arbitrator of what is and is not allowed under the US Constitution.

57. A: The Sherman Antitrust Act outlawed "every contract, combination ... or conspiracy in restraint of trade or commerce among the several States, or with foreign nations." Option C describes trade within states; because the Sherman Antitrust Act does not address such trade, option C can be rejected. Options B and D each describe a use of the Sherman Antitrust Act; i.e., the Act was instrumental in breaking up both the Standard Oil trust and the AT&T monopoly. However, neither of these particular uses are as influential as the general outlawing of acts restraining trade between states; rather, it was the general prohibition which made these particular applications (and others) possible. This eliminates options B and D.

58. C: It is not true that the Second World War came to be known as "The War to End All Wars." Although this appellation sounds more fitting to WWII, it was actually the description given to the First World War. Of course, at the time of WWI no one knew that WWII would take place, so at that time the phrase seemed a suitable designation. Moreover, world leaders then wanted to avoid another world war in the future and thereby formed the League of Nations to prevent such an occurrence. When this proved unsuccessful in preventing WWII, the United Nations was formed. WWI was the worst war the world had ever experienced at the time, but when WWII broke out, it was far worse than WWI. It is true that in the Second World War, nations mobilized all of their resources—both military and civilian (A), to the point that there was no more distinction between the two. This war also claimed many more civilian casualties and military casualties (B) than previous wars. Very large contributors to the great numbers of civilian casualties were the Holocaust, wherein millions of people including Jews, Catholics, Jehovah's Witnesses, Romani, Poles, Soviet POWs, Freemasons, homosexuals, and people with disabilities were killed. Further, the Second World War was the first war in history to detonate nuclear devices (D), when the United States under President Harry S. Truman bombed Hiroshima and Nagasaki after Japan refused the unconditional surrender terms demanded by the Allies at Potsdam, Germany.

59. B: The debates of 1858 resulted in Douglas's victory over Lincoln in the senatorial race. However, his performance in the debates helped make Lincoln a viable candidate for the presidency, and he was elected to that office two years later.

60. D: Machinery and transport jumped from 34.3 to 42.0 percent in exports and from 9.7 to 28.0 percent in imports. Chemicals increased exports slightly, from 8.7 to 9.0. Imports declined slightly, from 5.3 to 3.6; thus Choice A is incorrect. Crude material exports declined from 13.7 to 10.8 while imports declined from 18.3 to 8.3, making Choice B incorrect. The decline in exports of food and beverages was just under 4 percent, while imports declined 7 percent; therefore, Choice C is not an accurate choice.

Online Resources

Due to our efforts to try to keep this book to a manageable length, we've created a link that will give you access to all of your online resources:

mometrix.com/resources719/vsolvaushist

It's Your Moment, Let's Celebrate It!

Share your story @mometrixtestpreparation